Fergie
Her Secret Life

Fergie
Her Secret Life

Allan Starkie

Thorndike Press • Chivers Press
Thorndike, Maine   Bath, England

This Large Print edition is published by Thorndike Press, USA and by Chivers Press, England.

Published in 1997 in the U.S. by arrangement with Michael O'Mara Books Ltd.

Published in 1997 in the U.K. by arrangement with Michael O'Mara Books Ltd.

U.S.   Hardcover 0-7862-1018-4 (Basic Series Edition)
U.K.   Hardcover 0-7451-5467-0 (Windsor Large Print)
U.K.   Softcover 0-7451-8766-8 (Paragon Large Print)

The text of this Large Print edition is unabridged.
Other aspects of the book may vary from the original edition.

Set in 16 pt Plantin by Minnie B. Raven.

Printed in the United States on permanent paper.

British Library Cataloguing in Publication Data available

Library of Congress Cataloging in Publication Data

Starkie, Allan.
    Fergie : her secret life / Allan Starkie.
        p. cm.
    ISBN 0-7862-1018-4 (lg. print : hc)
    1. York, Sarah Mountbatten-Windsor, Duchess of, 1959–
2. Nobility — Great Britain — Biography.   3. Large type
books.   I. Title.
    [DA591.A45Y6784   1997]
    941.085′092—dc21   96-52772

TO
MICHAEL AND LESLEY O'MARA

Contents

Acknowledgements

Roles can change amazingly quickly. One moment you may be a successful business-man with powerful friends, the next you find yourself on your knees scrubbing the linoleum floor of a prison library. In the first case you are surrounded by people calling themselves your friends; in the second you are lucky to know a handful of people brave enough to acknowledge your existence. My thanks, therefore, are limited to a small number of friends.

I would like to thank Andrea van Wijk and Margot Schäfer, the first employees and last survivors of Oceonics Deutschland, who remained by my side when our partners deserted us and when I could no longer even pay them.

The frantic thirty minutes a week which constitute the visiting period in Höchst Prison is a daunting experience which few of my former 'friends' were willing to endure. I want to thank the four people who cared enough to interrupt my solitude with their kindness.

I was lucky enough to be befriended by a

man whose kindness, generosity and humour lightened my months of confinement. His bravery, and the shining example of his unqualified love for his wife, impressed and inspired me. He sits now in an even more dismal prison in Singapore, a human sacrifice on the altar of the incompetence of his superiors. I will never forget Nick Leeson and the friendship we forged as we endlessly circled the prison yard.

When I began this project it became clear that each potential collaborator wished to twist my book to fit his or her own agenda. John Bryan wanted to fashion 'the stake to pierce the heart of the Vampire'; the Duchess of York wished the truth to remain hidden; a literary agent saw the book as a modern *Gone with the Wind*, with the Duchess cast as Scarlett O'Hara. I began to lose hope that anyone cared about the truth, until a gentleman of the press named Geoffrey Levy helped me. He never exploited the opportunities created by my vulnerability, but as a result of meeting him I was introduced to Michael O'Mara. It seemed as if Fate had been particularly generous to me. Michael's reputation for being as honest as the day is long is actually an understatement. He immediately understood what I was trying to say, and took a chance and trusted me. When the Duchess of York tried to suppress this book he fought with fairness, honesty and strength for our right to free speech.

As we were drawn more and more into the fight to release this story, Lesley O'Mara kept the project moving forward, leading the team with unfailing confidence. I would like to thank all those at O'Mara for their dedication to seeing this project through, with a special mention of Toby Buchan, for his wisdom, diligence and dedication, and Shelley Klein for her hard work and professionalism. Special thanks, too, to Carolyn Mallam for her endless patience and support, and to Andrew Morton. I would also like to thank our army of lawyers, including John Linneker, Niri Shanmuganathan and their team at Taylor Joynson Garrett, Suzanne Reeves at Wedlake Bell, and Michael Korde at Dr Groepper and Partners. And thanks, too, to Dr Zipser-Ebner for helping me to understand the past.

Finally, I would like to thank my mother, for being just as proud of me in prison blue as she had been when I wore West Point dress gray.

Publisher's Foreword

The Duchess of York made strenuous attempts to stop publication of this book. John Bryan made it clear he would prefer not to see it on the bookstalls either. Why, in the face of such opposition, does someone who has been a close friend of both sit down to write his version of their life together?

Allan Starkie paid a high price for his friendship with these two volatile characters: the five months he spent in the solitude of a German prison cell was the least of it. It comes as no surprise, therefore, that in the long hours available to him during his incarceration, and in the months after his release without charge, he meticulously recorded the experiences of a four-year entanglement.

The Duchess's reaction to the news that Allan's book was to be published was swift and costly. She secured an injunction to prevent its publication, even though she did not know what the book contained; in reality this story relates as much to her former friend, John Bryan, and to Allan, as it does to herself.

In the end reason prevailed and this book

was cleared for publication — but not before a great deal of money was expended in the defence of Allan's right to tell his own story.

It was only by a series of coincidences that Allan Starkie, a New Yorker and former soldier, with few English connections, became involved in this extraordinary affair. A graduate of the US Military Academy at West Point, he had a distinguished career in military intelligence, serving in Panama, Korea and Africa. Later he was appointed one of President Reagan's social aides; but at that point he gave up a promising career in order to give his parents the support that only comes with a realistic salary, the sort the US Army could never provide. He went into the construction business in Manhattan.

As a young cadet, Allan Starkie had represented West Point at the debutante balls in New York. He was the man, stiff-backed and polished, who marched behind the debutantes carrying their state flag, while tuxedoed young men like John Bryan and David Rockefeller languidly trailed after the girls as their civilian escorts. Socially, there is a big difference.

A few years later he found himself on the other side of the fence — on John's side, the side of old money and blue blood. Together these new friends trod a gilded path, enjoying all the benefits and amusements of being attached, in their different ways, to a member of the royal family. An aide to former US Treasury Secretary William Simon, who figures later in this story, told him: 'You are living a charmed life. You are mingling with royalty and you are running a large company. Keep a record of it, because it's only a phase, it can't last for ever.'

He kept diaries, written at the end of each day, into which he poured his experiences and observations. For a former spy he was remarkably unsecretive about what he was doing: when the diaries' existence became known to the Duchess and John Bryan it was assumed by everyone that he had become the triumvirate's official scribe — each person urging him on because they wanted their movements recorded for posterity.

The Duchess of York, acutely aware of her place in history, encouraged Allan to keep track of her life with as much detail as he could, declaring: 'One day you'll write such a marvellous book about it.' John Bryan, in his turn, always hoped Starkie would write his biography. But Starkie was not writing their life so much as his own, trying to make sense of four crazy years which were to have such a dramatic impact on all three lives.

As much as anything else, his chronicling

of events was a way of seeking an explanation of what went wrong. At West Point he was taught that loyalty is paramount; and only after he saw his loyalty betrayed, as readers will see as they read this book, did he even begin to question the actions of the ill-starred lovers.

His is a very modern story about the abuse of an ancient institution. Remarkably, he tells it without rancour. It makes what he writes all the more powerful and persuasive.

Chapter 1

The Buckingham Palace secretaries flitted in and out, curtsying each time they made their entrances, searching for a slide-projector for our meeting, returning with tea and coffee in fine bone-china cups. It was a warm summer's day and the tall windows were open, giving out on to the front courtyard of the Palace. Beyond the Victoria Memorial stretched the Mall and the rest of London, bathed in sunlight. From below came the sound of muffled orders, and of guardsmen's boots stamping on gravel.

She sat before me, magnificent in a red Ralph Lauren dress decked with a double row of brass buttons. The blue-grey eyes sparkled mischievously, as if to say, 'How am I doing so far, Starkie?' — her demeanour suggesting that I knew she was simply playing a part, and that it would be great fun if I played along. Yes, there were moments when the Duchess of York was undoubtedly regal. In Buckingham Palace she possessed a vital sensuality which seemed to reanimate the stale air and invigorate the long corridors and their countless portraits.

15

Our voices were drowned suddenly by the noise of drums, and we were offered the unique experience of witnessing the ancient ceremony of Changing the Guard from inside the Palace. The German banker by my side almost wept, he found the moment so moving.

For me, pleasurable as the occasion was, it represented no more than another in the series of roles I had seen the Duchess of York fulfil in the past months. On her husband's warship I had observed how perfectly she played the part of an officer's wife: friendly but distant to the sailors, playful with the junior officers, respectful of the Duke. In a Mayfair nightclub, or at a party in a marquee behind her rented home, she would dance up a storm, tell ripe jokes with the best of them, and manage to make each guest feel as if he or she were the only person she wanted to see.

During charity trips in the depths of Albania, Poland or Bosnia I saw her comfort children so ill and dirty that the nurses would not touch them. Fearless on horseback, she turned into the quintessential countrywoman the moment she slipped on her riding boots. At business meetings I watched her dazzle a room full of hardnosed New York tycoons with her ideas and enthusiasm. I have seen

16

her in her rare moments of happiness, and in the depths of the dejection in which she normally lived.

Never was she lower than in the months following publication, in 1992, of the photographs which showed her topless in the South of France, romping by the swimming pool with John Bryan. This captured moment, which fused the couple together in the public's imagination like a freeze-frame image from some Gothic horror movie, ruined the lives of both of them, and I saw the terrible mark this public humiliation left on Sarah. That autumn, she looked worse than I have ever seen her; listless and disheartened, she gained a lot of weight. In the evenings I would see her wandering aimlessly round Romenda Lodge without makeup and with a towelling sweatband round her head, wearing an oversized man's shirt and tights which emphasized the extra poundage she was now carrying round her hips and thighs. Her eyes were tired, and she looked as though her soul had gone.

Here was the other side of the coin, the obverse to the upbeat, power-dressed businesswoman; before me was the portrait of a woman no longer quite in control, drinking and smoking too much. At night she would down a handful of sizeable vodkas, then take to the wine. Her cigarette butts littered the house, despite her desperate attempts to give up.

At this juncture she felt she was in a trap: her country hated her (or so she thought), the press was at her throat, she had burned her bridges for a man she did not even love, and she was lost. Fear and lust had forged her misalliance with John, but the frenetic pace at which the love affair grew had been driving it towards disaster almost from the start.

The Duchess was often a positive force for good, but if I could point to one factor which contributed to her downfall, it would be her vacillation. At the height of their affair Sarah and John would talk thirty or forty times a day on the telephone. She would then say to me, 'Tell him not to call me so often' — and if he complied with this dictate, she would simply call *him* more often. Many similar examples of her turnabout nature litter the narrative that follows.

For those drawn into the Duchess's circle, however, there was a special feeling of belonging, enhanced by her use of secret nicknames and obscure references which only the participants would understand. In front of blank-faced officials from Coutts, the royal bankers, she would turn to John and say,

'Did Mr Rose tell Mrs Rose cherry trees yesterday, Otto?' Translated, that meant, 'Did I tell you I love you?' As a mannerism it was charming; it made everyone who was close to the Duchess feel that they were in some way special. She would take a word or phrase someone had used and turn it into a code which would then become part of the vocabulary; thus this small group came to feel that not only were they living in her world, but that she was living in theirs.

There may have been a moment in her life when things had been right for the Duchess, but when once I asked her, 'When were you happy last?' she could only answer that there had been times, many years ago, when she had believed she was happy, simply because she did not know better. It is my view that her mother's abandonment of Sarah blighted her life and distorted her view of how to live it. For a while, when she was taking Prozac (a new anti-depressant drug, called 'America's happy pill'), there was an upswing; but for the most part she was constantly fighting her depression while searching for something in which she could believe. One escape route was through work, and she would construct very long working days into which she packed public appearances, business projects, and elaborate family arrangements. In all the time I was close to the Duchess I remained deeply impressed by the amount of energy she would put into these different areas of her life; but when the work was over, the energy gone, she would crumble and fall into a depression. True, there were good days, but there were many more bad ones.

On the good days, we planned and plotted together, got drunk on Concorde (she travelling as Sarah Starkie), shared our regrets and depressions. Yet I cannot define her by any one of these images, only as a composite of all of them; because behind the many guises lies the essence of the Duchess of York — her insecurity, her vulnerability, and her compulsive need to be accepted and respected.

My first contact with John Bryan came in June of 1989. I had been working in London for several months, setting up the offices and operations of a specialist construction company which had won a large portion of the Canary Wharf project from the developers, Olympia and York.

One day I took a call from an old friend named Charlie Reid; we had worked together on two high-rise buildings in New York, and had become friends. Now he was in Frankfurt, where he was responsible for the new high-rise MesseTurm, the towering office block which was to be the tallest building in Europe.

Charlie talked about the project, then mentioned that he had given my name to a couple of people and recommended me to them. He added that the interiors contractor was a newly established construction division of an English oil-support company called Oceonics. The management, according to Charlie, had no idea what they were doing, and had stumbled into this enormous contract simply by producing a bid that was so ridiculously low that the general contractor could not refuse. The latter, Hochtief, had indemnified itself against what it regarded as the inevitable failure of this fledgeling division by writing savage penalty clauses into its contract with Oceonics. Clearly the English company needed help, but I told Charlie I was not really interested. 'Do me a favour, Allan,' he replied, 'have lunch with these guys. They're a couple of crazy millionaires, but the old man is a real industrial hotshot. It's a free lunch, anyway — and I promised them.' I reluctantly agreed that if they called I'd meet with them.

Two days later I answered the phone, or tried to.

Before I could finish saying 'Good morning', I was hit by the fastest-talking sales pitch I had ever come across, 'Hello, my name is John Bryan and I am deputy chairman of Oceonics Group Plc. We are an oil-service and defence computer company who have recently decided to diversify into the international construction industry specializing in exporting American techniques in high-rise construction to the European market.'

If you can imagine that sentence said as one continuous word, you can picture just what it was that confronted me. I interrupted: 'Look, I don't want to be rude, but I'm very busy — can you just tell me what you are selling?'

'I'm not selling anything, I was given your name by someone — I promised not to reveal who — and was told you might be interested in meeting with me.' He invited me to meet him and his father at seven o'clock that evening at his apartment. The oddest thing about the whole business was that I agreed to do so.

Cheyne Place is a little strip of houses at the tail end of Royal Hospital Road in Chelsea. It is so small that even some London taxi drivers have difficulty finding it, as I was to discover that night. Across from the ancient Physick Garden is Number 5, a brick building with a glazed front door painted telephone-box red. Next to the door is a panel of doorbells, one of which carries a blue plastic sticker with the name 'Bryans' — meaning more than one Bryan.

There were indeed two Bryans there, John and his father. Tony Bryan's actual string of names is Anthony John Adrian Bryan, and he called his only son by the same four names. At this time both AJABs were residing at Number 5, thus the plural Bryans. They enjoyed being thought of as a team. They were pleased when people referred to them as 'the Two Bryans', while sentences such as 'Have you heard, the Two Bryans are living in London?' would cause them great delight. My appointment was with both.

After being buzzed into the small lobby I made my way to the back of the building and took the tiny elevator, also bright red, to the top floor, where the Bryans lived. The apartment actually occupies the topmost floor of three adjacent town houses, and the living room encompasses the entire upper floor of the centre house. The back wall is of glass, opening on to a long terrace with a breathtaking view over the Physick Garden towards the Thames.

The apartment was rented furnished, so

23

John could not be held responsible for its contents; indeed, I doubt whether he ever noticed them. The living room had a large fireplace with a huge red painting above it — just a canvas covered with red paint — and there were two sofas of exactly the same red as the front door, the elevator and the painting. An old Steinway grand piano served as a combination telephone table and filing cabinet, while a narrow sixteenth-century dining table was decorated with another two or three telephones, more files, and two ultra-thin Asprey briefcases, one in brown and one in black. These sleek accessories scorned the notion that they might be burdened with massive reports; indeed, they were constructed to hold no more than two 'bottom lines' each. In five years I was never once to see a morsel of food on that table, nor hear a note of music from the piano, nor see a single fire in the fireplace. One wall held bookshelves, with a space let into them to accommodate an old grandfather clock, which remained broken or unwound for those same five years.

A door on the right of the living room led into a labyrinth of four rooms used as offices and guest rooms. The other notable features of the apartment were a jacuzzi bathtub, and an antique carved four-poster bed — which was effectively where this story was to begin.

On this, our first meeting, I was met by the Two Bryans as the elevator door opened. My initial impression was of two men of almost identical dimension and dress, both well over six feet tall, slender, and dressed in exquisitely well-tailored dark blue suits. They were both smiling widely. 'Hello,' said the younger one. 'How do you do?' added the older. On a second glance, however, I realized that they were somewhat different. Tony Bryan looked like a cross between an elongated Fred Astaire and someone Hollywood might have cast as 'The Chief Executive Officer'. Elegant, charming and completely at ease, he exuded an air of old-world stability that soothed and encouraged. By contrast, the younger man was bursting with energy, and could barely manage to stand in one place long enough to shake my hand. He had regular features, blue eyes that seemed as if they were laughing at a private joke, and was bald on the top of his head, though he had let his hair grow rather long on the sides and back. His appearance somehow made me think of a pirate in a business suit.

This was John. For those destined to see him only in newspaper clippings it would be hard to explain either his magnetic charm or his charisma. Yet you can sense it immediately when you are with him. It gives you the feeling that not only is John Bryan a winner, but that he can suspend gravity and disbelief; indeed, that he can accomplish anything.

Tony Bryan's air of steadiness and strength was not accidental, for he understatedly boasted many accomplishments. He had been born on 24 February 1923 in Saltill, Mexico, of English parents. As a child he was sent to boarding school in England, first to St Richard's prep school, and then to the Roman Catholic public school, Ampleforth. At the outbreak of the Second World War his family had been in Canada, and he had therefore joined the Royal Canadian Air Force. A Spitfire pilot, he was commanding a fighter squadron at the age of only twenty-two, and was awarded the Distinguished Flying Cross for his remarkable exploits during low-level attacks on German airfields in Occupied Europe. Eventually he was shot down over France, and even now as a hobby flyer carries a toiletry bag in the cockpit, joking that the worst part about being shot down behind enemy lines is not being able to brush your teeth.

After the war he attended Harvard and married his first wife, Lida — from this, the first of four marriages, John and his two sisters were born. Tony Bryan's second wife was Josephine Abercrombie, then, in the 1950s, one of the richest women in America, and through whom he was able to acquire for himself a seat on the board of her enormous company, Cameron Oil. In the nineteen prosperous years that this second marriage lasted, he was appointed to the boards of Chrysler, ITT, Federal Express, and the Pittsburgh National Bank, as well as becoming a trustee of Carnegie Mellon University and of the Pittsburgh Ballet Theater. A good marriage, then.

Even so, it didn't last, and was replaced with a short-lived union with Pamela Sakowitz, whose husband's sister, Lynn, was the mother of Steve Wyatt. But Steve and John were closer than a rather spurious 'cousin-age-by-marriage': they had gone to high school together in Texas.

John did not flourish in the constant emotional upheaval. A difficult pupil, he was thrown out of so many boarding schools that Tony Bryan once told me that he saved his best suit for two occasions only: to meet bank presidents, or John's new headmaster.

To a certain extent, it is possible to understand why he had such difficulties as a child. His mother, Lida, was eccentric and erratic, and for a time she was institutionalized as a result of her over-dependence on Valium; the drug had helped her to the conclusion that her husband had assassinated President Bush. But Lida had spirit: on the day she was taken into hospital she snapped at the administrator, 'I have been invited to five parties tonight and this isn't one of them!'

With the ultra-rich Josephine Abercrombie as his new stepmother, John's path through life was assured. He travelled to his new schools by private jet, and was later to qualify as a pilot and fly his father's planes. On one occasion when father and son were flying together, they decided to practise landings on the Delaware River (the plane was an amphibian — that is, able to land on water or runways). One or the other pilot had forgotten to retract the wheels, however, and on contact with the surface of the river the plane flipped over and instantly sank. The cockpit filled with water at an alarming rate, but when John looked over at his father as they lay on the riverbed, upside-down and belted in, Tony Bryan appeared to be occupied with removing a small piece of fluff from his lapel. When the two men finally made it to the surface they were hauled out by a man who greeted Tony by name; the senior Bryan had dealt with their rescuer the previous week, when he had crashed his other plane. So John inherited his father's cool — and his forgetfulness.

With the introductions out of the way, I was escorted to the dining room table, which was covered, as it always was, with papers. We sat down, the Two Bryans side by side across from me. Although they were ostensibly interviewing me, instead of asking questions they began an enthusiastic presentation of a very autobiographical nature. Within minutes I had been told how successful they were, and indeed who they were. It was clear that they had not prepared themselves for this meeting, and perhaps were not even sure why they had arranged it.

This in no way detracted from their enthusiasm, however, as they spoke with glee of their board memberships and the degree of faith that business icons like Lee Iacocca and Harold Jenine had in them. Finally the flow of anecdotes began to slow down, and the conversation moved on to Oceonics, the reason why they had invited me. John launched into a monologue, a good deal of which was about him. Eventually he got closer to the point: 'I had the financing from the Kuwait Investment office to make a 15 or 20 million-dollar acquisition of a UK oil-services company, Oceonics Group Plc. So that was my first acquisition and it was very exciting, by March [of 1987] I was running the company and living in England, it was just wild.'

It transpired that Oceonics wanted to diversify into construction and was about to be awarded a large contract in Germany — the contract for the MesseTurm interiors. They were about to establish a German company and were looking for new management — which was where, thanks to Charlie Reid, I came in. Finally, after having listened to the two of them for perhaps two hours, Tony Bryan asked his first and only question of me: 'Do you speak German?'

'No,' I burst out thankfully. This seemed to sadden the older Bryan, while John remained nonplussed. Then he said, 'So what, Pop? He'll learn in a couple of weeks.' As far as they were concerned, I was their new German chief executive officer.

We had a considerable number of meetings during the next seven months. I resolutely refused to allow the Bryans to hire me, but first out of curiosity, then out of a growing friendship with John, I continued to meet with them.

At one point I even accompanied John to Frankfurt and watched him gaze in horror at the growing mass of concrete as the Messe-Turm took shape. He recalled later, 'I looked up at this thing and I said to myself, we don't have a single construction employee, how the hell are we going to do this?'

As we arrived back at Heathrow I was allowed to watch John proudly perform a magic trick that was to cause him grave damage just four short years later. We jumped into a cab and John said 'Car park please'.

The cabby was rather disappointed with the shortness of his journey. 'Don't worry,' explained John, 'I'll give you an extra five pounds if you let me have your parking ticket. Just say you lost it — the attendant will remember that you just drove in.'

Incredibly, the driver agreed. As we drove off John proudly announced that he had saved over £100. At the time his expenses were reimbursable from his company, so what made him do it? I believe it gave him a thrill to think that he was superior to the rules that govern mere mortals.

After our initial meeting at Cheyne Place, the Bryans had asked me, as a favour, to go to Frankfurt and just look at their operation, interview their staff, and make an analysis of the budgets they had drawn up. This I did — but what I discovered was that the contract they had pitched for would lose them millions straight away; the operation was so amateurish that they had not even budgeted for labour costs. I went back to England and reported to the Bryans: 'Not only will this project bring down your company, but it's going to destroy the reputations of everyone concerned. I don't want to get involved with it, but I'll give you the name of someone who might.'

That someone was a fellow West Point graduate and ex-Harvard Business School man, Chris Miller. The Two Bryans interviewed him, and offered him the job. I was asked to have lunch with them one last time, during which both father and son kept on talking as though Chris and I were a team. I still refused to join them, not least because I was enjoying London life and my work at Canary Wharf, but I agreed to go over to Frankfurt at weekends and act as a consultant on the MesseTurm project.

On Mondays I would fly back to London, and in the evening report to John at his flat in Cheyne Place, keeping him up to date with whatever progress was being made. He had some difficulty in following what I was saying — all five telephone lines in the flat would be ringing simultaneously, and he found it hard to concentrate. But he liked and trusted me, and when he liked and trusted someone there would be huge smiles of agreement and a welter of congratulatory phrases. To him, I was the solution to his problems, a saviour

— and a fellow American. He would drag me to Oceonics board meetings in Aldershot, and ask me to report on the Frankfurt project as if it were my responsibility.

We were also mixing socially more and more, having drinks and dinner together, and discussing his plan to sell off the German division of Oceonics before it collapsed. Then I learned that Tony Bryan and his partner, Dennis Sokol, had bought a hospital company, HCI; in fact, the international division of HCA, the largest hospital company in the world. Now, at last, I saw a future with the Bryans, and made my decision to join them.

Chapter 2

It is hard to know which of the two — John or the Duchess — wanted it more, but each for their own reasons tried to draw me into their relationship.

The Duchess established a close rapport with me, and through that hoped, perhaps, to gain a greater measure of control over John Bryan. For his part, John regarded me as his partner and, never really able to split business from pleasure, felt it quite natural that I would be his partner in this, his greatest adventure.

They pulled me into every facet of their lives. Already John's business partner and best friend, I was soon fulfilling a similar role with the Duchess. After their affair was so spectacularly uncovered I became John's proxy, his 'loyal second', chaperoning the Duchess around the world in his place; one day competing with her in an equestrian event, the next embarking on a charity trip to Eastern Europe. Sarah and I developed business ideas, worked on several writing projects, and even established a charitable foundation together. But all the while the real agenda was their reliance on me as an arbitrator in their relationship, a mouthpiece for the words they were too frightened to say directly to one another.

Even now the affair is over, it is difficult to state with any certainty that they ever loved each other. For the Duchess, John Bryan satisfied a number of needs: she regarded him as her charismatic 'shiny fish', the consummate charmer who was also — in her eyes at least — a social equal. He provided her with satisfying sexual experiences, and he represented himself to her as wealthy, self-possessed and confident at a time when she needed support. Put together, these factors combined in her to create a sensation akin to love. Not the wild, abandoned excitement she had experienced during her infatuation with Steve Wyatt — but something strong enough, at least, to last four years.

For John, the Duchess was a passport to instant fame. For a man whose stated ambition was to be recognized in restaurants, such a relationship exceeded his wildest dreams; overnight, he became a household name. The Duchess had 'years of international experience', children he loved, a staff of servants he commanded as if his own, and a sexual appetite he relished. Desperately hungry for a short cut to the fame and wealth which, through his father's marriage to Josephine Abercrombie, he had witnessed in his youth, John clung to this relationship with an obsessiveness which sometimes, kneeling and weeping before her, he would scream out was eternal love, even as he saw the affair dying around him.

Both came from broken homes, and both had distant fathers and eccentric mothers who emotionally abandoned their children. Aware of the similarities of their childhoods, the Duchess once told me that a carpenter working on the Long Island home of John's mother, Lida, remarked that the little boy was 'cute'. 'Take him home with you for a couple of days' was Lida's reply, an offer which the amazed carpenter accepted. When Tony Bryan left Lida for Josephine, it was indeed odd that he should have been awarded custody of the young John, but the distant father was too busy running his business to allow this distraction to alter his lifestyle.

Sarah's mother, Susie Barrantes, is startlingly similar to Lida. She had been married for eighteen years to a well-connected but ultimately unsuccessful cavalry officer, Ronald Ferguson, who — though pitched out of the Life Guards as a captain (awarded an outgoing promotion to major, he never served at that rank) — was able to forge a career for himself as 'polo-stick-in-waiting' to the royal family. Later Ferguson's own marital indiscretions — with a polo sponsor, Lesley Player, and with various women at a seedy West End massage parlour — were to create a national scandal. But it was Susie who caught the headlines first, when she fell for an Argentinian polo opponent of her husband, Hector Barrantes. Their love was a *coup de foudre* and she ran away, abandoning a fifteen-year-old daughter, Jane, and her thirteen-year-old sister, Sarah, to a gruff and distant father. I once pretended to read Susie's palm and told her she had the propensity for falling head-over-heels in love. Her eyes became moist and she told Sarah that my skill was astonishing. But her infatuation with Hector (and her abandoning of her family) did undoubtedly create in her younger daughter a need for love.

Starved of affection and reassurance, both Sarah and John developed a charm they used as both weapon and shield. They became seduced by the idea of one another, narcissistically fascinated by the mirror-image each saw in the other. Then, as the affair progressed, they identified faults in each other, becoming obsessed with changing or 'improving' the other. 'We must be like two cherry trees supporting one another, intertwined as we grow towards the sun,' is how the Duchess described it to me once in the early days. John at the same time would say, 'Allan, I am getting her finally to confront herself and to want to become an honest, ethical person.'

From narcissism to criticism, from self-love to self-hate they moved, until their anger and disgust with one another spiralled to the point where the Duchess dismissed John as 'the biggest mistake in my life', while John now regards her as 'white trash' and 'a vampire'.

The truth was that the love of Sarah's life, always, was not John Bryan but Steve Wyatt. It was with Wyatt that she broke her wedding vows, while pregnant with her second child and with her marriage barely three years old. And since her real affection remained with this other American, the stepson of Houston oil magnate Oscar Wyatt, Jr, it made what happened next — the destruction of a marriage, the final denting of a royal reputation, John's own bankruptcy and social disgrace — all so futile. She never really loved John Bryan. He was simply the stand-in for an absentee lover, and he always knew it, but that knowledge did nothing to quench his insatiable lust for Sarah and what she had to offer.

In March 1990, only four months after having met Sarah, Steve Wyatt introduced her to John Bryan. Accustomed by now to the use of 'safe houses' for their clandestine meetings, the lovers gave a dinner party in London and, as a former schoolfriend of Steve's, and a cousin-by-marriage as well, it was inevitable that John would be invited. Wyatt, warming to the pleasures of having a royal concubine, ordered that his friend should observe protocol and arrive before the Duchess. This nettled John, who deliberately turned up late, long after Sarah had arrived. Introductions were made and John, either nervous or irritated, made a jokey comment and moved on.

During dinner he had a chance to observe her more closely. From her photographs in the newspapers he had drawn the conclusion that she was not particularly attractive, but in the flesh he found himself rapidly warming to her. She was six or seven months pregnant and looking 'sexy'.

Wyatt seemed to be enjoying showing off his girlfriend to the assembled company, but John felt strangely uncomfortable: 'These people were a bunch of forgettable losers.'

After dinner it had got worse, however —
Steve invited a group of people to troop by
and look at her, 'like it was some kind of
spectator sport'. He had been astonished at
the sight of these people, most of them becoming increasingly drunk, ooh-ing and aah-
ing and sitting down next to the Duchess.
Disgusted, in the end he had gone to find
Sarah's detective, and asked him to do something to get the guests to leave. 'I couldn't
believe the way Sarah and Steve behaved,
just showing off in front of garbage, in front
of people you wouldn't say hello to ordinar-
ily.'

In the relative privacy of the safe house,
all inhibitions had tumbled. The lovers,
proud of their possession of each other,
needed to show themselves off to somebody,
anybody. But if John Bryan, ever a stickler
for the *comme-il-faut* in others, was contemp-
tuous of the company, he soon mastered his
emotions. The rapport with Sarah as they
started to talk, the sexual chemistry, was in-
stantaneous.

They started joking together and when
Sarah asked where the bathroom was John
showed her down the stairs, and they stood
chatting, uninterrupted, for ten minutes.
John was hooked, and immediately became
protective; he ordered the other partygoers

to keep quiet about the Duchess's presence there that night and became enraged when one said, 'Oh, no! I'm going to dine out on this evening for the rest of my life.'

During this period it was the Duchess who sought to make public her friendship, though not her affair, with Wyatt. She had encountered him during an official trip to Houston, Texas, in November 1989 while staying as a guest of his mother and stepfather at their massive neo-classical mansion in River Oaks. Already seeking an exit from her three-year-old marriage, she felt comfortable in these extravagant surroundings — and was instantly attracted to the son of the house.

Back in Britain, a month later, she paid a visit to Leeds to attend a performance of the musical *Show Boat*. Her return flight was cancelled due to fog, and hasty arrangements were made for her to stay the night at Constable Burton Hall, near Leyburn in North Yorkshire. As it happened, Steve Wyatt was already there as a house guest, and the couple ended up spending two nights together under the same roof — even though the Duke of York was waiting for Sarah at Sandringham. It would not have taken long for Prince Andrew to learn the truth; and in a public outing a couple of weeks later photographers were able to capture the sudden change in mood towards his wife. Leaving Harry's Bar in Mayfair after a party, Sarah tripped and fell. The normally courteous Andrew walked resolutely on, leaving his seven-month pregnant wife to pick herself up and chase after him.

Her Royal Highness the Duchess of York gave birth to Princess Eugenie, a sister for the nineteen-month-old Princess Beatrice, on 23 March 1990. Six weeks later she flew with Wyatt, Beatrice and two royal detectives to Morocco, where the couple spent the next five days together.

Meanwhile John Bryan was plunging ahead with his dual ambitions of becoming a Master of the Universe and conquering London's *beau monde*. He flew to Frankfurt, New York, Edinburgh, Moscow, San Francisco and Houston in the space of a month. On his return his routine would include muscle-toning sessions with his personal trainer Josh Saltzmann, furious games of squash, then nights spent in Mayfair and Chelsea, escorting well-born girls on his climb up the social ladder.

It may be that behind his motivation lay a desire to beat his father Tony. He was forever on the lookout for 'the deal of the century', 'the motherlode', though there had never been a hope that he could match his father's socially enhanced business success. On the squash court, he was, in his mind, trying to better his father's victory in the US National Championships, another goal he could never achieve. Only in the social arena did he come near — his previous girlfriend had been Geraldine, Lady Ogilvy, the daughter of a peer and the ex-wife of a future peer, with powerful connections embracing the press and the royal family. For a time his best friend had been Mick Jagger, whom he would see in London and New York — until Jerry Hall warned her husband that John was 'a bad influence', in itself a comment guaranteed to open doors. In New York he routinely dined on Sundays with Truman Capote, and he claimed to me that he had repeatedly declined Andy Warhol's pleas to paint his portrait.

This pedigree, combined with family money and his father's business contacts, allowed John to present himself, if only in short, high-energy bursts, as a very successful young man. As long as nobody questioned what he would be doing when he got off the next plane, or who was on the other end of the mobile phone which never stopped ringing, he did indeed present an impressive front.

Months after their first meeting, John's interest in the Duchess of York had not waned. He received periodic reports from Steve Wyatt on the progress of the clandestine affair, and in October 1990 he was invited, as a friend of Wyatt's, to the opening party of Sunninghill Park, the Yorks' recently completed and heavily criticized modern house in the grounds of Windsor Great Park. To John it was clear that this was a party to pay homage to Steve and Sarah, not a house-warming. Certainly a large proportion of the guests seemed to be made up of Steve's friends. There was a band, and Elton John sang some songs. Then Prince Andrew came over and introduced himself to John; it was the first time the pair had met.

It was clear that the Prince knew what was going on, but he made an effort with his wife and her guests to make everyone feel comfortable. But, said John, 'She was acting so bloody obvious.'

Earlier that day Sarah had paid a tearful farewell to her stepfather, the polo player Hector Barrantes, at a memorial service arranged by Lord Vestey. Her voice had shaken with emotion as she read the valedictory 'Death is nothing at all, I have only slipped away into the next room.' The mood was still with her as she stood to address her party guests, John recalled sourly.

She gave a little speech and talked about Hector Barrantes, but John found the sentiments cloying: 'It was supposed to be a housewarming, not a wake. It was morbid to discuss something like that so openly.' Furthermore, he added, it was obvious to anyone there that she was treating Andrew with 'incredible guilt' — her constant references to her 'wonderful husband' were, in John's view, 'too over the top'. 'Everyone in the room knew she was with another man and that she was treating her husband like absolute shit, rubbing his nose in it.'

The partygoers drifted away after midnight, shaking their heads at the awkwardness of it all.

The next year, 1991, was a busy one. I had joined John on the board of Oceonics Deutschland and the company was expanding. We won project management business in Warsaw, Moscow, Spain and Portugal.

John's relationship with Geraldine, Lady Ogilvy was over and he drifted through a number of short-lived affairs. The relationship of the longest duration during this period was with Flora Fraser, daughter of the novelist and historian Lady Antonia Fraser. She was also a cousin of John's secretary,

Julia Delves Broughton, so it was all rather cosy and convenient.

Flora seemed more taken with John than he with her; at one point he explained apologetically to me that his 'sort of girlfriend' was going to join us for dinner in Frankfurt. By way of redress he added, 'but she paid her own way over here'. I found Flora to be probably the most intelligent and sensitive of his women. The relationship was therefore doomed.

There seems to have been little communication between the Duchess and John from the days of the Sunninghill housewarming until the end of 1991. By late autumn, however, it was becoming clear that, for a number of reasons, Steve Wyatt would have to return to America. His affair with the Duchess had reached such a pitch of intensity that they had convinced each other that she should divorce her husband and marry her lover. This astonishing development, after less than four years of marriage and with a baby of eight months, would have caused untold damage to the reputations of all concerned, yet it was only averted by accident.

Though a member of one of America's richest families, Steve himself had little money. His attempts to make it big in the oil business, in which his stepfather, Oscar Wyatt, was a colossus, had not been successful. In the summer of 1990, just before the Iraqi invasion of Kuwait which triggered the Gulf War, Sarah, at Steve's behest, had hosted a dinner party at Buckingham Palace for Dr Ramzi Salman, head of Iraqi oil sales. The incident created a furore when it became known, not least because Oscar Wyatt was a heavy purchaser of Iraqi crude and was at the time negotiating for a significant Iraqi investment in his own US-based refineries. London ceased to be as welcoming to Steve Wyatt as once it had been — and besides, he needed to make money if he was to realize his ambition of marrying the Duchess of York and of keeping her in the style to which she had become accustomed. He therefore resolved to return to America to make an independent fortune, a decision accelerated by a letter from the Inland Revenue.

As Wyatt prepared to leave for the States, the Duchess did something which, with hindsight, is open to more than one interpretation. She invited John to lunch at Le Caprice, a *bon ton* restaurant behind the Ritz Hotel in London.

The agenda was simple: she wanted to ask John his advice on her *Budgie* books. He, however, read much more into the event:

'We had a couple of glasses of wine and we were flirting madly, absolutely insanely — just giggling, laughing, flirting.' John's expertise in book publishing and associated matters was zero, and Sarah must have known it. After a few moments devoted to 'business' they talked about skiing, Christmas, mutual friends. The attraction was extremely strong, and yet John recalled: 'Steve and she had definite plans to get married, no question about it.' This, according to John, was the motivation for her to leave Andrew. Wyatt was desperately short of funds at the time, and Sarah knew that his stepfather had said that he would never give him a penny as long as he lived. 'So Steve was working towards making some money, but Sarah was paying most of his bills — she was supporting him in a big way.'

Wyatt had told Sarah that he would return from America once he had made his fortune, but in the meantime she was already feeling sorry for herself over being abandoned. John sensed as they talked over lunch that she felt neglected by everyone — by her husband, by the Palace, and now by Steve.

Although they made no plans to meet again they began to call each other on the telephone. From November to the first week of December they spoke often, and soon the calls developed a suggestive, then an erotic, tone as Sarah got into the habit of calling John from the bath: 'She would call me from the bathtub all the time, whenever she was in the bath she would call me . . . that is a pretty erotic thing when you are sitting in the bathtub.' Eventually John found he was getting 'pretty hot'; 'you know it was just very erotic stuff, you don't call a man from the bathtub if you are not ready to go to bed with him.'

During the Christmas holidays they were unable to speak frequently as John was in Vail staying in the ski-lodge of his stepmother, Josephine Abercrombie. The Duchess meanwhile had her last Christmas as a participating member of the royal festivities at Balmoral, then went skiing in Klosters. John sent her a Christmas gift from Vail, and they planned to meet again after the holidays.

By this time John was heavily fantasizing about the Duchess. His short-lived relationship with Flora Fraser was over, and in the vacuum left by her departure he relied on the services of various prostitutes; he visited Sudfuss, the poshest brothel in Frankfurt, and took a blonde and brunette off to bed.

In the first days of 1992 Steve Wyatt made his final departure plans. It was understood by all that his departure for America did not signify the end of his relationship with the Duchess, merely a strengthening of it. Once his fortune was made, he would return to claim his bride. On 12 January he and John met for a farewell lunch in London. By the 16th, John was being mentioned on the diary page of the London *Evening Standard* as a close friend of the Duchess: 'He may prove more dependable than Wyatt,' the piece commented, not entirely without irony. On 23 January, just eleven days after bidding farewell to his close friend, John Bryan took the Duchess of York to dinner at La Tante Claire. It was no coincidence that the restaurant was just a minute's walk from his flat in Cheyne Place.

To start with, the conversation centred on Steve. Both the Duchess and Wyatt had been extremely emotional at being parted, especially Steve; he was desperate to get married to Sarah, and for them to have a child. But after a couple of glasses of wine, the Duchess appeared to put the thought of her future husband behind her, and when John suggested retiring to his apartment across the road she readily agreed. They sat in the living room next to the piano and, John said later: 'I kind of grabbed her and she put her head on my shoulder, I had a couple of bottles of champagne, we were both getting drunk, and we'd had a wonderful dinner.' And then he gave her the first kiss. He was, he admitted, nervous — 'I mean she was married to Andrew and keeping that going.' He knew, too, all about her affair with Steve Wyatt, and yet 'here she was jumping into bed with me' not many days after Steve had left. To John, this seemed to be remarkably incautious. 'I couldn't believe that anyone behaved with such reckless abandon, and I guess reckless abandon is something that I am no stranger to. . . .'

Earlier that same day, Sarah had arrived back from a semiofficial visit to Florida. She flew into Britain in a maelstrom of bad publicity — and something worse; something far worse. The *Daily Mail* had broken the story about 120 photographs of Steve Wyatt, the Duchess and Princess Beatrice which had been taken while they were on holiday in Morocco. Overnight, a scandal of monumental proportions had erupted. One of the photographs showed Wyatt clutching a delighted Princess Beatrice in a rather fatherly way.

Lesley Player, who accompanied her, recalled Sarah vanishing, prior to the homeward flight, into a VIP suite at Miami airport and screaming 'like a banshee' at her father as he inadvertently interrupted her phone

51

calls. Finally the door of the VIP room opened. 'Holding her head high, but looking pale and biting her lip, Sarah emerged,' Lesley wrote. '[Her father] hastened over, put an arm around her shoulders — and then to our consternation and embarrassment she burst into tears. The two of them walked together through the departure hall, and I saw Sarah wipe her eyes with a wan smile and a shrug.' one of the calls, according to Lesley Player, had been to Prince Andrew, but 'the conversation with her husband had ended abruptly.' It is now clear that the words which signalled the breakdown of the Yorks' five-year marriage were spoken during that transatlantic telephone call. Andrew told her that a decision had been made to end the marriage; it was not his decision. Sarah's hysterical behaviour in the first-class compartment on the inbound 747 — throwing bread rolls and peanuts, cutting eyeholes in an airsick bag and wearing it on her head while making telephone noises — indicates the depth of her shock.

Steve Wyatt was slowly sliding out of the Duchess's reach, and she was on notice that her marriage was over. What she now urgently needed was an accomplice, someone to protect her against the storms and buffets ahead; someone — unlike her father — who was immune to the pressures Buckingham Palace can bring to bear. Who better than John Bryan, who was largely unmoved by what he called 'the royal stuff'? That night, frozen out of the royal family for her infidelity and — worse — her indiscretion, Sarah prepared to give herself to him, safe in the knowledge that however smart he thought he was, he was not as smart as she.

I am convinced that, to this day, John Bryan remains unaware of the Duchess's stratagem that night. The end of his reminiscence about their dinner together is nothing if not breathless: having kissed her, he found himself both surprised and disconcerted, wondering whether the Duchess knew right from wrong. He knew right from wrong, he said — then added, with breathtaking understatement, that he also knew that this was 'probably highly irregular'. 'I knew what the whole thing was leading to . . . it was obvious . . . then we were just trying to make our way to the bedroom as fast as we could both go.'

That night, their lovemaking was limited by the wish of the Duchess. She was to remain insistent on stopping just short of full intercourse out of what she felt was loyalty to Steve, and these limitations remained in effect until June of that year.

The weekend following I took John fox-hunting on Dartmoor. During the train journey back to London, he talked to me of his feelings for the Duchess. 'She is everything that I want for a wife, except she is a little older than I ideally would like,' he said, quite seriously. I pointed out that she was still a very married woman. 'Yeah, she is,' he said with a smile — as if that would soon be changed.

Chapter 3

Three weeks later, in late February 1992, John introduced me to the Duke and Duchess of York. After that night of passion in Cheyne Place his relationship with Sarah had moved swiftly into top gear, and by now he felt confident enough to introduce his new friends around.

With the furore over the Steve Wyatt holiday photographs still raging he began to feel that his grasp on Sarah was strengthening. The Duchess, in an ill-contrived exercise in damage limitation, spoke through her friend Pilar Boxford to a British newspaper, denying any impropriety with Wyatt: 'We were not intimate friends,' she lied. Pilar added that the Duchess was angry over the way the matter had been publicized: 'But she is dealing well with the situation. She has had a lot of bad publicity in the past but I am assured by her there are no grounds whatever in this case for the criticism she has endured.'

To the world at large, it looked as though the Steve Wyatt affair was no more than an injudicious friendship which had got slightly out of hand. If the highly tuned antennae of the London press's royal correspondents led them to suspect that the relationship was more than platonic, they did not dare say so. And however well-informed they were, or boasted they were, they had no inkling of Sarah's mad plan to run away with Wyatt and become his wife.

Now, suddenly, that plan was in limbo: Sarah was in London, Steve was in Washington, energetically renewing his bachelor lifestyle in the apartment which she had paid to decorate, and the glare of adverse publicity meant that it was unlikely they could ever meet again. John's moment had come, and he knew it.

That February he organized a dinner party at Annabel's, the exclusive Berkeley Square nightclub where royalty can drink and dance the night away unmolested by the attentions of the common herd. It was here, twenty years earlier, that Prince Charles had taken Camilla Parker Bowles in his arms for the first time; here, too, that other male members of the royal family have danced slowly with women not their wives.

John's idea was to introduce two powerful German bankers, Graf (Count) Krockow and Karl Otto Pohl, a former President of the Bundesbank, to the Duke and Duchess. Unfortunately, both men declined the invitation and John was left with the difficult proposition of either cancelling the dinner or replacing the guests. He opted for the second choice, and his older sister Pamela, known as Baby, and I were drafted in as substitutes. The Yorks invited Julia Dodd-Noble, an old friend of Sarah's, her husband Paddy, and an attractive blonde named Lizzie, who was there to distract the Duke.

I was dressing at my hotel when John called in a state of agitation to say that the dinner had been pushed forward an hour, and I was to leave straight away. As I arrived outside the entrance to Annabel's in Berkeley Square, a large black chauffeur-driven limousine pulled up and the Duchess stepped out, followed by the Duke. She was wearing a gold dress and heavy makeup, and looked very striking, if slightly exaggerated. It was the first time I had seen her in the flesh. The Duke, dressed in a dark suit, walked beside her, while passers-by and the doorman, recognizing the royal couple, seemed transfixed by them. These were still the days before their separation had been announced, and in this period 'Fergie' was everywhere, not just in the media, but on teacups, postcards, key chains, and almost every other kind of souvenir. She was, in short, instantly recognizable.

I let them go ahead of me, then walked into the cosy ambiance of Annabel's, where John was waiting for us with his sister hovering close by. The Duke, with no inkling of any undercurrents, walked up to his host and greeted him with a big smile and a jocular remark. John smiled in return, and turned to greet the Duchess. I was then introduced to them both, bowing as I had been instructed. We sat down and waited for the others to arrive. The Duchess sat next to me and said, 'So John dragged you kicking and screaming here tonight?'

'Yes, he did,' I replied, then, thinking that this probably sounded rude, added, 'but of course I really wanted to meet you, Ma'am.' There followed a slightly nervous period of rather stilted small talk.

Then, since all the guests had arrived by now, we entered the dining room and were shown to our table, which was not far from the dancefloor. The Duke sat at the far end, with the Duchess at the other end. John sat to her left, then Paddy Dodd-Noble, then Baby on the Duke's right. Julia Dodd-Noble sat to the right of the Duchess, with me next to her and Lizzie on my other side, on the Duke's left. The seating in all parties either organized by or for the Duchess is extremely significant: it is generally intricately planned and suggests the play that will unfold during the evening.

Tonight was no exception. The Duchess wanted information about John, and she thought that I would be a good source. She had placed Julia nearby in case she herself missed something I said, and to verify her own deductions. Baby and Lizzie were meant to serve as distractions for the Duke, both to entertain him and to prevent him from interfering with the other end of the table.

The strategy was a successful one, not least because the two girls made an artful job of oiling up to Prince Andrew.

With the apparent success of the distraction campaign, the Duchess was free to speak openly and to begin fulfilling her agenda. Shortly after we had taken our seats John, with a radiant smile, and the Duchess with shining eyes, bent their bodies as close to one another as possible and began whispering. Their extreme closeness actually prohibited their usual custom of playing footsie, and they had to make do with rubbing their calves together.

Finally the questioning began: 'So Allan, you have a really special friend here?'

'Yes, he is one of a kind,' I answered.

'Why is that? How come he is so successful?' she queried.

I had expected something like this when I had realized how insistent John was that I come: I knew that a woman like the Duchess would not be satisfied with a simple answer.

A week earlier, John and I had rented a large black BMW in order to travel to a business meeting. Although in no particular hurry, John had wanted to see how fast one could drive between Rostock and Hamburg. I decided to use this story to explain him to the Duchess.

'Ma'am, John is a big, black BMW with all his lights blazing. He is in the fast lane with his foot down on the gas and absolutely no intention of releasing it. Many cars will veer off to the slower lanes, but some will remain ahead of John, either by choice or because they are travelling too fast to down-shift into the slower traffic. He will push these cars faster and faster — faster than they ever intended to go, and far past where they intended to stop. You see, he does not lead his companies in a conventional sense, he pushes them to achieve more than they would if they tried to follow his lead.'

At the time I believed every word of it, and my sincerity was obvious. The Duchess's eyes shone moistly with delight and pride. It would be some years before we were to learn that the obverse of this metaphor was that

John, thrilled with the speed, had no idea of the direction in which he was travelling or that he was pushing the cars ahead of him until they all ran out of gas.

We interrupted our mutual admiration to dance. I had initially declined to dance with the Duchess after watching John twirl her around the dancefloor, but Julia insisted that I accept; after all, she said, 'It isn't every day that a Duchess asks you to dance.' After we left the floor an incident took place as she danced with John, in which a man danced over and attempted to stomp down on her foot. The royal bodyguards reacted immediately and the man was thrown out. Shortly afterwards, the royal couple departed, though most of the others stayed on. As I left, my last sight was of John and Baby dancing wildly, shaking their arms over their heads, two creatures trained their whole lives for just this type of event.

In the weeks that followed there remained an uneasy truce between the Duke and the Duchess of York, and their supporting factions. Their reactions to the as yet unannounced separation were different. The Duke remained at home at Sunninghill, apparently happy enough still to share a bedroom with Sarah. She, for her part, having secured my loyalty as her 'new best friend', started to make her dispositions. From the moment she had allowed herself to be seduced by John to the official announcement of her separation, made by Buckingham Palace on 18 March, there was a mere eight weeks. Much needed to be accomplished, and John was the man to do it.

Though the term was to become one of universal derision, at that time John was indeed Sarah's financial adviser. He saw ways to maximize profits from her *Budgie the Helicopter* books, and he set about the project with gusto. This enthusiasm met with approval from Andrew, naturally enough concerned at the cost of maintaining a semi-detached wife.

John now had unlimited access to Sarah at Sunninghill Park, and in the ensuing weeks he became a more or less permanent fixture there. Indeed, their friendship, notwithstanding Sarah's recent, and widely publicized, entanglement with another American, earned a degree of acceptance within the royal family.

During the ensuing months the happy couple travelled extensively together, making at least six trips abroad, and shared undisturbed intimate moments daily at Sunninghill Park. John even showed an uncharacteristic degree of faithfulness to the Duchess — in mid-March he told me that one of Andrew's former girlfriends had come on to him at a party, but that he had refrained from inviting her home because the Duchess was already waiting for him at Cheyne Place. That would not have deterred the John Bryan I had known until then. But he seemed satisfied, even though in some respects their sexual relationship remained incomplete.

The couple would spend all day together at Sunninghill, then drive into London to dine at their favourite haunt, La Tante Claire. 'It was intimate every time,' John recalled, 'I was in lust.' According to him, she had told him that she was getting divorced, and he believed that her plan at that stage was to divorce the Duke and marry Steve Wyatt, meanwhile enjoying an interim relationship with John Bryan.

However perplexing this was for John — and given the restrictions imposed upon their lovemaking, it should have struck him as a very odd basis for a relationship — nevertheless he ploughed on. On reflection it is clear that at this juncture Sarah was exercising a non-verbal form of control over him, drawing him in close to her without letting him gain the upper hand in the relationship. A psychiatrist would argue that although this was a way of making herself more attractive to a man, it had very little to do with sex: it was to do with power and control. To a lesser extent Sarah was now playing power-games with the other two men in her life as well — using John's closeness as a weapon to taunt the still-faithful but exiled Steve Wyatt, and showing her still-admiring husband that she was attractive to jet-setting figures like John and Steve. Over the years, her Machiavellian skills have received little credit, but here they could be seen in their true colours.

As much as anything, John became Sarah's father-confessor. For six years she had struggled against the sneers of the other royals and the Buckingham Palace hierarchy — 'Vulgar, vulgar, vulgar,' spat the Queen's former Private Secretary, Lord Charteris, in an off-guard moment — and the very real prospect of at last being freed of their influence allowed her to vent her anger and frustration at their snobbish airs. To them, she was simply the girl with a past who came up from the servants' quarters: Major Ronald Ferguson may have been useful at fixing up polo matches for Prince Charles, but it was absurd to think that a daughter of his could marry a prince!

Chief among Sarah's *bêtes noires* was Sir

Robert Fellowes, the Queen's Private Secretary and, although a cousin of hers, a ferocious critic; but she told John that she felt she was hated by all the Queen's children, though the Queen herself remained courteous. Prince Charles was ambivalent: Sarah had brightened when she heard that he had told his wife, 'Why can't you be more like Fergie?' but felt let down when she realized that Charles had probably said it more to hurt Diana than because he actually liked Sarah.

Although in most cases a husband on the point of separation from his wife would take unkindly to the presence of another man in their house, the Duke of York continued to warm to John. Sooner or later the talk would turn to divorce and Andrew — oblivious to the fact that after he packed up for the evening and went to bed, John and Sarah would enact their version of making love in his study — sought his rival's advice, and the two spent hours talking about the divorce.

Explanations as to what had gone wrong were something the Yorks both chose to avoid. The Queen wanted them to divorce quickly and was willing to offer them incentives: if her plan was to succeed, the couple would argue that, from Sarah's perspective, Andrew had neglected her as a result of his naval career, while from the Duke's, the separation would be on the grounds of her (unspecified) unacceptable behaviour. But Sarah did not want an open discussion as to the reasons for the failure of their marriage; and this in turn elongated the progress towards divorce, because the perfectly valid argument that Andrew had spent only forty-two nights at home in the first year was never deployed.

John recalled: 'Andrew felt that if he could let a lot of time go by maybe he could get back together with Sarah. He thought that time was on his side, when in fact it was against him. I told him he would have a much better relationship with his wife if he got it done now.'

John's advice included backdating the time they had been separated to speed the final divorce, but Andrew, who was caught between a rock and a hard place — his wife and the Queen — vacillated. John's 'philosophy' for Sarah, meanwhile, was for her to be seen 'leaving in an orderly way rather than the way she did it which was just get kicked out — what dignity is there in just getting thrown out?'

The arm-wrestling continued, but by early March of 1992 it was clear that an announcement would have to be made. Things did not go according to plan, however, for just as Buckingham Palace was gearing itself up to make public the fact that the marriage of the Duke and Duchess of York was over, the *Daily Mail* stole their thunder. Sarah, revealed the newspaper, was seeking an official separation from Andrew, and had approached lawyers for their advice.

The leak to the *Mail* caused untold fury at the Palace. Chaos ensued. On 19 March BBC Radio's royal correspondent, Paul Reynolds, and five other royal correspondents were summoned and given the official statement announcing the separation. In addition, the Queen's Press Secretary, Charles Anson, gave Reynolds a private five-minute briefing. The words he used so shocked Reynolds that he immediately went on air on the BBC's *World at One* news programme to declare: 'The knives are out for Fergie at the Palace.' He went on to report that the Palace believed that Sarah had ordered a PR firm to brief the *Mail*, and that in retaliation he had been told, in terms no Court official had ever used before, how unsuited the Duchess was to public life.

There had been no PR firm, and Anson was forced, through gritted teeth, to make a public apology. Now things were out in the open, John allowed a little light to fall on his own role as an honest broker in the affair. Or, to put it another way, he started briefing the press. Bursting with self-importance, he paid a visit to the London home of the *Daily Mirror*'s indefatigable royal correspondent, James Whitaker.

'At that time he was masquerading as merely a consultant to the Duchess,' Whitaker recorded in his book *Diana v Charles.*[*]

Cocky and determined, he maintained he was acting as a broker in the negotiations between the Queen's solicitors, Farrer's, and the Duchess of York's over the financial terms of the settlement. He described Farrer's and their senior partner Sir Matthew Farrer as 'a bunch of assholes' and he claimed to be playing a central role in the negotiations. 'They can't do a damned thing without me,' he bragged 'and the Queen has said I have got to be involved at every single level of negotiation. My word is final.'

Up to a point: in fact it was the Queen's word which ended the matter, but not before she had consulted her Lord Chamberlain and Private Secretary. Short of other candi-

[*]Signet, 1993

dates on whom to put the blame, the Princess of Wales was generally held to have been responsible for the press leak. Her competitiveness where Sarah was concerned, and the fact that she was known to hate the Duchess stealing newspaper column inches from her, made her the obvious culprit. Ironically, the feeling between the two wives of Windsor was mutual. According to John, Sarah was jealous of Diana, and when Charles said to his wife 'Why can't you be more like Fergie?' she took that right to heart. 'She said, yes, I should have been the one to marry him, and she got everyone in the household to say, yeah, yeah, and pretty soon Sarah was convinced that she was the one for Charles and that she should have ended up as Queen of fucking England.'

John recalled that such was this jealousy that whenever Diana made an appearance on television, or got good press coverage for some event she had attended, Sarah would actually burst into tears — 'she'd cry for two days'. Nor can it have helped that a national opinion poll at this time found that Sarah had done 'most damage to the RF' (royal family). At the other end of the scale, Diana topped the poll.

Life at Sunninghill, post-separation announcement, continued in its bizarre fashion, with John arriving most mornings. The Duke, a serving naval officer, was none the less at home for much of this period, and the two men maintained an uneasy rapport. Before he learned what was going on between his new friend and his wife, Andrew would occasionally produce a girlfriend for John; slowly, however, the realization dawned on him that when he went to bed, or retired to the distraction of his video player, he, the Queen's favourite son, was being cuckolded in his own house.

Chapter 4

With or without John Bryan's influence, an amicable settlement was arranged between the Yorks: a suitable home would be found for the Duchess, bank overdrafts of £300,000 would be secured, and no attempt would be made to separate her from her daughters. In return, she was to remain silent in the terms and conditions agreed, even though this meant turning down a multi-million-dollar offer from America to publish her personal account of life inside the royal family.

More directly, John assisted Sarah's future financial security — or so it seemed at the time — by securing a contract with a television production company called Sleepy Kids to turn her *Budgie* books into a cartoon series for television. With merchandising rights for Budgie toys and games, she could expect to make at least £2 million and possibly as much as £5 million. This one deal confirmed in Sarah's mind that John was a major player, a man who could deliver what he promised. It was their finest moment together.

In the middle of April 1992, largely to escape the hammering she was taking from the press, the Duchess planned a holiday in the South Seas. John had been told by a friend that the Indonesian island of Banda was a tropical paradise, so that became their chosen destination. With his usual inattention to detail, however, he had failed to discover that the local volcano had wiped out most of the paradise, leaving their hotel with no running water and the beach strewn with lava, an7d thus unusable.

In order to dupe the press, it was decided that the Duchess would travel without John as far as Thailand. Reinforcing this ruse, John told his circle of friends and his business acquaintances that he would be undergoing sensitive meetings with government officials in Rostock. He even tried to have his telephone calls and fax messages diverted so that they would be automatically transferred to his hotel; sadly, however, post-volcano Banda lacked the technical sophistication to effect this.

And so John disappeared to the South Seas, leaving a host of people looking for him in eastern Germany. John's father called me asking for his number in Rostock. Unconcerned by the international manhunt, John phoned me, and I told him of the growing number of people who suspected he was not where he claimed to be. 'Good,' he laughed, 'now jump on the first plane to Bali and get out here, man — it's great!' He handed the phone to the Duchess. 'Starkie,' she exclaimed. 'Come on, Starkie, money talks and bullshit walks!' I had no idea what this meant, but agreed to join them and bought a ticket. But before I could fly out, they were discovered — a tourist had recognized and photographed them, and a reporter from the *Daily Mail* had identified the people in the photographs. One showed John carrying Princess Beatrice on his shoulders, an early reminder of the Steve Wyatt photos, which were then still fresh in the public's memory.

John remains unabashed at the duplicity of it all. The false trail they laid took them from Thailand to Bali, and from Bali to Banda. Taking the precaution of ordering separate rooms, the couple enjoyed the full delights of a honeymoon, barring one thing — Sarah's restriction on full sexual intercourse was still in place. The civic leaders of the small island had promised that their famous guests would be left alone and that no special fuss would be made, but hosts of warring rowing boats thrashed through the water in front of them, their crews yelling and screaming, by way of greeting. The entire population, it seemed, was waiting for them at the airport, and a band of warriors performed a dance of welcome.

Sarah and John went scuba-diving, then took the little princesses off to neighbouring islands where the beaches still had sand. Accompanying them was Sarah's friend Julia Dodd-Noble, and after a few days the whole entourage returned to Bali for a further week before flying home.

John believed that Prince Andrew was 'heavily into denial', while the public still only knew part of the truth. 'John just denies flatly there was any kind of romance going on,' said his loyal friend and former flatmate Whitney Tower. 'He went to the Far East with her because he had certain connections there, and he was a go-between to convey her wishes to her husband. He called me a couple of times for public relations advice when the reporters were camped outside his house and it was really hitting the fan. I just said, "Be honest with them, the more you say, the more they're going to trip you up. I suggest coming out with something that isn't going to offend anybody." '

Back in Britain, meanwhile, there was mounting pressure for Sarah and the children to be found a new home. Finally a company called Expat Home Minders came up with a house which, in principle, seemed to meet most of the Duchess's needs. Called Romenda Lodge, it was situated in the distinctly unregal environs of the Wentworth Golf Club in Surrey, but it was reasonably close to Sunninghill Park and to Beatrice's school in Windsor.

Oceonics was called on to make an estimate of the work needed, and received the contract to carry it out. John was excited by this and promised that our firm would receive a 'By Royal Appointment' title — an impossibility, since royal warrants are only issued in the names of the Queen, Prince Philip, Prince Charles and the Queen Mother. Early in May we set up our first meeting on the project, John having called me in Frankfurt and asked me to meet him at a restaurant in Ascot on the following day. I was so disturbed by the lack of preparation, however, that I did not even try to get there; instead I came to London a day later and arranged a meeting whereby a fashionable architect friend of John's could meet Nina Campbell, who had been responsible for the decor at Sunninghill Park.

I made the architect promise that he would represent the interests of Oceonics, rather than his own, and that he would maintain proper confidentiality. In the event he did neither, and stories appeared in the press. I never spoke to him again. Nevertheless we refurbished the house to HRH's satisfaction, and Nina rented reproduction furniture in mahogany for the dining room, with a large desk and overstuffed chairs and sofas for the drawing room. The walls were hung with the Duchess's own watercolours, mostly landscapes, and a number of family photographs.

The result was cosy. As I drove through the gates to inspect the finished work I had a chance to assess the place. One passed through a gate in a black iron fence and down a long, tree-lined drive towards the house, the drive ending in a gravelled circle with a fountain in the centre. The house itself, mock-Tudor in style, was rectangular, with a façade of brick and exposed beams, and was built primarily on two floors, though there was a small attic apartment, which was to be used for the nanny. On the ground floor a hallway ran the length of the building, ending in French windows which opened on to the back garden. To the right of the hallway was the combined lounge and study, to the left was the dining room, with beyond it the nursery and, next to that, the kitchen. The top floor had six bedrooms and two bathrooms, while outside there was a swimming pool and pool house, as well as a small wooden children's house and swings. The entire property was fenced and patrolled by the Surrey Police, and Sarah moved in on 15 May.

On the night she moved out of Sunninghill Park, her possessions and the children's toys bundled up in two unmarked vans, the Duchess was taken out to dinner by her husband. But next morning it was John who was at Romenda Lodge to make sure she was settling in comfortably. She brought with her a nanny, Alison Wardley, and a maid borrowed from the royal labour-pool.

At Andrew's insistence she took their daughters up to Balmoral, where the whole family spent the weekend together as though the separation was just an everyday occurrence — something which was to characterize the Andrew-Sarah relationship all through her affair with John, and, today, continues to do so. But already Sarah's mind was filled with the prospect of a trip to Argentina with John, ostensibly to visit her mother, Susan Barrantes.

Susie was in financial difficulties, having run up debts amounting to millions of dollars, and John had offered to help sort out what he called 'the family disease'. Accompanied by a detective, he and the Duchess flew to Buenos Aires in June, then went on to the Barrantes family ranch, where John had the opportunity to try his hand at polo.

The Duchess described the ranch to me as 'erotic' and often told me stories of what life had been like during a six-month stay she had enjoyed there before her marriage, recalling nights spent in the open air, grilling a steer over a fire under the stars. Clearly the place held powerful romantic associations for her and, perhaps unsurprisingly, it was here that she finally allowed John to consummate the act of love. The limitation she had imposed thus far had been an indication of her continuing love for Steve Wyatt, and its lifting symbolized the shift in her priorities from Wyatt to Bryan. It had been just five months since Steve had left Britain, pledging eternal love and promising to return to make her his bride; five months since she had told him she would wait for him for as long as it took.

John and Sarah, now finally bonded, flew up to New York before heading for London, taking in Au Bar, in which John was a partner, and the stores of Fifth Avenue. Making an attempt at discretion, the Duchess stayed at the Carlyle Hotel while John lodged at the prestigious Union Club, where his name would one day be humiliatingly posted for unpaid subscriptions.

Two weeks later the couple were airborne again, flying to Paris for meetings with officials from the Banque IndoSuez. 'I am now in the final analysis of portfolios for the management of her money,' John importantly told the press. The two princesses joined them in France on the following day, and were rewarded with a trip to EuroDisney. John remembered: 'They opened the rides for us at night. They had a whole security force, but the Disney ones were better.' They stayed at the New York Hotel, close to the park, where they were given a huge suite — 'the kids had a great time, Disney brought all the characters up to their room. . . .'

It was not all family fun, however. On the night before the couple had spent the evening at the Ritz Club, where they drank champagne with their dinner and took to the dancefloor: they danced all night 'and had a great time — those were some of our best times. . . .' It was also, he remembered, 'all pretty dirty. . . . we were making out on the streets of Paris, just making out on the streets . . . then we realized, what if someone is watching? We were just crazy. . . .'

Next day, when cornered by the press, John had this to say: 'It is ridiculous to suggest we are having a romance. I know the Duke very well.'

Such was the success of the Paris trip — discounting the moment when a fellow British visitor to EuroDisney turned to the Duchess and asked caustically, 'Is this another freebie, Fergie?' (it was) — that Sarah decided she would throw a surprise birthday party there for John a couple of weeks later. She flew over a dozen guests including her private secretary, Jane Ambler; meanwhile John's sister, Baby, lured him to Paris on a false pretext and took him to L'Orangerie, where the rest of the guests were waiting to applaud the arrival of his thirty-eighth year. Later the party moved on to Castel's, the French capital's most glamorous nightclub — but 'We went to some club, God knows which,' was John's recollection of Sarah's minutely detailed plan for that night.

The Duchess and her American financial adviser were sighted in London a few nights later when they attended an Independence Day dinner at Mosimann's, the exclusive dining club in Belgravia. Fellow guests included Michael Caine, Jeremy Irons, Bob Geldof and their wives, and the retired US baseball star Keith Hernandez. As was the form when they were in Britain, John and Sarah arrived and departed separately.

In July, relishing the sense of fulfilment their deepening relationship brought, the happy couple took some friends for a cosy weekend in Scotland. The trip itself was unremarkable except for how it ended. Steve Wyatt, having managed to sort out his tangled tax problems, had returned to England, and was waiting for the Duchess in one of their 'safe houses'. Unbelievably, Sarah asked John to drive her from Scotland to Stratford-upon-Avon where Steve was waiting for her. Even more unbelievably, he agreed.

For John Bryan, this was the most testing moment in their six-month-old relationship. He was conscious of the continuing hold Wyatt had over the Duchess, and despite his brave words was extremely worried at the prospect of the two meeting up again. But the Duchess insisted, and together they motored south. As John remembered it, 'basically I told her to go back to him.' He told her also that he didn't care — 'Steve was the great love of her life and she was going to spend the day with him so I took her down there and dropped her at the house.'

He knew that Sarah either had to get over Wyatt, or marry him. That night she called John as she was leaving Stratford: she and Steve had danced and had dinner together, she said, before going on to tell John 'what she would constantly tell me every month after that, "I have finally got him out of my system." ' For his own reasons, however, John had been confident that Wyatt would be unable to have sex with the Duchess on this occasion, and so it proved. But he was appalled by Steve's treatment of her: 'He would go out with other women all the time and tell her how ugly she was and how fat she was and that she should go on a diet. He treated her the way she likes to be treated, which is like shit.'

Though the Steve Wyatt episode had passed in Sarah's life, John still remained in his shadow. He once complained to me of a lunch she had with Wyatt and the Duke of York in 1993 to which he was not invited: 'She told me I couldn't come, she made up a big lie why I couldn't.' A week or so later Nigel Dempster, the *Daily Mail*'s diarist, rang John to ask him about the lunch, and the fact that the press had reported it rankled with him.

The memory of this triggered in John his fundamental view of the woman who was to make him world famous: 'I was consistently lied to, she treated me as if I weren't smart enough to know that it was all lies — that's what bugged me more than anything else.' Her biggest mistake in life, he said, was not her 'appalling disrespect', but the fact that she always underestimated people's intelligence. She was the most transparent woman he had ever known: every journalist knew what she was doing because if she didn't tell them herself it was obvious anyway. She lied to the press constantly, and that was how she treated her whole life — she had no self-respect. He had repeatedly told her that she even underestimated the intelligence of her own children — she should just tell them the truth, and not lie to them all the time. 'I don't go around telling everybody how honest I am all the time because at times I am a little dis. . . . I am not honest all the time, but at least I am aware of it.'

Whatever his feelings now, at the time John was smitten by Sarah, by the life she led, and by the possibilities which both offered to him. Little did they know it, but the honeymoon was nearly over; it would take only one more holiday for their lives to be changed for ever.

There was to be one last moment of calm before the storm. John and Sarah flew to Italy, where they rented a car and drove to a friend's wedding. There, after the party, they drove on alone and in disguise to Marseilles where they spent a very romantic weekend.

It was to remain the fondest memory of

their time together, and in the horrifying days ahead they clung to the recollection of it as a drowning sailor clutches at a lifebelt.

Chapter 5

The Duchess of York's relationship with John Bryan falls into two halves: before and after the South of France. The pre-honeymoon period extended from January to June 1992; the honeymoon between the trip to Buenos Aires in June and the couple's ill-fated trip to St Tropez in August. After that, the relationship changed and continued to change, buffeted by circumstances and damaged by the conflicting ambitions each had for the other.

It was to be another four years before Sarah would be stripped of the rank and title of Her Royal Highness, but this epic act of monarchical exclusion, unprecedented in British history, has its roots in the decision she and John made to take a holiday — their sixth that year — in the South of France.

Even now, John's understanding of what happened is incomplete. He claims to be puzzled that anyone should have known that he and the Duchess were holidaying together, but by then I believe he had adopted the head-in-sand mentality which affects many of the royal family, as well as major celebrities the world over: I am wearing dark glasses, therefore I do not exist.

'I reserved this house at the very last minute, so there was no way anyone could know in advance — it was reserved on a Thursday and we arrived on the Sunday. I wanted to make sure there was no risk of anyone finding out,' he told me. What he did not know, but might have guessed, was that as his King Air private jet touched down at La Mole airport, near St Tropez, two local photographers, having been tipped off by police, were already in place waiting to take their pictures of 'La belle Fergie' as she stepped on to the tarmac. One of the Scotland Yard bodyguards who flew in with the couple came over to the photographers and told them to get lost. So, from the moment they arrived, Sarah and John were aware of a Press presence — indeed, the Duchess had even gone so far as to don headscarf and dark glasses — and in any event *Nice-Matin* printed the airport pictures next morning.

Sarah had had to report their whereabouts to Sir Robert Fellowes, the Queen's Private Secretary, because she had with her the two little princesses, fifth and sixth in line to the throne, to whom she constantly referred as 'my lifeline'. The Palace knew, therefore;

apart from that, though, they believed that their holiday plans were a complete secret — John had not even told his secretary, Julia Delves Broughton.

None the less, the couple's ability to deceive themselves over what happened, and why, continues to this day. Paranoia, a constant feature of their relationship in later days, had already come into play. 'Oddly enough, in this case there was one major difference,' recalled John. 'The bodyguards were requested not to get local backup.' Normally, for such a trip abroad an officer is sent in as an advance guard. He notifies the local police, who are asked to work on the perimeter, while the men from the Royalty and Diplomatic Protection Service do the close-in work. On this occasion, however, they were specifically asked not to get the support of the local police, and John was sure that this was on the orders of Buckingham Palace, and that it was a major violation of the normal protocols and procedures. 'Now why,' he asked me, 'would anyone do that? Because they knew that somebody was going to be there and they didn't want them to get caught.'

Such a conspiracy theory does not wash, however. There was no percentage to the House of Windsor in exposing itself to worldwide ridicule by the publication of photographs of one of its members caught *in flagrante delicto;* nor, in my estimation, are the people who work at Buckingham Palace subtle enough or Machiavellian enough to work out such a scenario. In addition, as the party made their way to the rented villa, they were followed by a motorcycle, and though the driver took evasive action to shake off his pursuer, it was pretty obvious where they were headed. They should have realized then they had been spotted.

Le Mas de Pignerolle, a pink-stuccoed farmhouse with a capacious swimming pool, set in the hills half a mile away from the road, looked secure enough to the Palace protection men, but they had reckoned without the careful planning of French photographer Daniel Angeli, known as the 'hitman's hitman'. 'They were using the biggest lenses, they had everything set up before we got there. Apparently they had actually come to the pool and measured where they would take the photographs from — they'd been there for days, scoping out the location and building a little fort,' recalled John.

Angeli and his associate went undetected as Sarah, John, and the little princesses began to relax and unwind. The five-bedroomed house was filled with laughter and excitement, and when the children were taken down to the beach at St Tropez John and Sarah would relax by the pool. 'We never did that [sex] outside,' John insisted. 'Though there could have been a few things that looked like it, like she had her hand up my bathing suit.'

At night the lovers would go into St Tropez 'in disguise', as John calls it: Sarah would put on sunglasses, put up her hair and wear a baseball cap. He seemed astonished when people still recognized them. Within hours the word was out that John — who, only weeks before, had been pictured holidaying in the South Seas with the Duchess — was with her under the same roof again. 'We knew the press were coming, but we thought we had gotten away with it.'

As a diversionary measure, John flew back to London, where he insisted to certain newspapermen that there was nothing going on between him and the Duchess, and that it was 'a Buckingham Palace smear campaign' which had started the rumours swirling. He hinted that, if he had been seen in France with Sarah, it was simply because he had dropped her off before flying on to Italy. Now he was back in London and Sarah was in France, so what was the problem? The Duchess, the girls, and the detectives had indeed stayed behind, soaking up as much sun as they could — for the next port of call was Balmoral Castle, with its endless days of rain and mists.

Still the couple had no inkling of what was about to happen. But as Sarah was flying north to Scotland, the *Daily Mirror*'s James Whitaker was flying south, from London to Paris. There he inspected the results of Daniel Angeli's sojourn in his hillside fort: eighty shots of the Duchess, John and the children by the pool. The pictures were explosive, though not for the reason the photo agency thought — the Duchess was topless, a world scoop, they claimed — but as Whitaker inspected the photographs, he saw their true significance.

For there, in the frame with the Duchess, was the man who, weeks earlier, had stood in Whitaker's drawing room vehemently denying an intimate relationship with her. The pictures depicted him kissing her, caressing her, lying on top of her and — most famously — sucking her toes.

This is the part John Bryan hates most. For in the ridicule that has been heaped on him since his association with Sarah began, two phrases come back to haunt him. 'Financial adviser' now has an awful ring to it; and 'toe-sucker' sounds horribly comical to him. 'I wasn't sucking her toes,' he growled. 'I was licking them.'

Whatever the nature of those attentions, however, it was enough for Whitaker. Within days, fifty-five of the photographs had been published in his newspaper, creating a world-wide sensation. The reaction in Britain was one of amazement and disbelief, for John had convinced everyone that his relationship with Sarah was perfectly proper. Now the couple's deception was exposed, ignominiously, for all to see.

This was not before John had attempted some deft footwork to get the publication of the pictures banned. He received a call from a journalist, Stuart Higgins of the *Sun* (of which he was later to become editor), who told him about the photographs. 'It made my heart stop in a way, but I wasn't aware of the implications. I said "So what?" — I thought how bad could they really be? But then he told me that some were topless, and others were of us together.'

Higgins's call was not altogether altruistic. His newspaper's main rival had the pictures, and he was trying to encourage John to seek an injunction to have publication stopped: since the *Sun* could not have them, why should the *Mirror*? Through the lawyer, Peter Carter-Ruck, John did try to get an injunction, but the bid failed in Britain, though he did have the small consolation of stopping publication in France, where privacy laws are stricter. He rang Sarah in Balmoral and told her there was good news and bad news. The bad news, he said, was that there were photographs from the South of France — according to him, she knew at once what that meant, and was 'really scared shitless'. He continued: 'And the good news is that I have lawyers on it and I think they can get an injunction, they have already got one in France. It looked like we were doing reasonably well.'

Once he had lost his bid to get an injunction in Britain, John gave an interview to Sky-TV News: 'All the reporters were there, hundreds of them. I gave a big statement about the Press Complaints Commission, about Lord McGregor's rulings and everything else I could think of. I wish I still had a copy of that speech, it was one of my greatest speeches.'

Though not statesmanlike, it did have a certain gravitas:

There is no doubt that my privacy and that of the Duchess of York has been grossly infringed by Mr Angeli, when he took the photographs, and by the publication of them in the media. Although the law in many jurisdictions protects the privacy of individuals, no such protection is available in England. This case provides a clear illustration of how distressing the consequences of this gap can be for those individuals whom the press persistently follow without regard to any consideration of legitimate public interest.

But no words could hide the facts: John had been caught with his trousers well and truly down. He made it his duty to contact the Duke of York to warn him of the impending disaster and to apologize. 'He was a real gentleman. He really is a good guy.'

The *Daily Mirror* duly appeared on Thursday 20 August, blazoning its picture scoop with the headline 'FERGIE'S STOLEN KISSES: Truth About the Duchess and the Texan Millionaire'. The captions dealt the death-blows: 'Poolside embrace: Arms entwined, Fergie and Bryan kiss and cuddle on a sun lounger at their holiday retreat.' 'Topless in Tropez: Fergie peels off for a session by the pool with her Texan pal.' 'Loving touch: Bryan kisses Fergie as she dresses daughter Eugenie after a session at the pool. Princess Beatrice looks on.' The night before

John had been shown a preview copy. The only utterance that came to his lips was 'Holy shit!' — he remained otherwise speechless, for the pictures were far, far worse than he had anticipated. Their publication created a national scandal, with copies of the 27p newspaper changing hands in Covent Garden for up to £2. Over four days the *Mirror* put on extra sales of nearly 2 million.

At Balmoral, the tension was unbearable. On the morning of publication Sarah came down to breakfast, to find all the newspapers laid out on a table in front of the Queen's plate. One of the servants present that morning remembers Sarah's reaction — not one of guilt, but of anger. 'She acted in the strangest way — you would have thought she was the person who had been wronged, as if she had every right to go on holiday with another man, kiss and cuddle him, and the only people who had behaved wrongly were the photographer and the editors of the newspapers who had published the pictures.'

As for her husband, one report suggested that he believed Sarah had been set up — John's influence here, undoubtedly.

In their wide-ranging book *Fergie Confidential*,[*] authors Chris Hutchins and Peter

[*]Pocket Books, 1996.

Thompson suggest that Andrew's theory may have had its roots in a bizarre Palace plot to have Sarah declared insane:

The Queen was asked to consider a suggestion that Sarah should be said to have suffered a nervous breakdown. The abnormalities of her earlier life combined with the stresses of joining the Royal Family had resulted in a severe disturbance, it would be said. Prince Andrew was told of the plan, which would make it clear that, due to illness, his wife had not been responsible for her actions for some considerable time. The plan then was to transfer Sarah to a suitable centre for 'treatment' and after a respectable period of time to restore her to the royal fold. Widespread irritation at her behaviour would thus, it was reasoned, have been replaced by public sympathy for high stress, a recognizable twentieth-century malaise that most families in the land could identify with, while many celebrities would have happily agreed, 'She is one of us'.

If there was indeed such a plan (which the Duchess truly believed, as is confirmed by the memoirs of the psychic Vasso Kortesis, whom she often consulted) then the Queen refused to buy it, and Sarah made her sorry way south, finally cast out from the royal fold. 'She was planning to leave at that time anyway,' said John manfully, 'because her children were meant to be doing something. There was nothing to say.'

Grim-faced, she returned to Romenda Lodge, the very antithesis of Balmoral's aristocratic grandeur. The public fascination for this latest scandal had not diminished. There was a riot at Heathrow airport because the crowds spotted a bald man and thought it was John. Small marble carvings of toes sold like hot cakes in Covent Garden, and some American opportunists produced candies in the shape of toes. Psychiatrists were interviewed on TV about the erogenous zones in the foot. It was a crazy period: on the second day, I turned on CNN and my screen filled with a shot of the telephone-box-red door at Cheyne Place. 'He is still in there. It's been 48 hours now,' intoned the journalist as if he were reporting a hostage crisis — which, in a way, he was. At one point, the TV showed John running out of the apartment, phone in hand, and as I watched my own telephone rang and I found myself speaking to him.

By 24 August it had become clear that the

only way I could get to see him would by lifting the siege of Cheyne Place. I elbowed my way through fifty or so reporters and technicians and through a forest of satellite antennae until I reached the door. Deciding to have lunch together, we climbed up on to the roof and then jumped from building to building in the hope of finding a convenient fire escape. In this manner we tried to discuss opening a new branch office for Oceonics Deutschland GmbH in Berlin.

John was very concerned for the Duchess, and especially because she blamed herself for what had happened. 'She is a rape victim, you know how rape victims are. If only they had not worn that dress, if only they had not walked down that dark street. . . .' But in a strange way the assaults of the media seemed to bring them closer together. It was Sarah and John *contra mundum*.

As for John, he was suddenly and improbably famous. Several years before, a mutual friend said of him 'His greatest motivation is fame'; if that were so, his dream had come true. He donned the cloak of celebrity as if it had been made by his Savile Row tailor. He loved to talk about how George Bush, during a briefing on Anglo-American relations, looked at clippings of John and sighed, 'Oh, not Tony Bryan's boy'. (It emerged that

Tony had accompanied Bush, then a diplomat, on his early trips to China with Nixon and Kissinger. During this time, Tony played tennis with Bush, to the resounding applause of tiny Chinese onlookers.) There were other advantages too: he had been generally successful with women, but after the South of France he became the undisputed god of love. Blonde heads swivelled wherever he went, men deferred to his quite palpable prowess. Although at this moment no one — not Sarah, not John, not I — knew what the future held, of the three of us, he at least was enjoying himself enormously.

One question remained unanswered: had the tip-off to the photographers been a part of a diabolical plan by Palace courtiers to discredit the already marginalized Duchess? Since, as I have said, and with the benefit of hindsight, that seems an impossibility, one then has to ask, who had the most to gain? While John Bryan lamented the 'awful publicity', his lawyer pointed out that 'This is all very good for [him], it shows he is good with the ladies, and that he has powerful friends.' Just how many people had actually been told of the couple's holiday plans? And who were they?

Once the initial shock had subsided, the

Duchess picked up the threads of her life. She had made a commitment to the publishers Weidenfeld and Nicolson for a book, which she would ostensibly research and write, about the travels of Queen Victoria. In early October, just six weeks after the South of France pictures had first appeared, she was ready to begin her research trips. It is at this point that my involvement with this story properly begins. John, now 'Prisoner of Romenda', to which he had fled from Cheyne Place, was, obviously, unable to accompany Sarah as she made her way across Europe, and asked me to take his place.

I agreed, and embarked upon a series of trips that would result in my forging an intimate relationship with the Duchess.

An extract from my diary of the trip gives some idea of what it was like to travel across Europe with the Duchess of York:

Day 1

Finally, to our great relief, she descended the escalator to the luggage claim. Yes, it was she, a little nervous perhaps, but here. She introduced me to Jane Dunn-Butler [her dresser], after the introductions to Anna [my secretary] and Ahmed [a Turk who worked as a foreman for Oceonics, and whom I had converted to driver] were made we waited by the luggage carousel until the modern stainless conveyor spewed out antique Louis Vuitton cases from 'the golden age of travel', as Vuitton would put it. They seemed incongruous reminders of the past as they emerged, surrounded by their plastic and canvas counterparts from our disposable world. Each bore a number, reminding one that once upon a time great ladies travelled with such numerous articles of clothing that the cases needed to be numbered to facilitate periodic inventory and accessibility.

We drove off toward Coburg. Four bodies in the car, but five people travelling together. (I mean John, both in spirit — as we talked about him a lot — and in reality — as HRH called him very often from the car phone.)

The moment we joined the autobahn that grey Sunday morning [18 October] the spirits of the Duchess began to lift. She felt free and safe. The movement had begun, the journey had started. That car was to become our refuge as we propelled ourselves through time, space and understanding.

Awaiting us at Coburg were Benita Stoney, the Duchess's co-author, Robin Matthews, our personal photographer, and Steph Hornet, his assistant. Now began our round of visiting castles with which Queen Victoria had been associated, the aim being to photograph the Duchess in each of these, usually in a setting connected in some way with Victoria. The three days proved to be a series of journeys from schloss to schloss, broken by photo-sessions, meals and nights in hotels. Sometimes there were problems; at one castle, for instance:

Despite an argument with the tourists who, in textbook German fashion, had decided that the rather dull carriage and sled museum had become considerably more desirable when closed to the public — the shoot went all right. I believed it could have been more imaginative. A picture of the Duchess standing by a sled is hardly something that brings to life Schloss Vestie and its importance to Queen Victoria.

At Ehrenburg, however, everything seemed to work much better:

As Robin and Steph set up, the Duchess aided by Jane and Anna changed clothes in Victoria's freezing chambers. I played my entire repertoire of four songs on a palisander wood piano commissioned by [Prince] Albert (as I began to play 'Greensleeves' the Duchess's sweet voice joined in, filling me with warmth).

The Duchess emerged in a stunning green velvet dress with a lovely green jacket. Robin asked her to stand in front of the red velvet sofa, under the golden Coburg crest. Her vital, sensual elegance, clad in deep green velvet, magnified and radiated through the faceted stone at her throat (a gift from John), seemed to revive that dead room. She sat regally on a piece of furniture that was a relic of a forgotten age, and almost magically she reanimated it.

We stayed in Ehrenburg that night, and I finally had the chance to talk to Sarah *à deux*. What I wrote in my diary that night, therefore, were my first impressions of her as we became better acquainted.

Upon returning to the hotel we ordered tea and planned to meet at 7.30 for drinks then dinner. The Duchess asked me to come down a little earlier. . . . [She] was waiting for me in a small booth, wearing a tight black sweater. I sat down next to her and we ordered our first drinks together. I looked into her eyes: blue-grey and very expressive. She has a way of fixing them on you that is attentive, trusting, and somehow vulnerable. When she is amused she will squint, almost closing her sparkling eyes, and wrinkle her freckled nose. Then she will let out a deep, seductive, short burst of laughter. At the end of such a performance who would not be hooked?

She began by thanking me, then started to talk about John. She loved him but was unsure about a number of things; she wanted to know if I would help her. In order to receive information she began by offering me some: 'You know that JB thinks the world of you?' I told her that we had a close relationship but that with John, close relationships do not last too long and often turn to hate. . . . As I finished the sentence I was shocked by the intimacy of the confession. . . . The Duchess has an unusual gift: in an incredibly short period of time she can win almost anyone's trust. She has a way of taking you into her confidence in a manner that suggests that she has never trusted anyone before, but can intuitively tell that you alone deserve to be. She then imparts confidences and secrets that seal the promise of trust that she has offered like a signature in blood. Those pleading eyes defy you ever to betray her, yet despite the intimacy of such a ritual the Duchess manages to remain somehow distant. She has not lowered herself to pledge brotherhood to you, she has elevated you by her recognition of your worth. Yet she has elevated you to a height where you can more easily serve her without ever being her equal. This preternatural gift is the Duchess's greatest asset and most terrible curse, for she is not able to sustain it for long periods.

The second day brought us to the castle that Queen Victoria called 'Dearest Rosenau', and here friction began to set in among our little group. I noted that 'By the end of the morning I began to realize that what appeared to be a coldness on the part of the Duchess was attributable to an incident involving Benita, one which put their relationship into question.' Benita, an accomplished historian, had mentioned that she was to start work on another book about Victoria. She obviously did not intend to invite the Duchess to co-author it, and through family connections, already had access to the Royal Archives at Windsor. The Duchess felt that she was helping towards Benita being accepted as a Victorian scholar, only to see her go off without even the courtesy of an invitation to join her in her next project. The Duchess had heard of this early that morning, and she was angry. Not knowing what had caused the coldness in her manner, I had called John from the car to ask him what he thought. He was sure she was not angry with me and said just be polite to her and she will come out of the mood. As a result I asked Benita to drive with Robin and replaced her with Anna, reuniting our team and offering the Duchess an opportunity for uninhibited communication with John, as we drove on to Boppard.

The mood in the car was subdued, the Duchess having been very hurt and her vulnerability was plain to see. We spoke of this, and of the need for an emotional regrouping and a definition of future direction. 'Those people [whom we had seen at another castle] were so nice to me' she said in a surprised voice. . . . 'Is it because of me or my title?' I answered that as they had never met her before she walked in, we must assume that their immediate warmth was very possibly a result of who she was. 'And what happens when I no longer have that?' I said something along the lines that people would still love her without a title, and she flared up, saying, 'I will never lose that. I will always be a Princess of the British Empire.'

The third and last day proved to be the best, both in terms of the castles we saw and the magnificence of their settings, and in terms of mood, so that our last dinner together that night was festive. The next day we dropped in on a castle in Cologne that Queen Victoria had visited, but by now our first trip was over and the Duchess was eager to get back to England. We drove to the airport and said our first goodbyes, each of us believing that we had made a new best friend in the other. When I got home I was greeted by the first of many messages from the Duchess on my answering machine. She wanted to thank me, to tell me I was completely wonderful, to ask why I wasn't there to bug her. As so often, the message was larded with jokes and breathless asides, interspersed with the odd obscenity. Next day, a box of conkers was delivered to my apartment, a reminder of my introduction to this very English game during our trip.

Chapter 6

The car stopped at the black iron fence and the driver pressed the buzzer. 'Mr Starkie has arrived,' he announced tersely. The electric gates slowly swung open and two guards motioned us in. Lurking behind the tall trees which lined the driveway were more guards, walkie-talkies in hand, silently looking on. We pulled up at the house and climbed out of the car. The Duchess herself opened the large wooden door to Romenda Lodge and smiled and hugged me, 'Oh Starkie, I am so glad you could come. Come in, I have a little surprise for you.' She escorted me into her study, which also served as a lounge and was dominated by a large desk against the window at the far end of the room. The desk was cluttered with hundreds of little things: pictures of Prince Andrew, decorated enamelled boxes, and miniatures in frames. In the centre of one wall the huge hearth, its chimney blocked off, formed an alcove in which the Duchess had placed the sofa. Above the sofa hung a large photo from our German trip of my driver, Ahmed, carrying the large Louis Vuitton cases while HRH leaned against a wall near by. The coffee table had an upholstered top which was cluttered with magazines, mostly with her picture on the cover. Several overstuffed chairs added a comfortable touch to a room that had a very cosy feeling.

John strolled in, greeted me, then sat down. 'OK boys, we're going to have a treasure hunt,' announced the Duchess with glee. 'You take turns looking around for your goodies and I'll say when you're getting warm.' After about half an hour of playing this game we had uncovered the numerous Hermès ties, toiletries, and other gifts she had hidden in the room. She can be extremely generous, and something more, creative in her generosity. The manner in which she gave us these things was unforgettable; indeed, one sensed the pleasure she got out of the planning and giving of presents. It was also a fairly simple way of winning affection.

Next I was introduced to her daughters. They were very young then, Eugenie only two and a half and Beatrice four, but their characters were already strongly developed. Before we began our meeting the Duchess had to drop Beatrice off with a friend, and I was left alone to watch *The King and I* with Eugenie. Later, when it was time to pick up Beatrice, the Duchess decided to take

Eugenie with her, and I pretended to look sad at the thought of losing her company. She noticed my face and said, 'Don't cry, you silly man, I will be back soon.' I was enchanted — and little wonder, for they are delightful children.

Finally the time came for our meeting. I handed out an agenda that I had prepared, and we sat down in the dining room, a long room with a large mahogany table in the centre, and a sideboard usually overflowing with food. The room was decorated then with several of the Duchess's watercolours, and a large cherry tree made of silver, with rubies as cherries, stood on the table. During the weeks prior to the South of France pictures the Duchess and John had developed a code for speaking about personal feelings during business meetings. 'Cherry trees' was the code for 'I love you', and this personal secret was immortalized in small statues and large cufflinks.

The Duchess sat at the head of the dining room table, with John to her right and me to her left. 'Before we begin I have a question,' she said. 'Allan, why are you doing this? What do you want out of this?' I answered, 'I would like to help you.' 'Why?' she persisted. It was a good question. 'Because I like you, and he loves you,' I answered, pointing to John. She seemed satisfied by this, and we started.

These meetings were, in theory, at least, to be a combination of business development discussions to plan and execute specific projects, strategic planning to decide on the direction the Duchess should take with her commercial projects and charity work, and very personal discussions over the relationship between the Duchess and John. Actually all these matters were so tied to one another that, in a sense, the agenda was very small. Implicit in almost every discussion was John's sometimes hidden, and often very open, question, 'When will you legitimitize our relationship?'

I had dubbed these conferences 'Fireside Chats', after President Roosevelt's radio broadcasts to the United States from 1933, in which he discussed topics of national interest and importance. These broadcasts had helped to calm the frightened American public during the Great Depression, and by the same token I hoped that we would be able to keep our meetings calm and constructive. I was, of course, wrong. The first topic of the very first meeting was how to create a future business strategy for the Duchess. There were hundreds of opportunities available to her that might have generated millions of pounds very quickly.

In October of 1992 the Duchess's overdraft was very small, and it was our belief that the divorce would take place the following spring, and that this would bring her a modest settlement which at least would repay her debts. This was, then, a good time to be picky about the type of business she wished to pursue. She was concerned not to profit from ventures that seemed unfitting to her rank, or ones that would discredit the royal family, and at that time she refused to accept many lucrative deals for these reasons, from playing Queen Boadicea with Peter O'Toole to modelling designer jeans for $1 million. In that first meeting, therefore, we decided to create a set of criteria by which we could sort through the various opportunities and select the most appropriate, without violating her sense of what was acceptable. We developed the following list as a yardstick:

1. Image enhancement/no loss of mystique
2. International
3. Dutiful
4. Honest/ethical
5. Helpful to social needs
6. Community help

This list was to be used until at least the beginning of 1995 in order to evaluate possible projects. We decided to test it on the two projects we had been discussing at this time. The Duchess had been asked to consider writing or sponsoring a book to help the Welsh coalminers, many of whose pits were about to be shut down. She was seriously considering the idea until we applied the criteria list to it, at which point she declined the project on the grounds that it failed in both categories 1 and 2.

Angels International, a children's charity, had asked her to give her name to a book to which the world's leading photographers would each contribute a photo of a child. The book would be without text and the funds would go to Angels. The Duchess applied her new litmus-test to this project and agreed that it fitted. As a result, I met several publishers in New York and London to determine if there was interest in the venture. They declined, however, and the proposal died.

We next discussed whether HRH should agree to do an interview with Maria Shriver, wife of Arnold Schwarzenegger and niece of President John F. Kennedy, for her show on American TV. The Duchess was against the idea, but John, with his usual persistence, convinced her that she could generate an additional $250,000 from the American sales of *Travels with Queen Victoria*. (Actually, the book was never released in America, but he was always very good at generating convincing statistics.) She finally agreed, after they had decided that the interview would begin with the Duchess saying, 'As you know, Maria, I have agreed to do this interview in return for your station donating $30,000 to brain-damaged children.' It was also agreed that she would not specify British children, in order not to alienate her American audience. This was to be my first exposure to the clever use of charity work as a means of providing a shield of respectability for almost any enterprise.

The Duchess had insisted on keeping an office at Buckingham Palace but now wanted a commercial one as well. John and she had decided to rent offices together, and we made a list of what they both required, deciding as a result to seek a complex of about 2,500 square feet with a private lift leading directly up to it. The Duchess wanted a room to store her wardrobe, which at the time was still at the Palace, and ideally a small apartment adjacent where she could dress. The complex was to be split in half by a joint reception area and a conference room. John and I had hired an in-house lawyer, a Texan named Jim Hughes, whose time was split between Oceonics and the Duchess, and we agreed that he would be given the task of locating the ideal office.

Finally, we discussed the strategic planning — that is, the Duchess's long-term aims — and she came up with the following list:

1. Healthcare/charity fundraising
2. Preventive research
3. Community recreation
4. Re-education through children's books
5. Arts

With the formal part of the meeting over, we turned to other plans. John and I had planned to go to a language school in Germany in January, and we now asked the Duchess to come along. She decided, however, against being seen abroad with John so soon after the St Tropez photos. 'So let's just be careful,' she said, 'it's only five months until I am completely free.'

When the Fireside Chat ended we were served dinner in the same room, during which Sarah began telling me how horrible things had been for her lately. She then did something odd, something which I was to see quite often later: she began to give me unsolicited information about the royal family. I believe that when she felt insecure she considered that this was her surest defence. She told me that the Queen had really pressed her to come to Balmoral for Christmas, even though she would not be allowed to stay in the castle with the rest of the family; she was to spend the time in a small farm near by. As the evening wore on and we got drunker she told me that Lord Mountbatten had had a crush on her mother, and had enjoyed watching Susie bloody the sides of her horse with heavy spurs. This, as it happened, coincided with a story I had been told about Mountbatten, who kept a photograph of the Queen in his study — the picture showed her spurring a horse.

Our first Fireside Chat had been a long and tiring experience, and I finally, and gratefully, drove off to bed in the early hours of the morning. As I left, I handed the Duchess a copy of my diary from our travels around Germany together. She promised to read it the next day.

A little over a week after the Fireside Chat I accompanied the Duchess on the second leg of our research trips together. I was surprised to realize that she had not called me once during the intervening week: a curious avoidance on a business level, but stranger still on a personal one. She had tried so desperately hard to win my friendship with her long talks, intimate confessions, and gifts. It seemed odd that now, when she seemed confident that she had that friendship, she would not want more frequent contact. I mentioned this to John. 'She got frightened,' was his answer. 'She has been constantly criticized for being so friendly; for instance, greeting all the servants in the Palace by their first names.'

That second trip in early November of 1992 was to Italy and France, where Queen Victoria had travelled regularly. My secretary and I arrived early at Milan airport and met HRH and Jane Dunn-Butler at the baggage recovery area. Sarah announced that she had read my diary entries from the last trip and wished to include them in the book verbatim. She also said 'Rostock is a done deal — your brother wanted me to tell you, isn't it wonderful? Call him right now.' Having known him for three years, however, I had learned to translate John's use of superlatives; 'a done deal' generally means that the project is 'being seriously considered'. In this case, even that translation would have been too optimistic. The Bryans' massive ego and negligible patience could not tolerate the slow process of building up Oceonics; instead, they required something large and impressive in their corporate quest for self-definition. An ageing diplomat named Dr Franz Josef Bach, whom John liked to believe had been Konrad Adenauer's Chief of Cabinet (there had been no such position), brought us the possibility of redeveloping the antiquated University Clinic of Rostock, in the East German province of Mecklenburg Vorpommern, prior to the reunification of Germany. The project required an investment of DM 800 million and complex co-ordination with local and federal politicians, lobbyists and institutions. Although destined to drain the frail resources of Oceonics, it nevertheless offered the Two Bryans endless material for impressive discussions at dinner parties. As a result, the deal became Oceonics' Holy Grail, and in the end remained the bankrupt company's unfulfilled dream.

We were expected by the other members of the research team, so I rented a car and drove through the fog to Lake Maggiore where, in the dining room of our hotel, we met up with Benita Stoney, Robin Matthews and Stephanie Hornet. After dinner we went bowling in the hotel's alley — Benita painted caricatures of Queen Victoria on the steamed-up hotel windows. During the days between the first two research trips I had worked on developing a new clinic in Moscow for Tony Bryan, and while in Russia I had bought a sixteenth-century bronze icon which I had decided to give the Duchess. Before she went to bed I crept in to her room to place the gift under her pillow, and was surprised to see a large picture of Prince Andrew on her night table. Some time afterwards I realized that she always brought this picture, later augmenting it with pictures of her daughters.

We spent the next morning at the Villa Klara, now the home of the Count and Countess Branca, who produce the Fernet Branca liqueur. After tea and small talk with the family we quickly shot the pictures, and were getting ready to leave when we were told that the Brancas had invited a large number of friends to a lunch party in order to meet the Duchess. We had planned on driving through the South of France until we found a hotel that we liked, and we were looking forward to starting our journey. Sarah pulled me aside and said, 'Make some kind of excuse, but get me out of here.' I returned to the Brancas and explained that we would be happy to have lunch, but must leave at two o'clock because of an important meeting we could not cancel. Still the Duchess did not seem pleased, so I asked Jane if anything else was wrong. 'Well yes, she loves being with you, Allan, she really does, and when it is just the three of us she is very happy, but she is a little upset with your secretary, Anna, after what happened this morning.' At breakfast Anna had complained to the waiter that her three-minute eggs were too runny, and I had offered to eat them. The Duchess was annoyed about the exchange between Anna and the waiter, and wondered who Anna thought she was in the first place. In the end, however, it was decided that Anna, despite this grave incident, might still accompany us.

We left our hotel in the late afternoon and headed straight for Nice. I drove with HRH, who generally navigated, in the front seat beside me, both of us mentally switched off. Jane Dunn-Butler and Anna slept quietly on the back seat and the Duchess really let loose: 'Tell me, Allan, what does John live on? Does he take a big salary from Oceonics?' I explained to her that he took expenses but no salary. 'Why, he should take a whopping salary, will you tell him to?' I told her I understood that John did not need a salary, and this pleased her. I guess she could tell what I was thinking, for after a few seconds' silence she added, 'You know I have two children to support, Starkie?' She then began to speak for the first time about her feelings for Steve Wyatt. 'It is complicated, he is almost out of my system but I can't help thinking about him. I called him last week and do you know what he said? He said that he was watching a football game and I should call back when it was over. Well, I didn't leave [Prince Andrew] because of him, I left because of the system. It was the honest, ethical thing to do.'

It was late and we were exhausted by the time we crossed the French border. We had switched over driving duties a couple of times and now the Duchess was navigating. She led me on a detour up a steep cliff, from where we could see the lights of Monte Carlo. (Later she found out that when Queen Victoria's coach had made this journey she too had made a similar detour and found herself looking down from the same place. Victoria also described the local trees as resembling umbrellas, just as the Duchess did, quite independently, in her own diaries. It was such incidents that would foster her growing belief that she was perhaps the reincarnation of Queen Victoria, though in time she replaced this theory with a belief that Beatrice was actually the true incarnation of the great Queen.)

We considered driving down into Monte

Carlo and having some fun, but decided it would be too risky: we had no reservations, and soon discovered that all the hotels in the area were booked. By chance, however, we ended up at the Hotel Bellevue in Cap Ferrat, where the Duchess felt the presence of Queen Victoria to be very strong. We decided to take the cheapest rooms, but when the staff recognized HRH they insisted on putting her in a suite, something which she could hardly refuse. After we had checked in, the Duchess went off to call John, and came back to tell me that he had said, 'Stay wherever you like: I'll buy you the hotel.'

That night, Sarah and I had our first real argument. During dinner she began to tell me all the things she was changing in John. It is true that she had already greatly influenced the way he dressed. Always well turned out, he and his father had long visited the same Savile Row tailor who made many of Prince Andrew's uniforms, but the Duchess augmented these fine clothes with a selection of shirts in shades John had never worn, and Hermès ties in patterns more colourful than the Two Bryans generally considered suitable. She also designed and had made an enormous selection of cufflinks, ranging from miniature golden Budgies to infinity signs representing their unending love. But in addition to these outward and visible changes, the Duchess now had plans to alter many features of John's personality. 'He needs to be more humble, he must listen more,' she said, and went on to list all the things she was working on in order to improve him.

I told her I believed it would be dangerous to try to change John too much, and that she ought to accept him as he was. 'That is because no one has given JB any real attention,' she responded. 'So the poor fellow needs somebody there just for him.' As we expressed our different views the Duchess worked herself up until she was in tears, and so we decided to call it a day and go to sleep.

The next day was warm enough to have breakfast on the terrace. I arrived to find the Duchess, her eyes hidden behind a pair of sunglasses, sitting beside Jane. We managed to get through a quiet breakfast, which was broken only by Sarah's announcement that instead of spending two or three days in the South of France we would be returning by train to Paris that morning. She could sense I was surprised and added, 'Oh Starkie, we can stay for a couple of days in Paris and go dancing, and have a real laugh, and we need to visit Versailles anyway for the book.'

As we checked out I said, 'I'm very sorry

if I offended you last night.' 'Oh, don't be silly, I like a good argument sometimes,' which was polite, if not very believable. While we waited for the train I looked over and saw two tears running down her cheeks; 'She has a migraine,' said Jane. We entered our compartment and I slid into the seat next to the Duchess. 'I need space,' she exclaimed, and left us to sit alone at the back of the train, sometimes crying quietly to herself, then immersing herself in her diary. About two hours later she seemed better and announced that she was hungry.

As we approached Paris the Duchess's thoughts turned again to John — 'He has a great body, sometimes he wears these really nice tight black jeans. . . .' Then, as we saw the lights of the city ahead, the Duchess suddenly said, 'Benita can visit Versailles alone and write whatever she likes — let's get on the next plane back to England.' So I escorted her to Charles de Gaulle airport and watched her get on the plane, then called John to give him the flight details and to suggest what he might wear when she arrived home. I returned to Frankfurt alone.

The next week brought no word from the Duchess. As Friday approached I told John that I found her offer of friendship to be insincere, but he reassured me: 'Oh no, she really likes you, it's just that she's afraid that the two of you got so close so fast. Just give her time.' So I agreed to accompany her on the last research trip, to Berlin and Potsdam, that weekend. I was, though, still hurt by her behaviour and remained rather cold to her on the first night. Setting out that evening, I even went so far as to put her into a cab, then loudly asked which of the other members of the group wanted to ride with her. When nobody offered, I closed the cab door and let her ride alone to the restaurant.

We visited — naturally — a number of castles, and at one of them the Duchess asked an old East German woman what she missed most since the reunification of East and West Germany. Her surprising answer was 'the children's books we had in the East'. The Duchess, always keen to react to a business opportunity, asked me to unearth old East German children's books so that we could republish them. (In time I located some; unfortunately, however, their overtly communist content made them unappealing to publishers.)

An incident later in the day caused me to remark, 'I knew you were in a bad mood.' She reacted as though I had struck her. 'I am not in a bad mood! Why do you say so?' I replied that Robin and I could identify her moods, so clearly were they reflected in her face, and that we could predict from them whether the photos would be good or bad; we had even come up with names for her various states of mind. This information infuriated her, and she went storming off.

Robin excelled at composition. As we prepared to photograph the Duchess in the forest with the castle at Potsdam behind her, he expressed regret that there was not a fallen tree on which she could sit. Unfazed, the Duchess walked over to a group of construction workers who were standing near by and, when they recognized her, offered them each an autograph on a Buckingham Palace letterhead if they would relocate a fallen tree to meet our photographic needs. They eagerly agreed, and the Duchess's resourcefulness is recorded in her book.

We returned to our hotel for lunch. Before I could order any food, the Duchess said 'Allan, John really needs to speak to you, you'd better call him.' 'All right,' I answered. 'Could you order me something? Whatever — I don't care.' 'Of course,' she replied mischievously. That morning at breakfast I'd noticed that Benita seemed a little unwell and, suspecting a hangover, had decided to tease her by eating herring and pickles. The Duchess had decided she would be Benita's instrument of revenge, and used my absence to order me the most horrible thing she could find on the menu. When I returned a whole smoked eel sat on my plate. Benita, smiling from ear to ear, asked me if I had seen the film *The Tin Drum*, by which she was referring to a scene in which a horse's head is used to catch eels, and is reeled in with the wriggling creatures clinging to it. I ate the thing to spite them both, then excused myself to be sick. Sarah later remarked that she was impressed that I had eaten it so as not to let her get the better of me. It marked, perhaps, the beginning of our love-hate relationship.

That night the Duchess, keen to show me that she still regarded me as her new best friend, had also decided that she needed my further services. Up until this point we had all believed that the divorce would take place in the spring. During the year prior to the announcement of the separation the couple had only been together for about forty days, and the plan was to count that as one of the two years of separation, which meant that by March of 1993 the two years would have expired.

We had all agreed to meet in the bar of the hotel and then go to dinner, but when the Duchess arrived she asked me to sit alone with her and talk before we met the others.

She began by saying she wanted to clear the air between us. 'Starkie, I understand that you are confused that I don't call you more, but it's John, he was so jealous after our trip to Coburg.' I told her that John had explained to me that she had been criticized for getting too close to people. 'Oh don't be silly, he is only looking for an excuse so he doesn't have to say that he is jealous of us, but I don't care, I will call you more. I told you, you are a spiritual friend the likes of which I never want to lose.' Then, saying she needed to get something from her room, she left looking tired and sad. When she returned a few minutes later I could hardly recognize her. Her mood had utterly changed — now she seemed relieved yet excited. 'Oh Starkie, it hit me when I was in the lift,' she said. 'I can't get divorced in March, I must wait out the full two years, that will only be one more year, sixteen months from now, then I can leave holding my head up knowing that I did the right thing till the end.'

'But why is that the right thing?' I asked, not really understanding. She had an answer for that, too. 'Look Starkie, there is a chance that Charles will not be allowed to have the throne when the Queen abdicates. That would mean that Andrew would be Regent until William comes of age. I have to do the right thing for Andrew; besides, the Queen Mother is not going to live very much longer and she really wants me to stay married until she dies.'

'But she seems healthy,' I protested. 'No, she has problems with her legs, and she just is not well.' 'Is that why you seem so relieved?' I asked. 'I feel relieved to have made the right decision but poor Otto [John], he is going to take this very badly. You will explain it to him, won't you?' I agreed that I would try. We went to the bar to collect the other people, who by now had waited almost two hours for us and were rather hungry as a result.

As the Duchess predicted, John was not at all pleased at the delay when I told him. It meant another year and more of waiting, and considering the abandon with which the Duchess had pursued the hope of marrying Steve, this was doubly painful for John — it was the first of a series of delays that would ultimately sour, then destroy, the relationship. John, furious, reasoned that he had helped her with her divorce negotiations and felt that she would be far better off shedding her husband as soon as possible. Naturally he hoped they would be able to marry shortly after the divorce, and he did not understand why he should have to wait. The Duchess explained her decision to him that evening, and for the next ten days they argued incessantly. Each would call me and complain about the other's position or behaviour, and I would pass on the messages. The Duchess was, however, true to her word, and did call me more, and I believed that she was finally behaving like a real friend. I was asked to come to England from my office in Frankfurt and take part in another Fireside Chat to discuss this issue, and having flown over on the 19 November, waited five days for the call to Romenda. It never came. During this period a change had taken place: the Duchess pretended to back down slightly from her position over the divorce, and so the arguments, and consequently the calls to me, stopped. I returned to Germany without even talking to the Duchess, let alone seeing her.

I was unable to get through to her until the day after I returned to Frankfurt. She sounded miserable and tired and asked me to call again that evening. I called John and said I would let her have some rest, and asked him to tell her that I would call the next day. John, naturally, did not give her the message and she was furious that I had not rung. Eager as he was that the Duchess and I should be friends, John still performed enough sabotage on our relationship to prevent it from growing into something he would have found threatening. Though I was his best friend, still he did this — and it was gruesome to see the way he undermined people whom he only liked a little when it came to the Duchess's affections. Looking at it from his perspective, though, I could understand his concern. The Duchess had taken up with Paddy McNally* when she had still been involved with Kim Smith-Bingham, she had begun her relationship with Steve Wyatt while still married to Prince Andrew, and with John while still very involved with Steve. This tendency to overlap relationships was a concern to John; although, in this case it was an unnecessary one. In the four years of their involvement I never saw any reason to believe that the Duchess was untrue to John. By comparison, one can only make a statistical guess at the number of his affairs outside their relationship.

The next day the Duchess called to invite me to a Thanksgiving party she was throwing at Romenda Lodge, so that I could meet her father. By now fed up both with her and John, I declined the invitation.

*Grand Prix millionaire, and a former lover of Sarah's.

The Duchess will usually withdraw if people pursue her, but if they show little or no interest, she will generally jump through hoops to win back their affection. After I refused the party invitation she called and pleaded with me to meet her in Warsaw three days later for a charity trip. Already patron of a number of charities, she was looking for her own charity in which she could play a more direct role. When she received an invitation from Theo Ellert of Angels International to go to Poland she decided it would provide good publicity, and might perhaps evolve into the personalized charity she envisaged for herself. She had decided to bring Robin and his assistant, Stephanie, from the Queen Victoria research trips, and she insisted that I had to come. Deciding to meet her halfway, I said that I would attend the party at the Marriott Hotel in Warsaw, but could not visit the orphanages during the following several days.

The reception in Warsaw was a small affair, and the Polish government chose to send only the deputy health minister to represent it. Nevertheless, the Duchess and I managed to get him alone for long enough for him to make us an interesting offer. A former spa town had been destroyed during the war, but there was now a plan to rebuild it. He offered it to us for redevelopment, hoping that the Duchess's fame would significantly help the project. But although we remained in communication with the minister for a number of months, the town was too remote to attract western European tourists and in the end we declined. The Duchess went off the next day in a van we had rented and I let our lawyer, Jim Hughes, and his wife replace me as her escorts. It was during this trip that Sarah came to know — and to be impressed by — Theo Ellert. As a result she decided that, after years of sponsoring other charities, the time had come for her to found her own. Together, she and Theo therefore established what at first they called Children in Distress, which they renamed Children in Crisis when they learned that the first title was already in use.

I returned to Frankfurt and prepared to go to the language school to brush up my French. (It was in this school, which was set in a small German town called Meersburg, close to the Swiss border, that I had used to listen to John tell me about his early erotic calls with the bathing Duchess a year before.) On the morning of my departure the Duchess called. 'Starkie, I have a meeting tomorrow with Michael Dover from Weidenfeld and they are treating me very badly, please come and straighten it out.'

'I would love to come, but I have language school and I really can't cancel', I replied. 'Surely there's an airport near by?' she responded, but I refused to change my plans and called John after she rang off. 'Allan, we must stay firm with this, she has to learn that we have commitments too,' he said. Ten minutes later he called back: 'Look, those assholes at Weidenfeld are treating her like shit, you really ought to help her. She is in a very bad way.' So I cancelled the school and flew to England.

The Duchess once bragged to me that she could field any question that was asked about her book on Victoria, even though she had never read it. I guessed the publishers were less impressed with this feat than she was, and indeed, during the meeting, which was at Romenda, Benita was favoured with much more attention than was Sarah. Midway through, the latter said, 'Would you excuse me?' and pulled me into her study. 'They are shitting on me, Starkie, see how they ignore me? Why don't they take me seriously?' She began to cry, and I felt sorry for her. We returned to the meeting and after some time had elapsed I said, 'I hope that it is clear to everyone that this is the Duchess's project and that Her Royal Highness, through her diaries and tapes, has provided an enormous amount of input for this book.' Michael Dover was no fool. He quickly chimed in with the appropriate praise, and from then on attempted to include the Duchess more in the conversation. Sarah, for her part, was delighted with the way I had righted the boat, and now saw it as essential that I take over the co-ordination of the book to ensure that she was never again neglected.

John was to join us for tea, but until he arrived the Duchess and I sat in her study and talked. During our trips she had often been on the phone with her jeweller, Theo Fennell, about a design for a Christmas present for John. She was influenced by those creative gifts, full of hidden meanings and secret compartments, which Queen Victoria had given to her husband, Prince Albert, and decided on a sterling silver globe which could be opened to reveal otherwise hidden photograph frames. The piece arrived as we were talking, and surprised her because it was both larger than she had expected, and so shiny that you could not be sure if it were a globe or a big silver football. I suggested that the oceans be sandblasted to create contrast, and that a small plane be added, as though flying around the globe, since John was, like her, an amateur pilot.

John arrived and we sat down to tea with Beatrice and Eugenie. On the seats of the adult chairs in the dining room had been placed miniature Chippendale chairs, on which were petit-point cushions with the girls' birthdates embroidered on them. The little princesses solemnly mounted their chairs and said in unison, 'Dear God, thank you for our lovely teatime, may we get down now Mummy, please?' It was decidedly cute. Then we had tea, and each time the princesses didn't want to eat John would say 'Whatever you do, don't eat the —.' They would giggle, then mischievously eat whatever they had just refused. Without doubt, John was deft with children.

By now he had relaxed into his role as full-time guest at Romenda: to all intents and purposes he and the Duchess were now man and wife. Their lovemaking was hectic and abandoned. On one occasion during intercourse the telephone rang — it was the Duke of York, calling to arrange a meeting. Sarah talked to him while the sexual activity continued, but then put her husband on hold while she took another call, this time from Steve Wyatt. 'People may think that sounds extraordinary,' said a laconic John later, 'but it seemed very normal at the time. Anyway, they weren't to know.'

The transition from Sunninghill to Romenda Lodge, from marital home to exile, had been more disturbing than Sarah cared to admit. Instead of calling upon the royal family's serried ranks of sage old advisers, many of whom would have been happy to ease her passage back into the real world, she began to rely ever more heavily on a variety of psychic mediums and fortune-tellers, including Rita Rogers, astrologer Penny Thornton, and a figure who was later to become notorious for tape-recording her conversations with the Duchess for financial gain, Madame Vasso. As well as these women she also had a regular Friday night appointment, by telephone, with a spiritualist guru in Los Angeles.

After one consultation the Duchess was bursting with excitement because she believed that Prince Charles was about to die. The Prince of Wales had survived one avalanche in the Alps, in which his friend Hugh Lindsay had died, but — or so the prediction ran — he would not survive a second. In a fever of excitement, she called Diana to warn her of her husband's imminent demise. Wherever this mad idea had come from, it was something Sarah was to cling to for months and years to come. She cherished a vision of Prince Andrew being appointed Regent, reigning as *de facto* King until Prince William came of age, with her — separated but still married — by the Regent's side. Indulging in this mental refuge, she also saw the moment when she would finally outrank 'The Blonde' (the Princess of Wales) and put her in her place. A refinement of this dream — assisted, it has to be said, by Prince Charles's negligent habit of travelling with both his sons on the same plane — envisaged Andrew as King. What could be more blissful than to be Queen Fergie?

Nothing her psychics told Sarah ever came true. Every time they were proved to be wrong, there was some spiritual explanation for it. The tasteless prediction that the Queen Mother would die very soon, because of problems with her legs, proved groundless. In fact, had they but known it, there was some substance to this fear — but magnificently, regally, the Queen Mother rose above the wishes and dreams of mere psychics by undergoing a hip-replacement operation, from which she made a triumphant recovery.

On the following day, 3 December, we met again at Romenda Lodge for our second official Fireside Chat, this time including Jim Hughes, the lawyer the Duchess now shared with us. On the agenda was the discussion of projects, budget, and new offices. Once again virtually all these themes were tied to the fundamental issue of when the Duchess wished to get divorced, and how openly we could work together until she did. She chose not to mention her complex concerns about the Regency at this meeting, but allowed John to believe that the divorce would still take place in March.

As a result, Jim was given the task of negotiating with the owners of Chelsea Harbour for joint offices. The Duchess requested that the negotiation be based on a 1 March occupancy with one year rent free, and membership of the fitness centre thrown in. I am certain that she never intended to move in with us, but felt that it was better to convince John gently of the need to delay the divorce, a strategy she referred to later as 'softly, softly, catchee monkey. Let them all dance around me until they are tired.'

We discussed new projects, beginning by harvesting the ideas from our last two trips. The Duchess asked me to call the Polish Health Ministry and continue discussions for what we called 'Polish Water', the redevelopment of the spa town we had been offered. She asked that Angels International be included, and that we build an Angels home somewhere in the town. By this time the Duchess was feeling stressed and asked that we bypass discussions about her budget. Since the last meeting she had tried to develop a small business plan on her own, and this she now presented to us, with apologies and uncertainty. John grabbed it and said, 'Oh darling, how cute, your first business plan. Allan, look — Sarah made us a little plan.' I said, 'John, it sounds like you want to hang it on the refrigerator door.' 'No really, I think it is so cute.' Sarah had been hesitant about showing us the plan and was quite concerned that we would not like it, but she naturally became quite offended when John treated it like a child's fingerpainting. 'Oh don't get mad,' he said, 'you should have seen Allan's first business plan!' 'Yes,' I added, 'John and I did it on a placemat in a steak restaurant, but it proved surprisingly accurate.' 'Don't worry, darling', said John, 'Allan and I will write up an outline business plan for you over the holidays.' She swallowed her pride, and we continued our discussions.

When the Duchess sold an interview she usually retained the copyright in the photographs that accompanied the piece when it was printed. We therefore decided that a royal photographic library would be created in which these valuable photos could be kept, to be hired out for appropriate fees. John offered to ask a part-time employee of the Duchess, Anne-Louise Dyer, to undertake this task.

Through family connections in Argentina, Sarah had learned that there existed the possibility of privatizing a large hospital in Buenos Aires. This seemed to be similar to the project we were pursuing in Rostock, so the Duchess was keen to get John to submit a formal proposal. On behalf of Oceonics he did finally send information to the Argentinian officials, but due once again to poor follow-up the plan never reached fruition.

Despite the decision to leave out the budget discussion, it was clear that some short-term project was necessary to generate cash. 'You need to write some more *Budgie* books, darling,' was John's suggestion. Sarah was not keen on this idea, but reluctantly agreed to write another two. Additionally, John offered to write a proposal for how she would identify acceptable ideas for future books.

Next we discussed the charity front. It was decided that a Duchess of York Foundation should be created. This would be a vehicle for the Duchess to concentrate on 'substandard healthcare institutions', focusing on hospitals and orphanages, and also a means of reimbursing her for her associated staff costs. The Duchess was to go on two to three trips a year to expose and aid such institutions. She proposed that her father, Major Ronald Ferguson, be hired as the project manager for the foundation — not an idea I wished to see go further.

Finally we spoke of the development of the Queen Victoria book. What Sarah saw as the humiliation she had experienced the day before was still vivid in her mind: 'Starkie, you must run this project personally,' she pleaded. It was decided that she would send the publishers, Weidenfeld and Nicolson, a letter appointing me as her 'co-ordinator', and that as Benita finished the draft of each chapter it would be sent, through the Duchess, to me. I would then make my changes and comments on plain paper and return them to the Duchess so that they could be copied on to her letterhead and faxed, as if her own, back to the publisher.

So ended our second Fireside Chat. At the US Military Academy at West Point, where I went to school, there is a saying that 'if something is done twice it is considered a tradition'. In much the same way, these meetings of ours had evolved into a tradition upon which we all depended.

Next day I returned to Frankfurt, to find

a long and effusively grateful message from the Duchess on my answering machine. Beginning 'Hi, Starkie, this is your red-haired friend. I'm really pretty and I've got big boobs,' it was a cute message, but it was to be the last that I would receive for a number of weeks. Again displaying that confusing tendency towards intimacy and then aloofness, she simply stopped calling for a while.

Meanwhile, John was running short of money. He had borrowed about a hundred thousand dollars from his stepbrother George, who trustingly sent the cash in a Federal Express package the moment John called. Christmas was approaching and he felt under a lot of strain. He had been accused at times of trying to peddle his South of France story to Fleet Street, and I had certainly been with him during the time when he used to tell any newspaper interested in 'the Story', 'We will do this like a construction bid, you tell me exactly what you want and how much you are offering for it.' He had explained to me that he was stringing them all along so that none of them would risk printing anything too damaging for fear of losing the big story. The bids that came in were for staggering amounts of money; one paper offered him £1,000 a word for anything he was willing to say. He never did sell the Story.

On 14 December I was invited to a Christmas Party at Buckingham Palace, hosted jointly by the Duke and Duchess of York. It might have been an Oceonics company party, so many of our people were there, for the Duchess had invited John's secretary Julia, my secretary Anna, Jim Hughes and his wife Bethany, and me. John, naturally, was not invited, although the event had been entered and ringed in his diary. Feeling sorry for him, we had scheduled an Oceonics London office dinner party immediately after the affair at the Palace. John waited sadly for us alone in the restaurant.

Arriving at the Palace, we walked through a portal into the courtyard and were then led into a large room which had been decorated for the party. The Duchess met us at the door and told us that the Duke had not yet arrived. The room filled up fast, and finally Andrew strolled in accompanied by his dog, Bendicks. There was a piano player and the Duchess made us compete in a Texas two-step which none of us knew. After a time I began to feel very sorry for John, and so I rounded up the Oceonics contingent and prepared to join him in the restaurant. 'It was good to make him wait,' said Julia Delves Broughton. 'The only time I can like him is when I feel sorry for him.' We were delayed as I tried to prise one of the female guests away from her hostess. During my years with the Duchess I had the opportunity to watch so much brown-nosing that I began to write down what I came to believe were the rules that govern it. Rule one was: regardless of how obvious the brown-nosing may appear to people who witness it, the recipient will invariably believe that it is sincere. This woman, however, turned out to be the exception that proves this rule. I caught the Duchess's eye as, with difficulty, she separated herself from the guest, who seemed to be caught up in an endless series of curtsies. Holding back her laughter, she addressed me in a flawless Texan accent and a perfect imitation of the woman: 'Oh, Your Royal Highness, I don't know how I am going to be able to say goodbye to you.' We both laughed, proving my second rule, which is that to see a well-performed brown-nosing job can be as rewarding as watching a convincingly faked orgasm.

On the following day John and I flew to Rostock for a meeting with the Minister President. However, with elections impending and the Minister President's coalition too weak for him to risk making any major decisions, he sensibly did not show up. We were left with his cabinet of bureaucrats. Our bankers had met us there, and with their support John made a speech about why the Land of Mecklenburg Vorpommern should set a precedent and allow private capital to finance a public development: 'The only question here is, do you want eight hundred million marks or not?' Unfortunately, this was not the only question. Our meeting turned out to be inconclusive, and the next day we returned to Frankfurt by train.

The evening before we left, however, we went out to a local restaurant, where we encountered two girls. Within an hour John had taken his to the cloakroom for a more intimate discussion, and after they had returned I was left alone with both girls while John went off to freshen up. 'Could you do me a big favour?' I asked. 'Tell me — what is his secret, why is he so attractive?' They discussed it for a few moments, then said 'He is so confident, he seems so . . . rich.' Neither girl had recognized John and he had not spoken of wealth; yet, somehow, he had implied it. He took one of the girls back to the hotel for further discussions.

On the train back to Frankfurt we had five undisturbed hours together. This was a rare experience for John, who could never be without a phone for more than a few minutes at a stretch. We used the time to discuss how matters stood with the Duchess. I told him of the concerns that I had at the time: my perception of her insincerity, her continuing emotional involvement with Steve Wyatt, the question as to whether she actually would agree to a divorce, and my belief that John's attractiveness to her would be vastly reduced when she discovered that he did not have a fortune. He addressed each of these issues. It was his belief that Sarah was in an emotional crisis close to a breakdown, and that virtually everyone had mistreated her. We had to be patient with her, and there was no need for her to find out that he did not have a private fortune until after he had made one.

I asked John to write down what his immediate goals were, and he listed: liquidity, financial security, more leisure time, and respect. (Ironically, I asked the Duchess to do the same several months later and her list was very similar.) With hindsight, what we did next may seem Machiavellian, for we then planned how we could manipulate Sarah to make her more committed to her relationship with John. Both of us were already aware of her obsessive need to be loved. I therefore suggested that he should execute a tactical retreat, designed to frighten her into thinking she was losing him; at the same time we would withdraw some of the support we were giving to her business development. He was enormously grateful for my help in this. Perhaps I should be very ashamed of what I did, but I am not. I was dealing with two incredibly manipulative people, and at other stages I employed similar tactics on Sarah's behalf against John.

When we arrived back in Frankfurt we conducted the usual ritual of organizing staff to track down the things John had lost on the trip. This time, however, we were unable to relocate his briefcase, which he had lost in the railway station. In addition to two business proposals, the elegant Asprey case contained an inscribed photo of the Duchess as well as some letters from her. (Later she would make him shred all her love letters, but at this time he was allowed to keep them.) I saw him just one more time before the holidays, at our Frankfurt office Christmas party. The truth was that he was becoming a stranger to his own company, only gracing it with short guest appearances despite the fact it was his main source of funds and he was its Chairman. On this occasion he spent less than two hours with his staff before catching a plane back to England.

We went our separate ways for the Christmas holidays. The Duchess agreed to accept the Queen's invitation and stayed in a house on the royal estate so that her children could be included in the activities at Sandringham. John flew back to the States and went skiing in Vail, and I went to New York. I called the Duchess once or twice at the house, and found her rather depressed. She had bought the Queen an expensive and elaborate tea container with a silver corgi on the lid, symbolically guarding the warm message engraved on the rim. Sarah, however, felt that her generosity had not been reciprocated. John called me after the New Year, furious at the way she had been treated. 'Now she will have to leave,' he said. Deciding to strike while the iron was hot, he asked that we should meet at Romenda for a Fireside Chat as soon as we all were back.

Chapter 7

The third week of January 1993 we were finally able to meet. Contact between the Duchess and me had been minimal during the holidays, but when I arrived at Romenda Lodge she seemed too frail for me to criticize, so I launched instead into reading the comments I had made regarding the last draft of the Queen Victoria book.

We had tea and after the table was cleared began the Fireside Chat. I had intentionally not prepared an agenda this time, and said that I felt that a list of topics from me was not necessary, since the only real issue was a personal question between the Duchess and John. Using this as an introduction, he renewed his push for a quick divorce. I suggested that she acknowledge John as her lover: 'Don't you see, it is the only way to justify the [St Tropez] pictures? It is natural for a separated woman to bring her boyfriend on vacation and for him to be around her children. Hiding the seriousness of your relationship with John makes it seem worse. . . . Besides, everyone knows you live with him.' To this she disagreed, however: 'The press has no idea how often I see John. They are not even sure if the relationship has continued. We must be careful, very careful — we can't make another mistake.'

We tried to discuss business and financial issues, but as I have intimated they only underscored the central theme of her acceptance of John. I began with the shared offices: 'Jim Hughes, our lawyer, has negotiated with Chelsea Harbour and we can have occupancy in March as you asked.'

'It's too soon, too, too . . .' she responded in a sad, drawn-out voice.

'Fine', said a frustrated John, 'we will rent the offices alone.'

At this she became livid. 'It's too bad for you, Sarah, huh?' she said sarcastically.

'How can we win, Ma'am?' I asked. 'You think it's too soon to share an office with us and if we take it alone you get angry that we are leaving you out.'

'I know John can offer me a lot of things, and that he is helping me, and I am very grateful, but I don't want to feel that I have to be with him because of the things he is doing for me.' This was an honest concern, but I tried to put in a good word for my partner by saying, 'I hope John would be attractive to you despite or even without the things he can offer you.'

151

'And why does he want to share an office with me and be my partner? — so that he can be partners with the Duchess of York,' she said angrily. John was furious and hurt but tried to remain patient, replying, 'No, I want to be partners with Sarah Ferguson.' The Duchess took this as an insult and shouted: 'Now don't be disrespectful, John — stop it . . . I am the Duchess of York.'

At this point I butted in and tried to explain. 'He means that he wants to be partners with you as the Sarah he loves, not because of your title.'

She looked sceptical, but calmed down a little.

It was a pathetic situation. In a way she was drawing comfort and a feeling of security from the illusion of financial support that we had created. But in actuality we were offering her a beautifully wrapped box with nothing in it, while criticizing her for wanting the box.

John tried to discuss cashflow again. 'Sarah, how are you doing with *Budgie?*' he asked. Still angry, she responded in a condescending tone: 'Which *Budgie* — one, two, three, what?'

Since Christmas she had been on a skiing holiday, and had then lain in bed for two weeks with flu. During this entire month, as far as I could tell, she had not worked on either *Budgie* or on my corrections to her Queen Victoria book. I suppose she was too depressed to do much work and I could understand that, but at the time I felt she was being unfair. We were wasting a lot of time because of her procrastination over virtually all of our plans. She did not seem to be able to help herself; and on top of this she was now very short-tempered at these meetings. Looking back on it, I realize that she was depressed and frightened. She told me later that she had never had any real independence in her life. Now, after experiencing the agony of separation in order to win some freedom, she felt trapped by John's constant attempts at control in the guise of support. Her vacillation, however, proved to be an integral and very destructive personality trait that was to haunt us throughout the relationship.

As the discussion ended I looked at the Duchess. It seemed clear that she needed to be alone with John, and they ordered me a taxi. I felt as if I had been drained of every ounce of energy; then, when no longer needed or useful, I had been quickly sent away. I wrote the Duchess a thank-you letter for her hospitality and went off on a short vacation.

I assumed, rightly, that John and Sarah

were getting on well after the Chat as I received no word from her for the next week. Early in February I went on a skiing trip to Switzerland with a girlfriend, taking the draft of the Victoria book with me, as we needed to produce captions for the photos of the Duchess. I faxed her a couple of suggestions but heard nothing back. Again I was left with the feeling that I was only of interest to her when I could be useful in dealing with John. Even the help I was offering and the friendship we apparently shared did not seem to provide enough motivation for regular communication. I sent John a letter telling him that, given all my other responsibilities, not least in keeping Oceonics running, I could no longer help her and she could finish the book herself — this might at least offer her the chance actually to read it. I did not give any thought to how she would react, but I should have done: it cannot be emphasized enough that the Duchess's need to be liked is obsessional. She seemed to draw her life-force out of whatever praise and love she could extract from people around her. She was able somehow to tell what other people wished her to be in any given situation, and alter herself to conform to their expectations. I called this 'the chameleon effect'. She not only agreed with this analysis but turned my term into a verb, and after meetings or parties would sometimes ask me, 'Starkie, did I chameleonize them or what?!' When the Duchess read my terse faxes and spoke to John she panicked.

What happened next offered me some new insights into the way the Duchess thinks. I had sprained my knee while skiing, and since Sarah had asked me to meet her in Munich, I had cut my vacation short; during which time the girl I had brought remained in Verbier and had a fling with a ski instructor. Then, of course, the Duchess cancelled. I returned her call, pretty upset about my 'ski accident' and the fact that she no longer wished to meet me in Munich. I kept in mind that she had cut our stay at Cap Ferrat to one night, cancelled our three days in Paris, and had now decided to cancel a meeting in Munich for which I had shortened my holiday.

I told the Duchess I was upset with her, and felt used, and then told her about the apparent faithlessness of my girlfriend. She jumped at the opportunity to offer advice. 'Oh Starkie, keep her. Look, you don't need to marry her, but she is something for you to have while you are in Germany. She is very decorative, just use her while you are in that beastly place.' I believe that the advice one is offered often says a lot about the person giving it: was this not an insight into her own relationship with John? Was he not just a merely decorative accessory, to be used during a 'beastly' period without any real intention of marrying him? Her reaction provided me with yet another clue to her personality. Giving advice, jumping in to help in a moment of crisis, is very much like giving a present. She was grateful for a chance to give me something, though, consistent with her other forms of giving, this too was not sustainable. Nevertheless, she enjoyed the momentary satisfaction of feeling my gratitude, and at the end of the conversation I found myself accepting her invitation to fly back to England in three or four days' time.

I arrived too late in the evening to go directly to Romenda Lodge so I stayed in London. I felt so relieved at our rapprochement that I stayed up all night finishing the corrections to the Victoria book. Early the next morning I called John and tried to coax him to have breakfast and then go with me to our tailor for fittings, but he had to decline because he owed the man money. It may seem indefensible that John and I kept up to the Duchess the pretence that he was enormously wealthy; it is also very sad that he felt that we needed to do so. In reality he was as generous with Sarah as he could afford to be, and had spent over a million dollars by this time on vacations, gifts, staff costs, and legal costs as a result of the relationship. He simply did not have any more, and was ashamed to let anyone know it.

The Duchess and I still had to write the captions for the book by the end of the week, so it was decided that we would spend the next day together undisturbed. She was very much in her Victoria stage at the time, so I found her a beautifully bound book of lithographs of Queen Victoria's Jubilee and took it with me to Romenda Lodge. It was obvious that she too wished to make peace, for she had bought me an antique holy-water receptacle. When we presented each other with our peace offerings John broke out into laughter: 'The way you two fight and make up, pretty soon you will be giving one another country homes and yachts!'

I spent the night at Romenda, and the next day we shut ourselves in the dining room to write the captions. She was brilliant: I felt as if we could almost read each other's thoughts, that verbal communication was something that only other people needed. As we spoke we took turns finishing each other's sentences, applauding each other for our brilliance, and generally feeling close. At the end of the day I felt that I had certainly misjudged her, and that the new level of closeness we had experienced would certainly redefine our relationship; her habit of blowing hot and cold kept one permanently alert and attentive. I flew back to Frankfurt feeling completely seduced by her personality. We agreed to complete the captions at the end of the week after a meeting with the publisher to discuss the jacket of the book.

Three days later I was back in Romenda Lodge to finish the captions. When I arrived I found that the Duchess was about to have tea with Prince Andrew and they invited me to join them. Later we finished the captions and I said that I would get my office to type them up and send them off to the publisher, allowing the Duchess to complete the remaining watercolours required for the book. After Andrew had left, John joined us for dinner, and we had one of the few calm discussions about their relationship. The theme this time was mutual jealousy. Each was jealous and insecure. The Duchess had reason to start to question John's faithfulness, and for his part, John was jealous of being left out of anything the Duchess seemed to do or say. For example, he was furious that two completely insignificant events from the previous week had not been discussed with him.

Since we were on the subject of jealousy and passion, I told him that I felt sorry for Prince Andrew, and that he must love his wife very much.

'It is not love, it is some kind of sick obsession,' John responded.

'It is no more obsessional than your relationship with Geraldine was,' I answered.

'That's right, that was also sick, but I am more mature now, and I know that I can live without Sarah if I have to, and that is the difference.' I wonder now if John was able to remember those words two years later, when their relationship was in its agonizing downward spiral and he still could not let go.

We went to bed late that night and the next day I returned to Frankfurt where I had the captions typed and faxed to Weidenfeld. What happened next was astonishing.

The publisher was shocked and horrified by the captions. He felt they were too auto-biographical, and could be interpreted as being anti-monarchy. Having said all this, Michael Dover added: 'We regard these as highly confidential, and we will keep them in our safe until this is resolved.' He then offered to have Benita, whom he described as a 'wordsmith', rewrite them in a form acceptable to his company.

I was furious. Of course the captions were autobiographical, and I believed they were really the only part of the book where the Duchess had been able to say anything at all. These large colourful history books, known as 'coffee-table books', do not generally cause a sensation or generate a lot of revenue. I was sure that the book would be more successful if the Duchess were able to make some comments about her feelings. I therefore gave Michael Dover her number in Torquay and suggested that he explain his position to her. Next I called her; she was furious with the publisher and said that under no circumstances would she allow those captions to be altered. Next day, my machine held a furious message from her, her anger directed at Weidenfeld and Nicolson ('those fucking people'), and also at Benita Stoney, whom she felt the publishers were grooming to steal her glory. 'We are not going to let them get away with this, Starkie.'

Apparently not only did the publisher wish to purge the book of those particular captions, but for 'technical reasons' they no longer wished the front cover of the book to feature a large photograph of the Duchess. I spoke to her again, and again she reiterated that she would not allow the captions to be altered. On her behalf I called Michael Dover to relay this message. To my astonishment, he said: 'Well, Allan, this is rather odd — the Duchess told me that she agreed that the captions were inappropriate and ought to be changed, and she was happy to have Benita rewrite them.'

'That is not possible, Michael,' I said. 'When did you speak to her last?'

'About half an hour ago. And by the way, Allan, she asked that I have the old captions shredded.'

I felt betrayed. These captions were something that we had done together and believed in together: writing them had been an experience that had brought us much closer. It was bad enough that Sarah had backed down, but not to tell me personally, and to allow me to make a fool of myself, was too much. Yet this type of incident was to repeat itself numerous times in my personal and business dealings with the Duchess. She would often get too carried away with her own enthusiasm to maintain the position afterward. Too embarrassed to confront the person involved, she would take someone else into her confidence and, under the guise of kindness, would encourage the new confidant to confront the old one. The pattern was so repetitive that after a time, when other people called me on behalf of the Duchess, I would automatically expect to hear of her withdrawal from some commitment or plan we had made.

The captions were rewritten, and my credibility destroyed to the point where the new version was not even sent to me. The Duchess, still pretending that she was fighting for our old position, left a message, in which she continued to inveigh against her publishers, whom she now characterized as 'a bunch of cunts'. On her instructions, Weidenfeld did then fax me the sanitized captions, and I called her back after reading them, as she had asked in the message. 'Starkie,' she said 'you keep a copy of the real captions. One day we will use them, you'll see.' They were strictly autobiographical, and far more interesting than the rest of the book. They were never used.

On the last day of February I was again summoned to Romenda Lodge. There were, it seemed a couple of reasons for the summons. The Duchess's sister, Jane, was in England, having flown over from Australia, and she wanted me to meet her; and the

Lesley Player book[*] had just been released and had caused a stir in the Ferguson clan. Susan, the Major's wife, was to be there for dinner as well, and the Duchess was interested in hearing my reading of the situation.

By the time I arrived Jane was already there. Tall, thin and attractive, her face is slim and pointed, with an aquiline nose that bends down when she smiles. She seems sensitive and somehow apologetic. Seeing the two together seemed to highlight Sarah's special charm: there was definitely a strong resemblance in appearance and mannerism, but whatever created the spark that draws one to the Duchess was absent in her sister.

Jane spoke of her life in Australia, her various jobs and overall lack of experience, and told us of her engagement to a man named Reiner Luedecke and how wonderful he was. Coming on to the real purpose of the evening, she admitted she had already gone to a bookshop and bought a copy of Lesley Player's book, and the moment Susan Ferguson arrived she sequestered herself upstairs with her stepmother so that they could share the horror of reading the book together.

[*]*My Story: The Duchess of York, Her Father and Me*, Grafton, 1993.

Several hours later a shaken Susan and an irate Jane descended for dinner. Major Ferguson's wife took it well, even trying to be humorous about it, saying that her biggest objection to the story was that she came across as the frigid wife.

John pointed out that by forgiving her husband she was reinforcing his behaviour and thus accepting it. He spoke, however, in weird therapeutic terms which nobody wanted to admit that they could not understand: 'You see, Susie, we are attracted to the screens, the thing that attracts both people is that they both have the same screen and after their honeymoon period the screens begin to wobble.' We all nodded respectfully at this.

John, although full of advice, had naturally not bothered to read the book himself. From a small portion of the serialization, however, he knew that Lesley had accused him of using cocaine in her presence.

A very odd aside is that John, who had slept with Lesley's friend, Catherine Loewe, had confused the two women in his mind and believed that he had been intimate with Lesley — as Major Ferguson and Steve Wyatt had been. He was so sure of this that he had mentioned it to the Duchess during their first dinner date, and was horrified when she told him that Lesley was her father's girlfriend. Although sworn to secrecy the Duchess nevertheless relayed John's misconception to her father, and then in true Sarah style invited the whole group to a weekend at Sunninghill Park. It must have been more complex than a Noël Coward play: John dancing with the Duchess, convinced that the other female house guest was a former lover; and a lovelorn Major Ferguson and a complaisant Sarah trying to manipulate Lesley back into the Major's bed. On this evening of discussions about Lesley's book everyone in the room was still under the misconception that John had also been one of her lovers.

Later, after Susan had left and Jane had gone to bed, John, the Duchess and I held a post-mortem on the evening, trying to analyse what had been said. I wondered if they did the same thing about me once I had departed.

Three days later I was back in England to meet a representative of Louis Vuitton on behalf of the Duchess. We were looking for spinoff projects from the Victoria book, and marketing for Vuitton seemed a possibility, since she had taken a set of antique Vuitton cases on our research trips, and had been photographed with them a number of times.

One of these photos was being considered for the cover of the book, which seemed like a great advertising opportunity for the luggagemakers. I met their head of marketing in John's apartment at Cheyne Place on 3 March, and showed him the photo. I was surprised by his reaction. It appeared that Vuitton was not sure if the Duchess was good enough for them: 'We don't need to be identified with celebrities in our advertising, but we might be interested in throwing a reception for the book in France. Before we agree to do this we need to investigate the way the Duchess is currently regarded, and also the academic credentials that qualified her to write the book.' Such was the snobbishness of a manufacturer of treated canvas luggage.

Two weeks after the abortive Vuitton meeting we conducted our next Fireside Chat. As I have pointed out, when in her chameleon personality the Duchess often made commitments to friendship or, sometimes, to working relationships that she no longer wished to keep once she had changed back into the Duchess of York. Apparently during one such episode she had spoken to a retired major-general whom she had suggested might become her chief of staff. When unsure about the direction of her life she would periodically recruit new people to 'run me', as she put it. This particular general was one such victim at the time of this Chat. Naturally she already regretted the offer, and delegated to John the task of breaking it to him gently.

Jim Hughes's capacity had been reached, and so it was decided that we would augment the Duchess's business and legal representation with another American lawyer named Barney Lindley. He bore such a striking resemblance to Barney Rubble of the Flintstones that he always went by that name; since John owned a company called Bedrock, he regarded the employment of our new recruit as fate. The Duchess liked Barney, who spent almost all his time working for her out of the Cheyne Place flat. She even took him to Savile Row and kitted him out in a suit more to her taste.

Although Barney was supposed to provide a link between the Duchess's operations and ours, it was becoming clear that she now wanted to separate her business from John's. She wished to gather together her own team who would manage and develop commercial projects. The Duchess said she was certain the increased strain in her relationship with John was the result of their working together — they must separate their romantic and business lives.

The major theme of this meeting, therefore, was the recruitment of people with
whom the Duchess could control her many
commitments while still pursuing commercial projects. The former controller of the
Oceonics Group, an accountant named
Jeremy Scott, had already been working on
a consultancy to both the Duchess and John,
and it was now decided that I should hire
him as her chief financial officer. Her former
PA, Christine Gallagher, had resurfaced after
a long absence, and she wanted to give her
either a charity or a commercial position. A
third secretary would be added for the
Duchess's and Barney's use. Naturally these
personnel changes drastically increased her
overhead costs. When it came to firing personnel she could no longer afford to support,
however, the Duchess responded, 'After the
divorce. I don't want to make any changes
right now.'

On the question of how and where this
growing organization was to be housed, the
Duchess surprised us by making a second
180-degree turn, now wanting once again to
rent joint offices. Jim Hughes was again ordered to negotiate with Chelsea Harbour.
This time the Duchess asked for an office
with a river view, deciding that her wardrobe,
along with her dresser, Jane Dunn-Butler,

and one secretary, would remain in the Palace.

Other than the advance payments for the Queen Victoria book and money from the sale of *Budgie* publishing rights in Holland, there was very little income being generated. The criteria developed at the first meeting were still in use and restricted the Duchess greatly; yet she was full of ideas. She wanted to write a book on famous women in history, using her friendship with people like Margaret Thatcher. She even had a secretary research what type of perfume Queen Victoria had used in the hopes of releasing it under her own trademark: unfortunately, it turned out to have been simple rosewater. In frustration, she had turned to her former lover, Paddy McNally, for advice, and for a recommendation of a good marketing man she could employ.

After the Chat, and despite an enormous list of topics to discuss, as well as my increasing business involvement and burgeoning friendship with the Duchess, I was once again surprised to find that she did not follow through with me. I therefore continued sending her faxes on operational issues, but they contained no personal sentiments, and once more this frightened her. To make matters worse, on 20 March one paper carried a story about John headed 'Is this man leading her to disaster?' which seemed to jog her memory of my existence. That day brought two long messages on my machine, in which, referring to herself as my 'red-headed friend' or my 'sick aunt', she first thanked and praised me for the Fireside Chat (though she said she thought from my fax that I sounded to be in 'a grump'), and then wailed on about 'damage limitation' in the light of that day's newspaper piece about John. It seemed that none of us — Sarah, John, or I — could break the patterns in which we were now set.

April was a quiet month. On the 13th we met with Weidenfeld's dust-jacket specialist, Harry Green, whose job it was to sort out a new image for the jacket front. We got the publishers to agree to put her photo in a small box on the front cover, but even this was changed; and the pretty picture of her with the Vuitton luggage ended up on the back.

Ten days later we met again for the April Fireside Chat. It was, as it turned out, a short and annoying meeting. I cannot emphasize enough how linked our business lives and the future of our company, Oceonics, were to the fluctuations of the Duchess's state of mind, her willingness to get a divorce, and her acceptance of John. Clearly these factors had soured in the thirty-four days since our last meeting, and she was now once again convinced that she needed her independence. She asked us if we could help find her an office of her own, which could also serve as a company flat, with Barney and Christine agreeing to live there. This would keep them available twenty-four hours a day, allow us to pay them a reduced salary (they would not pay the rent on the flat), and perhaps even breed a new generation of thralls. Jane Ambler, who had been her secretary until recently, was resurrected and allowed to work from home, and a PA in Buckingham Palace was to take the calls that were currently going to Cheyne Place. This was the third change in direction in as many months, and it was extremely frustrating. The meeting did not last long.

In the background, almost forgotten, Oceonics was growing quickly and had turned very profitable. A large German finance house, Hypo Bank, took notice of us and decided that it would like to purchase 25 per cent of the company. In the course of our discussions with the bank John was so distracted by other matters that in the actual negotiation he left the conference room five times in three hours in order to call the

Duchess. Each time he returned, the annoyed bankers had to explain where we had left off. The deal turned sour, not surprisingly, and John gave Sarah the impression that I blamed her. On 11 May she sent me a furious fax. Parts of it had been obliterated, but the overall message was clear: I was thoughtless, had blamed her unjustly, had lied about the number of times I had tried to call her. She was sorry I felt as — according to John — I did, and that she failed in my eyes all the time, but I should try to see her side before making cruel or harsh judgements. Finally, if I chose to see her on the following day, I would see that she was not such an ogre.

After receiving this fax, I confronted her on the phone. Once she checked out my version — that I had not blamed her, and had indeed tried to contact her several times — and convinced herself she had been misinformed, and had reacted unfairly, she apologized, and left a sweet message on my machine. We were, it seemed, the best of friends again.

Two weeks after this episode we had our May Fireside Chat. Barney had found a suitable office/flat, and began by giving the details.

'Oh no', said the Duchess, 'if you could

all be kind enough to wait until September we can go with the joint offices.'

This was a record. She had literally changed her mind each month for four consecutive months. I say this not because the time wasted on searching for offices was so great, though it was, but for what the fickleness of her decisions represented. Our lives were in an endless state of flux, and her inconsistency simply typified it.

Increasingly ideas were thrown up and then half-heartedly pursued, only to be discarded. Typical of these were the purchase of a publishing company to produce the various books we were considering, a national exhibition of children's art tied in with *Budgie*, and the Duchess's promise to help Oceonics find a new equity investor. For this we were to pay her a commission, and give her an option in the company and a seat on the so-called board. She even authorized us to write a letter to a potential investor, stating that she was a director and member of the Oceonics 'board'. As a limited company, German law prevented Oceonics from having an official board, but the Two Bryans found this unsatisfactory and created one anyway, inviting John's brother-in-law Guy de Sellier, the veteran British industrialist Sir Ronald Grierson, the indefatigable Dr Bach and myself to join. From this point on, for the next three quarters, I included the Duchess in our board meeting papers as if she were already a member.

I had brought a set of Oceonics' board papers to the Chat and read them to the bemused Duchess. She stared at me with a funny look on her face and, with her eyes twinkling, waited until I finished, then said: 'Starkie, I am impressed that you were able to tell me all that without cracking a smile. I appreciate it, it was very kind of you to pretend that I understand.' She really did lack confidence and this suited John's goal of keeping her dependent upon him or, as he put it, 'barefoot and pregnant.'

But she was pleased to be a member of the Oceonics board, and believed that I had actually registered her as a director of the company. Convinced that such a registration would ultimately become public, I refrained from doing so — much to her delight when, two years later, we liquidated Oceonics. At the meeting, however, she asked how much she would get as a director's fee. We told her she would receive large commissions for securing Oceonics new business or new investors.

The Duchess loved to mingle with people from all levels of organizations in which she had an interest. Listening to the inevitable complaints within the ranks is a sure way to feel well liked. From such confidences she would invariably discover some member of each organization who was wonderful, special, and could assist in running her life. At this time, her charity Children in Crisis was going through some internal struggles in which individuals relying on direct communication with the Duchess were trying to undermine their boss, Theo Ellert, who was both very able and loyal. From this mêlée emerged a woman named Deborah Oxley as the latest royal champion. It was not quite clear what accomplishments she boasted, but the Duchess felt that she should be elevated to the role of assistant to Barney Lindley and John Bryan. In the meeting, therefore, it was decided that Deborah would fly out to Frankfurt where I could interview her for this role. I am not sure of the logic behind this, but in the world of John and Sarah, travel equates to work. As it happened, Deborah Oxley didn't get the job of assistant but, perhaps not surprisingly, she was soon promoted to manager of CIC, ousting the capable Theo.

I spent the next two weeks in New York, trying to find a publisher interested in buying the American rights to the Queen Victoria book. Simon and Schuster had published *Budgie* so I met with its Chairman, Dick Snyder. He said outright there was no market in the US for *Travels with Queen Victoria*: 'Look, people here know she isn't a historian but what she *is,* is a mother. She should develop her image as an authority on motherhood, then write books from that perspective. Americans like her but they don't understand the South of France pictures, I mean her being topless, and with the children there, Americans don't understand that, she needs to explain it to them in a magazine article about motherhood.' He contacted *Family Circle* magazine which, naturally, was interested. Before I left Dick said something prophetic: 'Tell her that Simon and Schuster have the best lawyers in this business. I can promise her that if she were willing to let us publish her autobiography we could ensure that she won any suits regarding confidentiality.'

I told him that might be so, but she would probably be frightened of losing custody of the children. 'If she moves here we could make sure she keeps the children,' he said expansively.

On 11 June, after my return from New York, we conducted another Fireside Chat. First we discussed the motherhood article and made plans for the Duchess and I to meet separately to write it. Barney was to write a legal opinion on how much she could write about her children without violating the terms of her own confidentiality agreement with the Palace.

When John had become involved in HRH's business and financial affairs, one of the pitifully few possessions that she had boasted was ownership of a penniless unlimited-liability company called ASB (the cryptic abbreviation for 'Andrew and Sarah Books'). John installed himself — and later Jim Hughes — as a director and used the company as their joint business arm until 1993. The cartoon deal for Budgie, for example, was made between Sleepy Kids and ASB. Still hoping to make some money with spinoffs from the Victoria book, we decided to try to get Weidenfeld to repay ASB for the expenses incurred during research in return for the Duchess's active support in marketing the book. We even decided to explore the idea of filming a documentary about the making of the book.

That weekend, the *Sunday Times* Magazine published a long feature story about John under the title 'Fergie's Rasputin'. John was upset: he called me and suggested I buy the paper, then asked 'Who is Rasputin?' —

he seemed amused when I explained.

The following day, the Duchess called me. Mondays are always bad for her — she feels a lot of pressure then, and is easily upset. She would often call me on Monday mornings so I could calm her down. After she had listed the horrors that faced her that week, I said, 'Well, at least you had a good weekend, according to John.' She seemed surprised, but responded, 'John had a good weekend, he thinks everything is wonderful just because I sucked his . . . finger.' We both laughed, not least because that was the extent of John's sensitivity.

Since Deborah Oxley was no longer a candidate for the job of John's assistant, Oceonics advertised the position and I narrowed down the recruits to two: the first was a bilingual American blonde named Sandra. John talked to her for less than five minutes before saying: 'Well, Allan says you are good. I don't really have any questions, let's get something to eat.' Within two hours he had taken the candidate back to his hotel where he did actually discover a question he wished to ask her. The answer was provided over the course of the night, and an exhausted, unshaven John walked into my office next morning to ask for an aspirin. He cancelled the other interview and went to the airport.

A few minutes after his departure Sandra appeared in my office with his passport and wallet; although never actually employed, she did nevertheless have the privilege of participating in the company ritual of recovering John's possessions.

By now the Duchess was getting so used to having me attend her meetings that she expected me to fly in for each one. Oceonics was beginning to feel the effects of the recession and increasingly I felt my duty was towards the company, so I declined a meeting she had asked me to help her with at the beginning of July. Thus began our second round of skirmishes with one another.

The trouble started with two messages on my machine, or two parts of the same message, in which she explained why she had been so hurt and angry when I had told her I could not be at the meeting. Her tone, however, made it pretty clear whom she considered to be the wronged party, and who the wrongdoer, and the effect was that the two messages, and the ensuing telephone conversations, set us again at each other's throats. Furious, I told John: 'She's your girlfriend and will probably be your wife one day, so I will be forced to see her at company parties — but that will be all.' He laughed

— he had grown used to these fights — and said: 'No, Allan, it will be somewhere between that and the three of us living together.' He then suggested that I come to Romenda and explain to Sarah the difficulties I was experiencing in trying to cope with her personality.

I wrote her a scorching letter and flew over to read it to her myself. She was waiting for me in her study and smiled nervously as I came through the door. 'Go ahead, Starkie,' she said, slightly impatiently. I read her the letter. In it I accused her of using me, of not being able to offer real friendship; and I had ended it by asking what was the point in founding a thousand charities if you were not really there for one friend? She listened quietly, then said 'Are you quite finished?' I told her I was, and added, 'I guess you would probably like me to leave now.'

'Yes, I think that would be best', she replied.

On hearing this, John popped out of his seat. 'Wait a minute,' he said, 'I am not going to allow it to end this way. It simply is not going to happen that my girlfriend and best friend don't get along. I will leave you two alone in here and I'm going to lean against the door so that neither of you can get out until you resolve this.' Then he walked out and very probably did put his weight against the door. Left alone, the Duchess was confronted with perhaps one of her greatest terrors: she was sitting in close proximity to someone who did not seem to like her. John's instincts were right. Instead of maintaining the high-handed and fatalistic façade she had produced in reaction to my letter, she began to explain the pressure she was under, the miserable period her life had entered, her dependence on me even though she simply did not always have the time to show affection and concern for me. 'Starkie, John is still very jealous of our friendship, and also you don't live in England. I mean, if you lived around here, I would be spending loads of time with you, probably three times a week we'd see each other and have fun.'

I decided to retreat from the hard line I had adopted, and said, 'All right, why don't we spend a few days alone together? We can talk about all the things we haven't had time for and we could write the motherhood article.' She seemed relieved. 'Oh Starkie, that'll be wonderful! I know! I know! I need to go to Paris next week — why don't we meet there and we can spend the weekend together?' I accepted gracefully.

Next Saturday I arrived in Paris as planned, and waited. And waited. By Sunday afternoon I was too angry to accept her belated suggestion that we meet for a couple of hours that evening and I returned to Frankfurt, meanwhile sending her an unfriendly note. I waited for her next move. It materialized on my answering machine ten days later. She was in France with friends, and had been for some time. Things had been awful, but were getting better, and she was going to get all her problems sorted out, would be much more positive, everything would be fine. But she gathered there might be some problems between her and me — could we talk about it?

We finally talked, and again patched things up. After her vacation she did seem a bit more reasonable and consistent, and by early August we were again very close. On 6 August we conducted what I dubbed a 'Fireside tag-team wrestling match'. The quiet three-way talk was a thing of the past: now it had evolved into a full-blown staff meeting attended by John, Christine Gallagher, Julia Delves Broughton, Jeremy Scott, Barney Lindley (to replace Jim Hughes, who had finally resigned) and Jane Dunn-Butler. (Jeremy Scott was an accountant whom John had made redundant from Oceonics Group Plc in 1990, and whom I had retained for Oceonics Deutschland as a consultant accountant. By the time of the meeting, I had integrated him into HRH's Fireside team, to such good effect that by June 1994 he had become her full-time employee and partner.) As a by-product of her eagerness to create a commercial staff while retaining her former royal entourage, the Duchess had converted her followers into what she hoped were businesspeople. So her former secretary Christine was now a project manager, and her dresser Jane Dunn-Butler was an assistant accountant. It was like taking a string of pit ponies and turning them out on a beautifully mowed lawn, in the hope that they would then be able to play polo.

John and I tried to convince the Duchess she should streamline the organization. She took this as a personal criticism and carefully recited all the duties that her office had to perform, from answering fan-mail to undertaking recces before charity trips. This lengthy justification was intended to show that she was in fact grossly understaffed.

The situation with her bankers, Coutts, was beginning to get desperate. The overdraft was growing, as Jeremy elaborately described, and had by this time reached £245,000 on the personal account, and £28,000 on the ASB account. Cheques for an additional £12,000 had already been drawn in the six days of August so far, and the remaining creditors stood at £96,000 against HRH and £30,000 against ASB. The grand total of the liabilities was therefore about £411,000, with no large source of revenue in sight. In consequence, it was decided that John would speak to Coutts and explain that an additional £35,000 per month for the next two months would be needed. Actually it was concluded that at the current rate of expenditure HRH needed £35,000 for fixed expenses and an additional £16,000 for variable costs: yet her monthly income from the Duke and other sources totalled only £8,000. What all of this meant was that, simply to break even, she needed a taxable income of £1 million per year.

We talked about projected sources of income for August and September: all that was likely was the remaining advance for the Queen Victoria book — £37,000. The Duchess launched desperately into a discussion of possible projects and sources of income: we spoke of TV documentaries, of creating a pseudo-autobiography in the guise of a book about a previous Duchess of York, of worldwide rights in miniature children's books, of books on Queen Victoria's children, of a *60 Minutes* interview in Australia to address children and their education, of selling extracts from the Victoria book to in-flight magazines, and even of autographed copies of the book being sold directly by the Duchess on mail-order television channels. Yet for whatever reasons these projects, like those before them, either failed to pass the stringent criteria that we had laid down, or were simply not pursued energetically enough. One could feel quite tangibly the Duchess's terror as the overdraft kept rising and the hopes of quick revenues failed, again and again, to materialize. The bank had been told by John in March that both HRH's personal and ASB accounts would be in credit by the end of the current year, and this no longer seemed possible. John, penniless but overconfident, as usual, stepped in and guaranteed a portion of the account.

Once this disconcerting Chat was over, I spent a little time with the Duchess and she gave me enough information to take a stab at a motherhood article, which I sent to both Simon and Schuster in New York as well as *Family Circle* magazine. Unfortunately only $5,000 was offered and the Duchess decided to kill the idea. The article was never published.

As August drew to a close I took ten days off to go to Lake Como for my birthday, and

I invited the Duchess to come with me. We had managed to stabilize our relationship, and were growing more fond of one another all the time. She seemed interested in joining me for a couple of days until she heard that I was going to be staying at a hotel called the Villa d'Este. At this she looked crestfallen and said, 'Oh, not there Starkie, I have such horrible memories of that place.' She had apparently been there in the past, with another boyfriend — 'he would make me wait out in the hall while he took other girls to his room.'

'How could you have let him treat you so badly?' I asked.

She shook her head and said, 'Andrew was the first man to act like a gentleman.'

'Were you never really happy, then?' I asked.

'I don't know, Starkie, it's a long time since I have been happy, it's hard to remember. Maybe I only thought that I was happy.'

Bearing these sad thoughts with me I took my leave and went without her to Italy. I was greeted at the hotel by a beautiful sterling silver pen set with an inscription engraved in a perfect copy of her own hand and in almost invisibly small letters. By comparison, John even forgot to send me a birthday card.

When I returned from my vacation I organized the mid-September Fireside Chat. Similar to the August meeting, it began with the tight-lipped Jeremy Scott reading a letter he had prepared about the Duchess's revenues versus her expenditure, essentially repeating that she was operating at a huge loss. She listened grimly. Then we talked again of the old projects — which remained pretty much where they had been the previous month — and of new projects which she'd had time to think up or which had appeared unannounced. One of the latter such was an offer from Phase 2, a French film producer sponsored by *Point de Vue* magazine, which wanted to make a documentary about the Duchess for French TV. Perhaps inevitably, the timeframe for the project was unrealistically tight.

John had been working for quite a while at producing the animated version of the *Budgie* stories, and had eventually found a small public company called Sleepy Kids, which had offered a deal whereby it would fund the development and marketing of the animated product, and in return for the rights HRH would receive 35 per cent of the future revenues after the investment costs had been covered. By this time the pilot programmes had been completed, we had watched the first video at Romenda, and the

Duchess — although not convinced that all the voices were what she had originally intended — had given John the OK to go ahead. By the time of this Chat, the project had matured to the point where the Duchess needed to get involved in the publicity. We discussed her launching Budgie as a cartoon-and-merchandizing character at the US Toy Show in February the following year.

In the meantime she was to give interviews to a few magazines to get the interest going. But as the video had begun to rise out of the ashes of the exhausted children's books, John Richardson, the cartoonist who had drawn the original characters, had come out of the woodwork to complain that he had been poorly treated in respect of the split of the revenues. When Sarah brought this up at the meeting, John insisted that he would give Richardson something to shut him up. At this the Duchess became very angry and said that we had to respect the cartoonist and listen to his complaints. John, who was feeling very pleased with himself at this time about the future of Budgie, first sneered, and then brooded for the rest of the meeting, until he got the idea that he and I should ignore the Duchess out of protest. Equally bored and distracted, I agreed, and we spent the rest of the meeting rewriting the words of 'My Way', renaming it 'I Did It Her Way'.

The words voiced our frustration. The Duchess was keeping us all in a state of limbo by neither going back to her marriage, nor letting it end. For his part, John was keeping the Duchess in a state of financial imprisonment, discouraging her from financial independence by sabotaging her self-confidence and criticizing the majority of potential projects, yet giving her the illusion that his financial safety-net would prevent her from falling very far. Each month from now on, the increased tension would be evident in these meetings, which by now had divided into two factions: the Duchess's team, and John and me. In this environment all we really accomplished was to hurt each other.

Chapter 8

In Britain during 1993, public opinion of the Duchess plummeted even further. Accident-prone and vulnerable as she was, there could be no rise in the public's esteem while she remained close to John Bryan. Meanwhile, her lover's own rehabilitation was hardly helped by the utterances of his stepmother, Pamela Bryan, who outraged royalists hoping for a reconciliation between the Duke and Duchess by declaring that John and Sarah would marry. 'They are an ideal pair, a match made in heaven,' she said.

'I am sure he will marry her,' she told the *Daily Express*'s reporter Philip Finn when he knocked on her door in Pennsylvania. 'She has everything he wants, and a high-profile position. They have so very much in common in their backgrounds which gives them a special kind of compatibility.' While this may have been true from Pamela Bryan's perspective, as it was from mine, in Britain it simply added fuel to the flames. The public saw no similarity between the shark-like, Savile Row-suited hustler and their downtrodden and directionless Duchess. But Pamela was not through yet: 'There are no family scruples about going after a married woman,' she observed. 'When I read what had happened between them, it was exactly what had occurred between his father and me. Just like his father he made an enormous play for a married woman. It must be in the genes — like father, like son. I was married when his father came chasing me.'

Some insight into John's own psyche was given by his stepmother's parting shot: 'He has not had a very easy time. He has lived in at least a dozen homes. He has had a stormy relationship with his father. Tony would say unkind things to him in front of the girls he brought home, even taunting him about going bald. I hated it. I would say "Leave him alone" but he would yell and berate John even more for little things, like not shaving.' Yet, she added, there was also a bond between the two men — Tony once gave his son unsecured, interest-free loans totalling $2 million to help fund his lifestyle through the acquisition of companies, and by the time Oceonics had crumbled, had pumped over $5 million into the company. More prone to regard his chequebook as a solution to all problems, Tony's neglect to offer John the discipline and guidance he needed made the financial loss all the more futile.

Despite this apologia, the public was not yet ready to embrace John Bryan. Running free, with no constraints and with no clear plan, he started to make some fundamental errors. Sure in the belief that the British press had no real idea of what was going on at Sunninghill Park now that Sarah had left, he called the Sunday *People* newspaper. In return for £20,000, he said, he would provide evidence that the Duke of York was engaged in an extramarital affair. Further, he offered to go through the Duke's personal address book: 'I will go in there and get it . . . a real steal,' he boasted to the newspaper. 'But I want [the money] on goddam publication, baby. I want immediate payment.'

He went on: 'I know 100 per cent he is going out with this girl and I know she has spent the night a lot at South York [the nickname for Sunninghill Park, after South Fork, the ranch in the TV soap *Dallas*]. I have some other details that are really big. I will produce a name. But I want twenty [£20,000] for this one, because I am going to be taking the ultimate risk.' In a further call he added: 'You must *never* reveal the source. I really am taking a fucking big risk.'

Earlier, John had been offered £10,000 for

Above, from left to right: Ghislaine Maxwell, Geraldine, Lady Ogilvy and John Bryan at a party in 1992. Prior to the Duchess, John's girlfriends had included Lady Ogilvy and writer Lady Antonia Fraser's daughter, Flora, also a writer. *(Fergus Greer)*

Below: Sarah and John at Lord Weidenfeld's birthday party at the National Portrait Gallery in June 1992. *(Richard Young/Rex Features)*

Above: The Duke and Duchess of York and the princesses enjoy a family day out at the Windsor Horse Show, May 1992. Meanwhile the separation was under way and her affair with John Bryan was in full swing. *(Alpha)*

Right: Compromising photographs of Steve Wyatt holidaying with the Duchess and the princesses in Morocco in 1990 were found in his flat in November 1991 and published early in 1992. *(Neils Obee/Alpha)*

Fergie with her 'financial adviser', as John was known at this time, on their way to Paris to celebrate his birthday, June 1992. (*Dave Parker/Alpha*)

Right: In August 1992, the publication of the 'toe-sucking' photographs of John and Sarah in the South of France created an international outcry. John later claimed that he was not sucking but merely licking the royal toes. *(Neils Obee/Alpha)*

Left: Sketching the Duchess in the Rhine Valley: the author accompanied the Duchess on several research trips for her book, *Travels with Queen Victoria. (Author's collection)*

Above, from left to right: John Bryan, Bill Simon, the author and Tony Bryan, John's father, at the Oceonics Deutschland reception to welcome Bill Simon as a partner. *(Author's collection)*

Below: The Oceonics team outside the World Headquarters in Frankfurt in October 1993. By March 1995 Oceonics was bankrupt. *(Author's collection)*

Above: The author with Sarah on a visit to Albania in October 1993. More of a tightly controlled publicity exercise than a charity trip, the Duchess was accompanied by *Hello!* magazine and a TV documentary unit. *(Alpha)*

Right: Promoting *Budgie*, the children's books featuring the adventures of a do-good helicopter, in the Netherlands, March 1993. *(The* Sun/*Rex Features)*

Below: The Duchess of York with Edda Holmvik, the author's fiancée, at Robert Splaine's stables in Cork, Ireland, December 1993. Sarah concealed the real purpose of her trip by claiming that she had come to see a victim of motor neurone disease. *(Author's collection)*

200

Above: Getting ready to jump at a showjumping competition in Cork, March 1994. *(From left to right)* Sarah, the author and Robert Splaine. *(Author's collection)*

Left: The author and Sarah pace the course before competing. *(Author's collection)*

Previous spread: The Duchess and the author visit Heather Blaze, the horse Sarah bought for Robert Splaine, to help realize her dream of securing an Olympic gold medal. *(The* Examiner)*

Sarah with her father, Major Ronald Ferguson. *(Dennis Stone/Rex Features)*

Above: Irene Majorie (here with John Bryan in Moscow, October 1994) and her husband, Franco, suggested to a desperate Bryan that he could make his fortune in Russia by buying raw diamonds or importing petrol. *(Stewart Mark)*

Below: Halloween at Romenda Lodge, 1994. Jane Ambler, Fergie's secretary, sits on the author's left. *(Author's collection)*

Above: The author with Edda *(right)* at Romenda Lodge, both dripping wet following a practical joke played by the Duchess. *(Author's collection)*

Below: Sarah promoting *Budgie* at the prestigious New York toy store, F.A.O. Schwarz, November 1994. A year later the publishers of *Hector the Helicopter* alleged plagiarism. *(Dave Chancellor/Alpha)*

The author with the Duchess on a trip to Frankfurt to open her children's charity, MIN, December 1994. (*Helmut Möller*/Bildzeitung)

Left: A signing session at Hatchards bookshop for *Travels with Queen Victoria.* *(Steve Finn/Alpha)*

Below: John Bryan *(far right)* aboard the *Kalizma* celebrating Massimo Gargia's birthday, August 1994. Massimo *(second from right)*, the flamboyant publisher of *Best* magazine, introduced John to the international jet set. *(Author's collection)*

The Duke and Duchess of York outside Annabel's nightclub in London following a cocktail party in honour of Clive Garrad, a wealthy East End businessman, whom Fergie wanted to sponsor Heather Blaze. Eventually he was to help buy the horse. *(Richard Chambury/Alpha)*

another story in which he claimed that the Duke had fondled a beautiful blonde businesswoman's legs beneath the table during a candlelit dinner at Sunninghill Park — and that Sarah had been embarrassed when the shocked guest complained. Though he was right in his assessment that the *People* was starved of exclusive royal stories, he miscalculated the paper's caution. They tape-recorded his allegations, checked them — and then published a full account of his deceit. There was not a shred of truth in either of the stories he was trying to sell.

Though the warning bells should have started to ring, John's exposure as a liar did nothing to halt his relentless pursuit of an easy buck. Soon after the *People* débâcle, Sarah's hairdresser Nicky Clarke informed her that the glossy London magazine *Harper & Queen* would like to feature her as their cover-girl. In truth, there is nothing that Sarah could have more devoutly wished: wherever she went in the world, on every newsstand she was confronted with magazines featuring her spectacularly beautiful sister-in-law Diana, the Princess of Wales. But rarely was the Duchess accorded the accolade of a front cover, and never in the world of the smart glossies.

Had John been away in Germany that week

doing what he should have been doing — tending to Oceonics Deutschland, the company which carried the bulk of his hefty expenses, but which had seen him only rarely in the past few months — all might have been well. He was not; and what occurred was nothing short of a major public-relations disaster. The then editor of *Harper & Queen*, Vicki Woods, a spirited woman with little time for the niceties of royal protocol, chose instead to record in print the progress to the eventual non-publication of the photographs.

'The Duchess seemed tempted by the idea of an interview,' she recalled. 'With hindsight it was clear she was tempted only by the photographs. Contact was through her terrier-like personal assistant Jane Ambler who was never off the telephone. Her Royal Highness would be bringing her personal manicurist to the studio; Her Royal Highness would be bringing her personal dresser; Her Royal Highness would be bringing her personal photographic agent.'

Though the photographer, Michael Roberts, is one of the most gifted in Europe, 'Her Royal Highness wanted a list faxed to her of all the A-list celebrities that Michael had ever photographed. And, finally HRH was very loath to be interviewed. She wasn't keen *at all*.'

Next, Vicki Woods was presented with a confidentiality agreement 'binding all participants in the upcoming photoshoot to Masonic secrecy *for ever,*' as well as a demand that the copyright in the pictures should pass to ASB, Sarah's company; the magazine was also asked to pay over £2,500 in legal fees. At this moment John stepped in: 'We spoke fairly frequently for the next day and a half,' wrote Ms Woods. 'Like every couple of hours. It was like arguing money and terms with a particularly difficult and out-of-it Hollywood agent about a major star.'

John's negotiating technique was recorded assiduously by Ms Woods who, having come to a decision about the exercise, was beginning to enjoy herself. 'You guys should be used to this kind of deal,' he blustered. 'You deal with celebrities all the time!' The editor pointed out that the Duchess was not a celebrity, but royalty. 'Exactly. She's not some dead-common fucking trashy little model!'

By eight o'clock that evening Ms Woods informed John that such were the difficulties in coming to an agreement that she was calling the photoshoot off, but twelve hours later John was on his car phone again, telling her she had wasted a brilliant opportunity. Then it was Sarah's turn to call the magazine's editor: 'It's awful dealing with all this protocol. . . . It's been so awful, and *guess* who's going to get the blame for it, *as usual.* . . . I'm a *serious person* and I'm not doing this just so that I can get free Christmas cards.'

All this was laid down with chilling accuracy in an article which damned, by their own actions, both Sarah and John; their venality, insecurity and self-importance shone through with glaring clarity. On the day after the article appeared, John's lawyer, Alasdair Pepper of Peter Carter-Ruck and Partners, issued the following statement: 'Due to recent adverse publicity John Bryan has decided to remove himself from day-to-day involvement with the media on behalf of the Duchess of York.' If only, the *Sunday Times* sighed, that were true.

If John was bad at handling the press, his treatment of staff, which left as much to be desired, was also becoming the subject of public comment. At the beginning of 1993 Jim Hughes, the Texan lawyer whom I had employed to assist the Duchess, had begun to show alarming signs of fatigue. Despite the fact that his wife Bethany had also been taken on the payroll as an assistant, Jim was ready to quit. He had written to me: 'I think it wise to express my frustration and dissatisfaction with the current situation. Without the development of new business prospects that will fund and justify [my] presence in London, I fear my responsibilities will continue to be as a lawyer on call for seedy press deals, negotiator with angry creditors of John's client [the Duchess], and little else. Not exactly personally rewarding and unlikely to result in significant financial rewards.' He went on to cite 'the continued distraction of John with the affairs of his client and my inability to pursue legitimate opportunities . . . because of the demands placed on my time by John's client.' I knew it could not be long before he quit.

If Jim's departure was a significant blow to the Duchess and John they probably did not know it, because staff were continually walking out on them. The difference in this case was that Jim Hughes was not a domestic servant, but someone who was in a position to make their lives easier and more profitable — if only he had been given the chance. But there was barely time to note his adieu: a Sunday newspaper carried a graphic account of John's treatment of one of the servants at Romenda Lodge, highlighting his displeasure with the way the butler had served a glass of Pimm's; soon the butler was to go the way of half a dozen other members of Sarah's staff since John had come into her life.

Mostly the staff were gagged by confidentiality agreements written into their contracts, but one domestic told the *News of the World* that John and Sarah were now effectively man and wife, and were forcing the Duke of York into a subservient role: 'The Duchess found reasons to keep the Duke out of the nursery and away from the girls as much as possible. She thought of the children as hers, not his. Andrew would have to wait until she was out of the house before he could play with his daughters. When he got the chance, he loved to play with them — but only when the Duchess wasn't around. One day they were playing in the bathroom and the water went everywhere. He picked up Beatrice and threw her into the bath and she was squealing "Do it again! do it again!" but he was petrified Sarah would find out. Every drop of water had to be mopped up and all the staff were sworn to secrecy. He thought he would be in for one of her roastings.' Certainly the Duke's role as father was becoming increasingly marginalized: once, after joining Sarah for Beatrice's school sports day, he was sent away while the Duchess hosted a mothers' party at Romenda Lodge — with John at her side. By now John was using his Cheyne Place apartment as an office and a place to take other women, but Romenda Lodge was his home. He even shared the rent payments at times.

All this did not go unnoticed at Buckingham Palace. Sarah was struck off the invitation list for the royal house party at Windsor Castle for Royal Ascot week, but then that may have been as much for her behaviour the previous year when, newly separated from Andrew, she had stood in the crowd with her children, embarrassingly waving at the royal procession of which she had once been a part.

John celebrated his thirty-sixth birthday in June 1993. The previous year he and Sarah had danced the night away in Paris; this year she wanted to do something different for her lover. She had remembered a scene from the 1957 movie *An Affair to Remember,* starring Cary Grant and Deborah Kerr, in which a glittering table in a magnificent room is laid for many guests, but dinner, when it is served by the retinue of waiters and footmen, proves to be for the two lovers alone. Sarah adored the idea of this scene and set up a marquee behind Romenda Lodge, had a dancefloor put down, found John's favourite music ('Unchained Melody' and 'My Way'), food and wine, and ordered a tableful of historic silver from Buckingham Palace. She told him she had invited all of his friends, including me, and added that it was a black-tie affair.

Such was the excitement with which she prepared her intricate plans for this major event that her grip on reality began to slacken somewhat. 'We'll make it like a fake Fireside Chat,' she told me. 'You fly in from Frankfurt — make sure you bring your dinner jacket in a garment bag so it looks as if you're really going to be coming to dinner — we'll have the Chat, and then you leave.' Slightly incredulous, I said, 'You mean you want me to take a couple of days off work and fly over, to come all that way *not* to be invited to the party?' None the less Sarah's idea was a tremendous success, and the couple made love long and passionately that night.

Birthdays aside, there now suddenly came a moment when things looked as though they might take a turn for the better. Though the British press continued to enjoy lambasting Sarah and her lifestyle, the United Nations took a more charitable view: it was suggested that her plight might be eased, and her life given some direction, by appointing her as a roving goodwill ambassador to its High Commission for Refugees (UNHCR).

On 11 June 1993 it was announced that she had secured the job, and the international standing which went with it, on the basis of her work helping children caught up in the Bosnian conflict. One newspaper reported: 'In her new role, Fergie will help raise awareness of the suffering of refugees. She will fly to world trouble spots, armed with a flak jacket, blue UN helmet and a diplomatic passport, giving her VIP status wherever she goes. Last night the Duchess said "There can be very few people who can fail to be moved by the tragic plight of the refugees around the world. That the number is increasing so dramatically is a major cause for concern. I am honoured and delighted to offer my support to their cause." Her remarks came as she collected an award from UN High Commissioner for Refugees, Sadako Ogata, from the refugee charity WomenAid at a London hotel.'

This was a major boost for the Duchess, and a chance to put some distance between herself and the welter of adverse publicity which was still rolling down the turnpike. She was to join the actress Sophia Loren, another new appointee, and together they would undertake high-profile work similar to that done by the actress Audrey Hepburn on behalf of UNICEF before her recent death. Sarah was told that her assignments would include visiting troubled countries like Bangladesh and Mozambique, but one observer wrote with prescience: 'The appointment will shock Buckingham Palace courtiers who have conspired against Fergie: this year they have already banned her from making a mercy mission to wartorn Bosnia. She was told she could not go because the Prince of Wales had an official visit already arranged.' Though stripped of royal duties since her separation, protocol still required Sarah to clear foreign visits with the Palace, though in lordly manner these courtiers always pretended to the press they did not know where she was or where she was going next: 'She negotiates her own arrangements,' they would comment snootily. When Sarah heard the news she called me in a frenzy of joy. 'Think of it, Starkie, I will have my own platform. It will just be me, and think of what I can do, and all the trips I can go on.' 'It sounds great, Your Royal Excellency,' I teased. Later, with a courtier, she joked how jealous this would make 'The Blonde' — the Princess of Wales.

So here, at last, was a chance for Sarah to do something of substance. Or was it? It took a fortnight for Buckingham Palace to recover from its astonishment that an organization as revered as the United Nations should seek out one of its castoffs to employ her in a high-profile international role. But once the royal juggernaut had started, there was no stopping it: in late July, Palace sources let it be known that the Duchess's UN appointment was 'entirely inappropriate', and a senior cabinet minister was pushed forward to reveal that Prime Minister John Major, although not empowered to veto the idea, was against it. There was no Shirley Temple* role available. Almost certainly the big freeze rolled out of Buckingham Palace and down the Mall to Downing Street, not the other way round. As the *Daily Express* commented, 'The royal knives are still out for Fergie.'

Confusion reigned, for though official sources had leaked the Government's disapproval — and that of the Queen — no one had bothered to inform the UN that the Duchess of York was suddenly unavailable. At the organization's HQ in Geneva, an official was caught off guard: 'The Duchess has not as yet turned up to be formally made an honorary ambassador. We expect her as soon as her schedule permits.' Her office also leaked its own comment to the press: 'She is now a free spirit and there is very little they can do to stop her. It seems sour grapes.'

As indeed it was. Next day, the UN had re-

---

*Shirley Temple Black (her married name), once a famous child star, became a politician, and, later, a roving ambassador for the UN.

covered its poise sufficiently to claim once more that it wanted Sarah: 'We won't be bullied by anyone,' said an official. 'As far as we are concerned the Duchess has the job and we are very proud to have her.' But by now the government disinformation service was cranked up: the Foreign Office had ordered her to cancel a trip to the former Yugoslavia two days after giving the go-ahead. The aim of the visit had been to launch an appeal for her charity Children in Crisis, and the Foreign Secretary, Douglas Hurd, had told her she could go to Croatia but not to Bosnia, because that would be too dangerous and would tie down UN troops. But forty-eight hours later, while Hurd was in Tokyo at a G7 summit meeting, his officials told her that she could not even go to Croatia. Though the reason given was 'security', UNHCR officials on the ground complained bitterly about the decision.

This was a moment when Sarah could have appealed to the British nation as a whole: it would not have taken much to spark a national debate about this opportunity to rehabilitate herself.

But it was July, and Sarah was in the South of France on holiday. Though the debate had raged hot and strong for a couple of days, by 30 July the United Nations, bowing to the combined weight of Palace and Government opinion, put out a statement: 'At this stage no other joint initiatives between UNHCR and the Duchess are planned.'

There were still a few matters to tidy up. The Foreign Office stated that Sarah's belief she had been offered a UN role was based on a 'misunderstanding'; this was countered however, by Mrs Pida Ripley, founder of WomenAid, who revealed the existence of a letter formally offering the Duchess the job. Conspiracy theorists pointed the finger at the Princess of Wales, who had impressed on Foreign Secretary Hurd that if anyone should be playing the international goodwill ambassador it should be her — and indeed, this idea was considered seriously by Hurd for some time afterwards. One last flurry occurred when sources at UNHCR suggested that the 'no other joint initiatives' statement was merely a tactical withdrawal and that the idea still had legs, but by this stage everyone had tired of it. Sarah, meanwhile, returned from her holiday to prepare for Princess Beatrice's fifth birthday party.

Her finest hour had come, and gone, while she was on the beach.

Back at Romenda Lodge, life was complete chaos. There were nine people in the house, but very often when one arrived it would be the Duchess who answered the door, or picked up the telephone and took messages for her staff. Sometimes it would be the nanny's boyfriend calling, and in the middle of a business meeting I would sometimes hear the Duchess say, 'She's busy just at the moment — can I get her to call you back?'

The staff *were* busy, but not necessarily at their duties. The nanny would often be upstairs while the children were running around crying downstairs. Once Beatrice fell down the stairs and lay there crying, while nobody seemed to notice. One of the house servants developed a relationship with one of the outdoor staff, a woman who believed that she was a fortune-teller and dream analyst. She thought she had discovered a similar calling in her lover. The pair would lock themselves away to further their arcane pursuits and would emerge to inform their employer of the latest cloud on the horizon. One of the pair had a vivid dream about John embezzling money from Sarah while having an affair with a woman from Belgium and in consequence refused to speak to John for days, so certain was he the dream was true. He told the Duchess and — for a moment at least — she too was convinced.

These people were Sarah's servants, but their domestic lives started to dominate her own. On one occasion she and I were in a meeting with lawyers in London when she was asked to take a call from the servant-cum-fortune-teller. The latter was in tears, crying that she'd had a row in the stables with her lover; in the background the Duchess could hear him shouting that he had been insulted. Our meeting ground to a halt while Sarah was forced to arbitrate between the warring factions at home.

At Romenda itself, it was virtually impossible to hold a proper conversation. While the Duchess and I were trying to discuss all-important money-making strategy, the door would open and in would stroll a member of the staff who, having curtsied twice, would inform HRH that they were out of toilet paper — what were they going to do, who was going out to get some more? The Duchess would handle this crisis and the servant would exit, while through the other door would come the children, bored. This perpetual state of barely controlled chaos appeared to make Sarah feel as if she were in control. It also kept her mind occupied: she did not welcome periods of time when her mind was free to think, because that would bring on her depressions. She was, effectively, encouraging the state of bedlam around her.

I tried to talk her into simplifying her daily routine, explaining that her life was in three separate compartments — her charity and public work; her commercial enterprises; and her domestic life. If she appointed one person from each to answer to her, or better still to answer to her private secretary, she would have more time to think and act. As it was, she took calls from everybody and listened to anyone who had a complaint — it was impossible for her to maintain a coherent path through life unless something drastic could be done to alter the shambolic status quo. At first my advice seemed to have some effect. She would say, 'Ah, yes, finally someone is running me, running my life, this is what I need.' But a couple of days later she'd be crying, 'It's *my* life, not *your* life — it's *my* life.' She didn't want the responsibility of running her own affairs, but she could not allow control to pass into another's hands.

The off-duty cook at Romenda was Terence Wilson Fletcher, who was also a portrait painter. The full-time cook, meanwhile, would bring her son to work, and the boy would be there for days on end, playing with Beatrice and Eugenie as an equal. This was refreshingly egalitarian, except that everyone was still expected to bow or curtsy on entering a room in which Sarah was present — there seemed to be no clear structure, even in a social context.

I often thought that life at Romenda Lodge was like an episode from *Fawlty Towers*. One of the women staff went to a party, ended up in bed with a fellow guest, and announced with pride the next morning that she was engaged to a Guards officer. The Duchess, fearful for the future of this union, spent time trying to persuade her not to do it, whereupon the poor girl broke down in tears and confessed to me that her father had molested her as a child. Life was just a series of bizarre scenes from soap operas, superimposed one upon the other, and never very far away was the domineering presence of John Bryan.

When the Duchess and I were working in the dining room, he would stroll in and scoop up a handful of Smarties or M&Ms from the dishes that were lying about, then wander round while chewing them with his mouth open, jingling the change in his pocket and making calls on his mobile phone. He would distract her and distract me, and all the while the servants would be running in and the telephone would be ringing and no one would answer it, until finally Sarah would burst into tears and run into the garden. It was then a question of which servant would rush out first to comfort her: usually Jane Dunn-Butler won the race with a sympathetic 'Oh, Your Royal Highness, it's so horrible! No one understands your suffering!'

It was a horror show, and by the end of a meeting I would be completely drained and would be grateful if the guest room was occupied and I could stay at a hotel. But on the nights I did stay, the evening would follow the same ritual. John and Sarah would have dinner and sit there drinking, using me as their relationship counsellor until they felt they had reached some new plateau of understanding. They would collapse, exhausted, and start cuddling and kissing, and I would beat a diplomatic retreat.

I became very fond of the little princesses; in part because I felt they were starved of attention. Beatrice was learning ballet and was dying to show off her newly acquired skills, but no one seemed particularly interested: I'd always try to find time to watch her practise her steps because it was important to her. If you showed either of the girls a bit of interest or affection they would latch on to you and not let go. Sometimes, when we were having our Fireside Chats, Beatrice would come in with a little painting, grab me and command: 'Come on, Starkie, out into the garden!' Once when we were out there she dangled down from the top of a swing, wanting to show me how she could kick her legs, but she lost her grip and fell, scraping her knees. I carried her back into the house because she was crying, but the Duchess said: 'Oh don't worry about that, she's just trying to get attention.'

I would hide little presents in the garden, then make the girls treasure maps. I gave both of them compasses so they could tell which direction to go in: Eugenie, as with all things, kissed hers and cuddled it. Beatrice threw it up in the air, made no attempt to catch it, and when it shattered on the ground ordered: 'Starkie, fix it!'

The little girls gave their love with generosity. Although Sarah has said that the most valuable time in her day is that magical hour at bedtime when she reads them fairy tales, that is probably the only time during which they have her undivided attention. It may be that she speaks fondly of that time because it is limited. Although at times she impressed people as a conscientious mother, she lacked emotional continuity in her relationship with her children, as she did in any other commitment. On foreign trips she would leave buying them presents until she got to the airport, then a frenzied search would ensue and totally inappropriate gifts be bought, just so they knew that she was thinking about them.

She was, however, jealous of others' success with her children. Once, Beatrice had a riding lesson with a member of staff and came back to boast about how well she'd done. When she announced that she would repeat her triumph the following day, the Duchess became extremely angry and jealously ordered: *'We'll* go out riding tomorrow.' Sarah, by this stage, was a single mother suffering all the pressures that other single mothers do; but I think she took little consolation from her children, and the relationship between all three inevitably suffered from this sad lack.

August came around and it was time for another Fireside Chat. Jeremy Scott produced the management accounts for the Duchess of York and ASB Publishing and it was just as we had feared — nothing had happened businesswise in the few weeks since the last Chat, except that the overdraft had grown at an alarming rate.

Listing the stalled projects was depressing. The French TV documentary, which could offer cash and kudos to the Duchess, had got nowhere. A projected interview with *TV*

Times magazine (kudos) had not moved forward; neither had an article for the French magazine *Point de Vue* (cash) or a signed piece for *Family Circle* (cash and kudos). Of nine projects only one was new, and that came to nothing. A month later we held a similar meeting, with similar results. The Duchess of York industry seemed to have ground to a halt.

Then, near the beginning of October, something strange happened — or it would have been strange, had it not been the Duchess. One night she was sitting at Romenda Lodge flipping through the TV channels when she came upon a documentary special fronted by a BBC journalist, Bill Hamilton. He was reporting from Albania, the tiniest of Balkan states with a population of 3.2 million, and until very recently the last bastion of unreconstructed communism. The conditions in Albania were appalling, even by Eastern Bloc standards, and having seen the programme, Sarah decided she must save Albania. She called Hamilton and said she wanted to help. Her idea of helping was a very tightly controlled publicity exercise to be witnessed by the cash-spewing *Hello!* magazine and a BBC-TV documentary unit.

It was a swift response to the UNHCR débâcle of only weeks before. Sarah wanted an international role, and when the UN job evaporated she was determined to create a niche for herself. She achieved this with remarkable ease. In Albania, the BBC cameras filmed people unloading brand-new cribs for needy children, the arrival of three lorryloads of sweaters and other clothing, and much similar aid besides. Anyone watching could have been forgiven for supposing that the Duchess had spent months setting up this well co-ordinated mercy mission; in fact, she had, with great good fortune, walked into a pre-existing situation that was ready to roll. With or without the Duchess, the aid package would have reached Albania on the very same day; from the charity workers' point of view she was simply along for the publicity, and they were happy with that. But it did not look that way on TV.

I had accompanied Sarah on most of her foreign visits since we had started researching the Queen Victoria book, and it went without saying that we would be travelling together on the mission to this strange and dangerous country. We spent many hours crushed together in the minibus which bumped us across Albania's rugged terrain and potholed roads, and she started to open her heart to me on the subject of a reconciliation with her husband. By now they had been separated for a year and a half and most press commentators had abandoned all hope of such a rapprochement; not, however, Sarah. She told me: 'One of the overriding reasons why I should go back to Andrew is simply to say "Fuck you" to all those people who said it couldn't be done, and all those people who have been backstabbing me. But it would mean returning to a joyless life, living as a nun and giving up JB.'

I told of my experience when, as an eight-year-old, I'd been taken to Woolworths by my father and told that I could choose between having a Crusader or a Desert Rat toy soldier. I had said I wouldn't choose either because whichever one I took home, I'd always regret that it had not been the other. Sarah exclaimed: 'That's it! No matter which way I go I'll regret it for the rest of my life!'

Then she added, totally unexpectedly: 'Allan, if it weren't for the children, the only answer would be to kill myself.' She said this not in a mood of depression, as she had many times in the past, but rather as if she had suddenly come to a clear and logical conclusion. It was a sentiment she was to repeat to me many times. Perhaps the sight of the hungry, sad, abandoned children she had come to visit brought back the black well of despair that haunted her from her own childhood; certainly there were many sombre moments during those days in Albania. We travelled almost the entire length of that benighted country in search of the orphans who had been relocated to an asylum for madwomen. The sight of these women living in sub-animal conditions is too horrifying to recount, but we finally found the children we'd been searching for and delivered up the gifts we had brought.

Sarah and I slept intertwined in the bus, and when we woke she joked: 'So, Starkie, after all these years we finally slept together!' We set off back to the capital, Tirana, where we were due to meet the Health Minister and the President, Sali Berisha. Half a dozen charities were trying to give help to Albania, but the Albanians themselves seemed unequal to the task of coordinating these efforts. During my time with Oceonics I had developed a concept I called 'Doc in the Box', essentially a prefabricated hospital that could be sent in containerized form equipped with medical supplies for a year and a team of Western doctors. Later I was to be criticized for offering up the suggestion to Albanian ministers, but they were under no obligation to commission Oceonics to provide the hospital; once they had grasped the concept, they could buy it in from anywhere.

Finally we were ushered in to our audience with the President. To my astonishment I discovered that the Duchess was extremely nervous. 'It's the first time I have ever met a ruling head of state,' she whispered. 'What am I going to talk to him about?' In the end she overcame this problem by asking the man whether he missed being a heart surgeon, his previous calling. If this seemed a trifle crass as an opening gambit, he did not show it. Indicating our official travelling companion, Vjellsa, a glamorous but not particularly well-disguised spy, he intoned: 'Every land has its exotica. You can report on our exotica, but what I'd strongly request you to do,' he went on, fixing Sarah with a steely gaze, 'is to go back home and speak to other members of your family and see if they can do something to generate interest in supporting us.' Sadly, the President was not to know that by now Sarah was no longer on speaking terms with almost all her 'family'.

One plaintive anecdote remains in my memory from our Albanian experience. When the Duchess and I returned to London we asked the Albanian Ambassador to come to a glittering evening in the City, which had been arranged to help raise funds for his country. The diplomat, a dignified man who was writing the first-ever English-Albanian dictionary in his spare time, lived in a borrowed flat and was so poor he could not afford a dinner jacket, and thus felt obliged to decline our invitation. Eventually the Duchess provided him with the necessary dress clothes, but even so he came to the party by bus.

Early in November, a ball was held in a modern hotel on Park Lane, to take advantage of the publicity we had attracted during the Albanian trip. The Duchess wore a stunning emerald green dress, very tight-cut, and with her hair done in a fluffy style which made her look the best I ever saw her. As usual things did not go as planned: though she had me as her escort, Christine Gallagher as her project manager, her private secretary and her father all there, she managed to get abandoned at the front door, marooned amid a sea of exploding flash-bulbs and shouted questions from the assembled reporters. She angrily pushed her way through the throng and had a terse five minutes with Christine in the ladies' cloak-room. The only bright spot was an unscheduled visit from *Baywatch*'s David Hasselhoff, who constantly referred to his famous TV series as 'Babe Watch'. I was glad when three o'clock came round and we could all escape.

Perhaps one should not be surprised at the spontaneous response the Albanian crisis had elicited from the Duchess, for she could be equally impulsive in her personal relations. She was constantly meeting new people and falling under their spell. One such was Eric Buterbaugh, a close associate of the Italian designer Gianni Versace. Eric had excellent contacts in QVC, the television shopping channel, and persuaded Sarah that she could make a great deal of money by selling goods on TV, following a path already well trodden by the likes of Ivana Trump and Joan Rivers.

Sarah became very excited by the possibilities, and the first product we discussed selling was her Queen Victoria book, which had failed to find a publisher in the US. The idea was that she would personally sign each copy sold, and such was our excitement at the thought of the millions of dollars that this would generate that I took a stopwatch and timed her signing her autograph to see how many books she could sign in five minutes. This idea came to nothing, however, so I then came up with the idea of selling Wedgwood plates adorned with an image of Windsor Castle, which still stood blackened by the disastrous fire of the previous winter.

At this point Sarah was still trying to maintain a relationship with the Queen, to what end it is hard to imagine, although she clung to her belief that Her Majesty had a sneaking regard for her. Be that as it may, the Duchess saw the selling of the Wedgwood plates as an opportunity to cement this alliance, and at the same time to give back something for all she had taken from the royal family. The plates would help raise money for the Windsor Castle renovation fund. It never occurred to her that if the press got to hear that she was personally profiting from an international appeal to save a world-famous monument, she would be crucified. All she could see was that a plate would cost £15 wholesale, there would be a profit margin of 100 per cent, and on top of that £1 would be added as a charitable donation to the renovation fund. Needless to say, this project died a death as well.

In the second week of November we gathered at Romenda Lodge for another Fireside Chat. By this stage the meetings had turned into a regurgitation of projects which neither generated income, nor were likely to. In this sterile atmosphere, John would manipulate the agenda so that the meeting became entirely personal to him and Sarah. In front of half a dozen people he would bark: 'When are you going to divorce this man? When are we going to get married?' This was intimate stuff which should have been dealt with behind closed doors. Almost invariably, his behaviour would lead to Sarah bursting into tears and fleeing the room, with the rest of us taking it in turns to lure her back in order to continue the meeting. In the time these Fireside Chats had been in existence, my feelings for the Duchess had fundamentally altered: in the early days I had thought she was exploiting John unmercifully and that she was simply a very lazy person, self-serving and parasitical. In the last months of 1993, however, it became clear that John had brought her to a point at which she was too frightened even to speak in these meetings. The Fireside Chat had lost its purpose, but no one wanted to admit it.

As the Holy Grail of marriage continued to prove as elusive as ever, John's savagery increased. On one half-baked project, yet another book or film about duchesses and princesses, Sarah had asked an aide to write a synopsis and send it to Duncan Heath, a powerful agent and friend of John's. Apparently the finished document had contained a number of typing errors, and was in any case not particularly well-written. In the next

Fireside Chat John had rounded on the Duchess and used this as an example of her organizational incompetence. He had then delivered an edict that nothing was allowed to leave her office, particularly to a man of the stature of Duncan Heath, without his personal approval. As a result of this and similar behaviour, she would attend these meetings fearful of what John would say in public, and even more frightened of what he would say afterwards.

One night we all stayed at Romenda Lodge, having agreed at a Chat that afternoon that Sarah should write a magazine article on 'A Day in the Life of the Duchess, together with her observations on motherhood', which various publications were offering thousands of dollars for. Next morning we came down to the dining room for breakfast, to find her sitting there, shaking, unable to drink her tea. She was clearly in shock, and when we started to discuss the outline of the magazine article she looked at John, then at me, and said: 'Well, I don't know.' Then she looked at him for a long time, but he refused to respond. Finally she said, 'JB, please . . .', then added after a pause, 'Please, if there's something you've got to say, say it now when they're here and not when the door's closed later on.' One of the other guests looked at me and whispered, 'God knows what he did to her last night when we were all asleep.'

During this period I witnessed a significant change in John. He was on at the Duchess the whole time, berating her, belittling her. Once he told her: 'I'm tired of your royal bullshit, you're a nobody, you're a nothing. You married a prince, but you're nothing. You hide behind all this royal bullshit and you're the most dishonest, stupid person I've ever met in my life.' At the heart of it, he sensed that she was flinching away from making the final break with Prince Andrew. He grew angrier at her procrastination over the divorce, and yet more livid at the thought that she imagined he was stupid enough to believe her excuses. He was furious that he was not allowed to be seen in public with her — and he knew that she responded to being humiliated.

This fitted in well with John's own attitudes towards the opposite sex. He used to tell Sarah: 'You're a tart, you're a slut,' and she would become extremely stimulated. She would call me up and ask, 'Does John fuck prostitutes?' and though he did, often, I would say, 'No, he thinks of no one but you.' Her response would be, 'Well, that's a mistake. I'd like him to fuck prostitutes, it wouldn't bother me at all.' Part of her role-play would be to quiz John about who had come on to him at parties, for she felt better about herself if she knew that women, attractive and sexy women, were interested in her boyfriend. On one occasion, perhaps unsure as to how far to go when she ordered him once again to treat her as a tart, John slapped her very hard across the face. As he related it, 'There was a second of just stunned silence,' and then it was as if a fountain was gushing where her eyes should be; tears poured down her face while she sobbed wildly, madly, for hours. John described this as a primal catharsis: certainly it frightened him, for her response was out of all proportion to the blow he had dealt her, and he asked himself if her reaction was less to do with his actions than with something that had happened to her in the past.

That last observation showed an unaccustomed moment of sexual sensitivity on his part, for as I observed John's relations with Sarah and the other people he bedded it gradually became clear that he actually did not like women. He had a particularly unusual habit which he described to me in great detail, and which involved his woman partner remaining fully dressed and sexually unfulfilled.

John used sex as a weapon. For the first six months of his relationship with Sarah he was almost completely faithful, and while things remained stable he was relatively loyal to her. But as the Fireside Chats became more strained, as his faith in her weakened, his acts of infidelity became more and more overt and increasingly bizarre. It was as though he wanted Sarah to know that he was taking his revenge with disadvantaged women, the implication being that they were her equals. He picked up a girl in Tramp, the Jermyn Street nightclub, who had only one leg. On another occasion he took a very small woman back to his flat where he triggered in her, by his unorthodox actions, an asthma attack. So frightened was he by her illness and its likely repercussions that he waited in the hall pretending to have called an ambulance: he had quickly come to the conclusion that if she died he would put the body in Barney Lindley's office next door, then drive to Romenda Lodge to establish an alibi. The episodes got worse and worse: John's sister, Baby, tried to find him a more 'suitable' partner and set him up with the daughter of a fabulously wealthy industrialist, whom they invited to the Bryan home in Watch Hill, Rhode Island. John took her to a bar, got drunk and forgot he was with her, picked up a blonde, and left his date stranded. Later he returned and humiliated the socialite by awakening her and then performing a perfunctory sexual act on her.

John and Sarah's relationship was not simply a combination of evasion and ritual humiliation, however. In its quieter moments it remained passionate and, as far as either of them felt able, committed. John took to ordering handmade pieces from a Chelsea jeweller, Theo Fennell. Theo did not come cheap: a pair of gold, ruby and diamond earrings cost £6,100, a small gold bangle £1,500. Sarah was as lavish in her gifts to John; neither could afford them.

Meanwhile, Sarah was not above using her charms in her attempts to reduce her backbreaking overdraft. She met an extremely rich Arab prince at a party in London in the autumn of 1993. She was aware that he had previously paid a great deal of attention to the Princess of Wales, though his interest had not been reciprocated.

Highly educated, he nevertheless liked people to believe that he did not speak English well. He enjoyed the company of Westerners, particularly high-born Western women, and had a reputation both for wanting to share his wealth and for prizing his friendships. On their first meeting, he invited the Duchess to a dinner party at his house in Mayfair.

Over dinner, he asked her, 'Are you my friend?' to which she replied, 'Of course, are you my friend?' In turn, the prince answered, 'But of course, and I would do anything for my friends. Is there anything I could do for you?' Without batting an eyelid, Sarah smiled and said, 'As a matter of fact there is. You could pay off my overdraft.' At that time, her debt to Coutts was hovering just under the £2 million mark.

Her host was not flustered in the slightest by this quite extraordinary request. 'Well, I could consider doing that for a friend,' he replied, 'but I don't see the point in doing that if you're going to fall back into debt again. I would like you to prove to me that if I do this, you'll never be in debt again.' This brought a protest from the Duchess: of course she wouldn't. She had all these projects coming along which were going to make huge amounts of money — they just needed time to come to fruition. After this, they would keep her solvent. The prince nodded, then said that he would like a member of Sarah's staff to present a plan to his own advisers to prove that this was possible. If it was satisfactory, he would help.

A business recovery plan was put together which demonstrated the incredible profits that would be generated shortly from Sarah's various enterprises, and this was duly submitted. The document apparently met with the prince's approval, and he again invited the Duchess to dinner, this time to his house in the country.

On the appointed night Sarah drove to the prince's house and was greeted by the sight of him wearing flowing Arab robes. Looking around, she realized that dinner was set out on a candlelit table behind them, and that the servants had disappeared. Her host opened and poured the champagne himself. The Duchess was left in no doubt that she was undergoing the first stages of a seduction; but the prince, though charming, she found unattractive, and it began to cross her mind that it might not be possible for her to pay back her overdraft in this manner. The prince told her that he thought he could help her, that he was her friend — and he leant forward and started to kiss her.

Sarah said later that once his lips had closed on hers there was no getting away; but somehow in the end she managed to break free (subsequently she referred to him as 'Rubber Lips' or 'RL'). Clearly the prince would not achieve his goal that night, and neither would the Duchess — but being civilized people, they continued the evening as though nothing had happened, and parted on good terms.

From this, Sarah expected either another invitation from her spurned would-be benefactor, or never to hear from him again. As it turned out, something quite different happened. In early December 1993, she discovered as she was checking through her bank statement that £50,000 had been deposited by the prince into her account. Sarah called me, excited at the thought of her £50,000 kiss, but made me promise not to tell John.

He finally found out, though, and was furious. Typically for John, once he discovered that there was money involved, whenever we had a major crisis he flew to wherever the prince was — Los Angeles, New York — and camped outside his door in the hope of raising some money from this man who had so generously thanked his girlfriend for a kiss. Despite this shamelessness, he always came away empty-handed.

Chapter 9

Travel provided the mental release Sarah was perpetually seeking. Though she had been in weekly psychoanalysis since the trauma of the South of France photographs, even taking along her sister Jane to share the experience, getting on a plane and flying away from the source of her problems was by far the most effective way of restoring her equilibrium. Soon after her return from Albania in October 1993 she took off for Nepal, where she trekked towards Everest on behalf of the MacIntyre Cara charity, with a number of patients suffering motor neurone disease in the party. A curious by-product of this trip was the acquisition of a Himalayan bearer, who was brought back to England and given a place on the staff at Romenda Lodge. Soon Yeltsin, as he was dubbed, who had undefined responsibilities, found himself answering the telephone — a bewildering experience for callers since he spoke no English at all.

In her absence, British newspapers speculated on the stability of her relationship with John: one report claimed that she had booted him out of both her love and her business lives, while another front-page story told how he had fallen for an unnamed twenty-six-year-old and that the distraught Duchess had gone on the Everest trip 'to forget'. It was a measure of the nation's thirst for news about Sarah and John that such stories were being fabricated, and they were all wide of the mark. Though the relationship had sailed away from calm waters, the pair were inextricably linked, both emotionally and financially.

Sarah was, however, still determined not to be seen with John in public. In her TV interview with Maria Shriver, transmitted in the US the previous year, she had disingenuously described John as 'a brother, really', much to his irritation: but she softened her stance sufficiently to attend the Bath and Racquets Club in London to watch him playing a squash tournament. Her presence in the gallery was duly noted and appeared in the newspapers shortly afterwards.

The frustrations remained, however. John took care of his with typical abandon: he was spotted in Shelby's, a Manhattan singles bar, at around this time. Sarah, a more complex individual, eased her psychological and emotional burdens by subtler methods — even if they sometimes bordered on the bizarre.

One day in December she was watching TV at Romenda Lodge when, flicking channels, she came across a show-jumping competition. One of the riders, who looked a little like Paul Newman, executed a stylish round atop a beautiful dapple-grey called Heather Blaze. She was transfixed. Within minutes she had called Jane Ambler and ordered her to tune in to the programme, look at the rider, find out who he was and where he was, and schedule a meeting. She had to see him. This done, she called me and, having briefly explained, blurted out: 'Starkie, I am going to win the next Olympic gold medal!' My reply, as diplomatic as I could make it, was, 'Well, you haven't ridden for quite a while . . .' but she cut in: 'It doesn't matter, it's my fate! I've found the horse, I'm going to Ireland to buy it, I've found the trainer, and you're coming with me!'

I flew to London, met the Duchess at Heathrow, and we flew to Cork to meet the latest objects of her obsessional nature, Heather Blaze and its rider, Robert Splaine. The trip was supposed to be a secret since it involved a member of the royal family entering Ireland, but we had to inform Buckingham Palace anyway. So, as we touched down at Cork, we were expecting to meet

Robert, but not the assembled Irish press corps, who had obviously been tipped off. Robert went to get his car while the photographers had a field day recording this unscheduled and — given the state of relations between Ireland and Britain — unorthodox arrival in the Republic. The Duchess was very much upset, almost hysterical. She had wanted this visit, which could not easily be explained away, to remain a secret.

Working in Sarah's mind was what the international press might make of a madcap dash to Ireland involving expensive security, and as we drove away she said to me: 'We can't be seen to be coming here just for a *riding lesson*. We've got to come up with another reason.' After a few moments' thought she picked up Robert Splaine's mobile telephone, called the Motor Neurone Disease Foundation (of which she was patron), and said: 'Hi, this is Sarah, I'd like you to do me a favour. In the next hour could you find me the name of someone who's been newly diagnosed with the disease, somewhere here around Cork?'

We arrived at Robert's place, the Corcorren Stables outside Cork, and Sarah mounted Heather Blaze while I was given a sweet horse called Henry. We went off over some jumps and Robert gave Sarah some instruction — despite a horsey childhood, she had not ridden for five years. At the end, flushed with the feeling of having been in control of the powerful mount (she only fell off once), she asked Robert breezily, 'Now give it to me straight — can I win the Olympic gold medal?'

This was rather like asking if she could win the Nobel Prize for Literature for having written *Budgie*, but Robert wanted to be polite. Anything was possible, he demurred, she just needed to recover the talent she had once had. If she really wanted to go through with her Olympic bid she would need two horses — one that could be kept in the stables at Windsor, and one in Ireland. He would then visit to give her instruction, or she could fly out to Ireland. In the meantime she'd need to ride several hours a day, carrying a mobile phone so that they could go over the things he was teaching her. The next Olympics, he added, were pretty doubtful, but perhaps she should be looking at the games that would follow four years later.

Maybe the prospect of some six years in the saddle merely to achieve a momentary whim was too much, even for Sarah, but she could not let it go that easily. She said: 'Robert, thank you for your honesty. What I think should happen is that *you* ride the horse in the Olympics. I'll buy the horse and sponsor you!'

To Robert, this was an extraordinary offer. A few days before he had been an accomplished but relatively unknown rider with no Olympic ambitions — now, after an afternoon in the company of a woman he had never met before, he was being offered royal patronage and money too. It did not take long for him and his wife to agree, but not before Sarah had told them: 'I want you to go ahead with this, but I want to warn you your lives will change — change in ways you can't even understand. You will be pursued by the press, you'll become celebrities in your own right, your lives will never be what they once were — all because of your association with me. Are you willing to go along with that?' Of course, said the Splaines, they'd had plenty of experience with the press, there would be no problem.

Her ambition fulfilled, if only in part, Sarah turned to the vexed question of explaining her presence in Ireland. She went out to call the Motor Neurone Foundation again, and learned that they had found a man newly diagnosed with the disease; they had called him and he was ready to receive his surprise visitor. She came back into the room smiling broadly. She had got her alibi.

The Irish police now escorted us in their squad cars through the pouring rain to find this poor man, who lived in a lower middle class development on the edge of the city. He was an upholsterer who, having retired, had taken his wife on a trip to Tenerife. While enjoying the sun he had suddenly discovered a stiffness in his arm; many tests later he was diagnosed as having motor neurone disease. There is no cure. The muscles in the body gradually seize up until the sufferer is completely paralysed, while the brain remains unaffected: you become a prisoner in your own body.

So we arrived at the house, where the couple waiting for us believed that we had flown all this way to see them. The idea was to let the press know that Sarah was on a charity visit and that she had taken the opportunity to ride with her 'friend' Robert Splaine — whom she'd met a mere two or three hours before. She started talking to the man, saying that in a way he was lucky that the disease had started in his arm because it would reach his face, heart and lungs last. Until now he had kept his emotions in check, but at this point he burst into uncontrollable sobs; then his wife started crying, between sobs saying to the Duchess, 'It's so good you've made him cry, he couldn't cry before.'

The return flight was difficult for me. On the way out the Duchess and I had enjoyed ourselves, looking forward to a day's innocent entertainment. She had even revealed what the world was not to know for another few hours: that the Princess of Wales was sensationally to announce her withdrawal from public life. But now I felt angry and sad and let down. Sarah's reaction was nothing if not pragmatic: 'You'll get used to it, Allan. There's not much you can do, but you help them any way you can.' In her own mind, I had no doubt, she had just done a wonderful thing but to me, because it was an alibi, all the goodness was sucked out of it. As far as I know, she never saw the man again.

That should have been the end of a miserable day, but it was not. Awaiting us at the other end was the extraordinary sight of HRH's butler carrying a Rastafarian wig: only then did I remember that Sarah was hosting a party at Romenda Lodge and that I had promised to attend dressed as a Jamaican.

The idea was a savage one: it was the middle of December, but the theme was 'Caribbean Beach Party', and guests were expected to attend in swimwear. We were ushered through the house and out into some canvas military tents, ice-cold from the night air, and with gas heaters that didn't work. There were rough wooden tables in a square with folding metallic chairs, tin bowls to eat from and a pot of stew in the middle. It wasn't a Caribbean party, it was a Mount Everest parry — the Duchess wanted all her guests to experience the discomfort she herself had been through a few weeks earlier.

As jokes go, it was just about tolerable for the friends she had invited, but also present were the motor neurone patients who had accompanied her to the Himalayas, some of them in wheelchairs and all of them suffering in the appalling cold. Addressing the assembled guests, the Duchess gave us her habitual four jokes, one of which involves a penguin and requires her to get on her knees and mime an act of oral sex.

I drove one of the motor neurone sufferers back to a hotel near Heathrow airport: he was due to fly back to Australia, and I think he had been somewhat stunned by what he had seen. But still, against all odds, he professed undying respect for Sarah and her sister Jane, whom he had met in Australia.

I got back to Frankfurt on 7 December, to find another of the Duchess's messages on my answering machine. She wanted to push on with another children's book project involving a character called Billy Bucket, which she was convinced could be really successful. But mostly she wanted to talk about our trip to Ireland, and the riding, and how nice it had been to see me on a horse, and how well I had ridden. She made no mention of motor neurone disease sufferers, in Ireland or anywhere else.

Now, it seemed, it was John's turn to ask me to accompany him on a solo venture. He had been nominated by the organizers of the Best Awards ceremony, an annual jamboree, sponsored by *Best* magazine, which for no apparent reason likes to give prizes to the jet set just for being themselves. Described as being dedicated to those who boast 'the most elegant of elegant lifestyles', the Best Awards had originally been created to honour beauty and elegance, but now tended to be bestowed on those considered by an international jury selected by the magazine 'to have imported a touch of elegance into their private and professional lives, whatever the field'.

An excuse to dress up, then, and to drink some free champagne in the company of others with nothing to do that night. But not in John's case — for some reason he took the whole idea of being nominated for the Best Awards very seriously, even though the unspoken reason for his invitation was no more than the fact that he had cuckolded the Queen of England's second son.

Perhaps he should have got a clue as to the merits of this occasion by taking a look at some of his fellow nominees. One such was Dewi Sukarno, former First Lady of Indonesia but more recently a resident of the Pitkin County gaol in Colorado, where she had served a custodial sentence for smashing a champagne glass into the face of fellow socialite Minnie Osmena. During her incarceration she had produced some animal sketches for a newsletter published by the Aspen Center for Environmental Studies; it was this creative gift which the *Best* committee wished to honour.

None of this mattered: John was heralded by the self-same committee as a 'celebrated international businessman', and in December he begged me to fly to Paris with him to collect his award at the Carrousel du Louvre. There was someone else who thought it essential that I be there, as was clear from a message on my answering machine. The Duchess hoped I would go — to support John and look after him, and also to make sure that he behaved.

It is worth recounting in some detail what happened in Paris that night, because it

changed John Bryan for ever. His upbringing
had been privileged, his early adult life pam-
pered, his fast track to the centre of things
effortless. But it would be fair to say that
everything he had achieved had been on
someone else's coat-tails. Tonight was no
different — he was here because of his affair
with the Duchess of York, not because of his
status as an international businessman — but
he was incapable of seeing it that way. This
award, he considered, had been won by his
own efforts — by the sheer force of his
charm, his looks and his personality.

I arrived at the Plaza Athénée hotel and
hurried to John's room, where I found the
celebrated international businessman naked
and shivering with fright as he prepared his
acceptance speech. He dressed and we hurried downstairs to drink champagne with Vanessa Redgrave, the model Naomi Campbell
and her mother Valerie, and John's nineteen-
year-old, leather-trousered niece Gwennie.
The glitzy cocktail reception offered a view
of John under stress: 'Don't stick your fingers
in my stomach, Allan, the photographers are
looking for stuff like that'; 'Hold my drink,
they are taking pictures'; 'Someone hold
these cigarettes for a moment.' Finally we
reached the table, where I discovered the film
director Roman Polanski and his new wife

Emmanuelle Seigneur, the Queen of Sweden, the late Shah of Iran's first wife, Princess Soraya, and Dewi Sukarno, as well as a host of models, actresses and aristocrats whose faces frequently adorn the gossip columns.

The awards ceremony proceeded at a deathly pace, but finally we were able to bid Vanessa goodnight and hail a cab for l'Arc, a stylish nightclub. Dropping Naomi Campbell's name got us in and a friendly bouncer cleared an area for us. Jessica Orsina and Prince Carlo Giovenelli danced over to us and the evening's entertainment started in earnest. Much later I left, leaving my credit card and what remaining cash I had with John, whom I last saw dancing with both Naomi Campbell and her mother. It reminded me of the night I had left him dancing with his sister Baby at Annabel's in London.

The next day we attended a gala luncheon at the Plaza Athénée. A highly entertaining Valerie Campbell was on my table, and we were joined later by a woman wearing heavy sunglasses, who began to regale us with a blow-by-blow account of her night's sexual gymnastics with the actor John Malkovich. With mounting horror it began to dawn on me that this was a terrible case of mistaken identity — the John she was referring to was John Bryan. Some highly complex manoeuvring was necessary in order to enlist this woman's agreement not to pass on what would have been a sensational story; it included, at the end, the promise of a trip to the Romenda Lodge Christmas party.

Christmas came and went, with Sarah spending a great deal of time with Andrew and their children. One London newspaper, *Today*, reported that:

> Fergie and her estranged husband spent many hours snuggled up in front of the fire at her home, Romenda Lodge, with Beatrice and Eugenie. They both travelled to Sandringham and Andrew embraced his wife warmly in front of the Queen and her family.
>
> Unlike the chilly example of Charles and Diana, Fergie sent out Christmas greetings for friends from herself and Andrew as well as the little Princesses.

Whoever had leaked this to *Today* warmed to their theme. 'It would not be over-egging it to say there was a feeling of romance in the air,' an unnamed source was quoted as having said. 'You'd never know that these two people are technically estranged.' The piece went on to suggest that Sarah and John's physical relationship had fizzled out, and that it was not beyond hope that the royal couple might get back together again. There could be no prizes for guessing which side of the estranged couple that came from; but even so, as soon as was decently possible Sarah escaped from the clutches of her in-laws and headed for the snow where she felt more secure.

And so the year ended, with no intimation of the storms and tribulations ahead.

Whatever did lie in the future, one thing was certain: Sarah and John's relationship, built on shifting sands, had moved on again. Not surprisingly, the trek through the Himalayas had altered the Duchess's perspectives and given her a new sense of direction. For the previous six months she had been taking Prozac to counter her massive mood swings and lurking depression; however, she had forgotten to pack the pills and had been forced to face nearly a month in the mountains without their support. The combination of physical exertion and lack of oxygen at those altitudes brought on a physical tiredness but also a sense of elation, and by the time she got back to her base camp at Kathmandu, and was able to call me on her satellite telephone, she was free of the drug's grip. 'You'll be so proud of me,' she boasted, and I congratulated her; but there was something else which had lifted her spirits: 'I'm looking forward to having my first orgasm in months.' Prozac, while stabilizing her moods, had robbed her of this particular pleasure. On her return from Nepal, Sarah had looked better than she had during the whole relationship. She had lost an entire layer of fat throughout her body — uniformly, for a change — and had clearly found her experiences very uplifting. In the company of her friend Allie Lobel, she had had plenty of time to reassess her priorities — and had come to the conclusion that it was time to divorce Andrew and marry John.

Her thinking went further: she and John needed to find a place where they could be happy together without the pressure of constant press intrusion. After they had talked it over together, they came to the conclusion that Switzerland would be their new home. Sarah calculated that if they relocated to America there was a strong chance that she would lose custody of her children.

Switzerland seemed an ideal compromise: ninety minutes' flight from London, yet sufficiently far away from the intrusive British press for her and John to be left in peace.

261

Switzerland also had mountains — after her Himalayan experience she was convinced that mountains had a very soothing effect on her psyche — and she pictured a glorious exile, rather like that of the Duchess of Windsor. A friend told me he could get John the necessary permits which would allow him to conduct his business from there and, happier than I had seen him in the entire relationship, he initiated a formal application for Swiss residency.

The crash, when it came, hurt him deeply. One day, a week or so later, Sarah told him: 'Oh no, I really can't do this, and I don't know what I'm talking about. It's too soon, it's simply too soon. . . .' It was typical of her vacillating, turnabout nature — but John did not see it coming. In his mind he was already married to Sarah; they had wiped the slate clean and started a new life. It was inconceivable that she could change her mind now.

From that point on the symptoms of the syndrome they were trapped in became more severe: the viciousness was more vicious, the lows more low — and, conversely, the highs more high. But after this John simply did not trust the Duchess any more. Soon I was forced to tell him that her plans to find a new home did not include him — she wanted a house of her own, for which provision had been made in her separation agreement, and John had talked enthusiastically about the possibilities. One day she called me and said: 'Look, Allan, you've got to help me with this. I don't want to live with JB. He's living with me every day here and that's the way it is, but at least he's got his apartment in Cheyne Place. Now he wants to give up Cheyne Place because he thinks it's silly paying rent for two places when we only need one. He wants us to work together at whatever home we live in and it's just too close, it's *pressurizing* me and I just want my own room and my own space and I don't want to live with him.'

She started to tell me that she wouldn't even mind if they were each to see other people, but then she retracted the idea almost instantaneously, deciding instead that he could remain as her boyfriend but that he must continue to keep his own establishment. Ideally, she said, she would like to see him three nights a week.

John's reaction when I told him was: 'Yeah, yeah, she's just saying that to you because she gets nervous and frightened sometimes, but she doesn't really mean it. She says these things for effect but you don't really understand her. You'll see. . . .' But it was he who had misread her — within six months Sarah would be confiding in me that she was going to cut loose from the relationship. For now, however, it was up to John to try to work out what was going on in the Duchess's mind. He confronted her with what she had told me, and she confirmed it. He came back to me and said: 'Well, fuck her — I'll just go and find another girlfriend and that'll show her.' And so for the next week or two he lived in his apartment at Cheyne Place, going out every night and bringing home whatever willing girl he could lay his hands on.

In the shadow of this rift we met at Romenda Lodge for another business meeting. For the first time, the agenda was broken down into two halves — projects for the Duchess to pursue, and projects for John to pursue. The two cherry trees, intertwined all this time, were beginning to grow their separate ways. Sarah had made it clear that the constant arguments about business were undermining the relationship, and she wanted something done about it. Anticipating her, I had made up the agenda, pulling John away from her and giving him his own projects to chase.

The Budgie animation was still the only serious deal that he had negotiated for the

Duchess, and by now it was becoming clear that it was not as clever as it might have been. Shares in Sleepy Kids, the animation company which had bought the rights to Budgie, rose tenfold in the months following signature of the contract — but John had failed to negotiate any stock options for the Duchess, so while Sleepy Kids almost instantly became a very valuable company, Sarah did not profit directly. Her deal was that she would get 35 per cent of future revenues, after Sleepy Kids' expenses had been recovered, once the animation was put up for sale to TV stations around the world.

Now that Sleepy Kids had realized the value of its newly acquired property, it approached the Duchess to buy out her 35 per cent share. The offer was worth £3 million, £1.5 million in stock and £1.5 million in cash. We urged her to accept.

John said to me after the meeting, 'I think it's probably worth more than that, but it's not a bad offer — I think she should take it and I should get half of it.' For since he had started negotiating on behalf of the Duchess, the question of whether he would take a management fee had never been discussed, and now it needed to be addressed in a hurry. I told John I would talk to the Duchess, adding, 'I'm sure she'll understand.' 'I'm not sure she will,' he replied, ominously.

So I telephoned the Duchess and said, 'Look, this isn't a social call, I'm actually acting as John's agent in this particular call. John says that now we're in a position to liquidate Budgie he'd like to clear up who owns what.'

'What do you mean, who owns what? It's mine.'

'Well John feels that half of the new money that's come out of Budgie should go to him.'

'Whaaaa? It's mine!' she squeaked. 'Budgie is my third child! Why should I give up a part of my third child to him?'

'Because he feels that he made it valuable for you.'

'Oh, I see. He doesn't want any of the old Budgie, no, because that's worthless — he just wants half of the new Budgie because it's worth something.'

I started to explain, but she interrupted: 'Hang on, tell me another way. Explain it to me in potatoes.'

So I did. 'It's like this. You had a potato, and you put the potato on your shelf and it started getting mouldy and old and you re-alized you were never going to be able to eat the potato or make french fries out of it because the potato was mouldy and old. So you had one mouldy potato on your shelf and this master cook came along and with his secret recipe made this delicious potato soup and now everybody can eat the potato. So what the cook is saying is "Can I please have half the soup?" '

The Duchess paused for a few seconds, then said: 'I knew it, it's just as I always suspected! He looked at me and became interested in me as someone he could make money from and *then* he fell in love with me later. This just proves it!'

I put down the phone, then picked it up again to call John and tell him her reaction. During the next four minutes the Duchess called and hung up several times, finally saying to my secretary, 'Tell him if he doesn't pick up the phone now I will never speak to him again.' When I did so, she berated me for having told John what she had said, but I replied: 'I told you at the beginning of the conversation that I was acting as his agent, and what you said really needs to be discussed. If you feel one-tenth of those things, you really shouldn't be together with him. That's your affair, of course, but naturally I told him.'

'Well, that was really stupid,' she barked. 'Let me see if I can fix things.' She called John and they made their peace, but the matter remained unresolved for several months afterwards.

Four days later we were back at Romenda Lodge for another Fireside Chat. By now the Duchess was in severe financial trouble, grappling with a huge overdraft that deepened as each month went by. John had told the bank that he would guarantee a substantial portion of the overdraft; so trusting were the royal bankers that they never asked for any collateral and simply took his signature as guarantee. Finally, when they wanted him to stand up for the money and it became clear that he didn't have it, they simply walked away shaking their heads. It never occurred to them to take action against him — or if it did, they were so embarrassed by their own laxity that they did not want it made public.

The overdraft continued to increase at the rate of between £35,000 and £50,000 a month. John just laughed and said, 'The bank is pregnant,' meaning it was too late, the bankers couldn't do anything. Within a two-and-a-half year period the Duchess's overdraft went from nothing to £3 million, and John kept Coutts at bay by producing successive business plans, recovery plans, lists of future revenues. Again and again he seemed able to convince the bank that it was not that the revenues didn't exist, but that they were delayed. Sarah's reaction to what was an extreme situation was remarkably calm. She looked at her overdraft as something which had nothing to do with banks or people; it was just a bad circumstance, like having a sick child.

Eric Buterbaugh was still pushing for Sarah to appear on QVC, the American TV sales channel. The Windsor Castle plate idea had come to nothing because Wedgwood wanted the fabrication costs of the plate up-front — the manufacturer's minimum run of 10,000 plates would have cost £150,000, which the Duchess did not have, so a cheaper alternative was sought. I then suggested that she paint a watercolour of Windsor Castle and have it turned into a limited-edition lithograph — or, better still, borrow from the Royal Archives a painting of the castle done by Queen Victoria. This idea went some way, though looked at from a distance it was most unlikely that the Queen would ever have allowed Crown possessions to be used for commercial profit by anyone outside her immediate family, as Sarah now was. In the end this, too, came to nothing, and the best idea Eric could come up with after that was to get people to pay £100,000 to have lunch with the Duchess. That had a predictably limited life, too, but it was a shame about

QVC — later I spoke to Ivana Trump, and she told me that she had made £165,000 in one minute, a record, selling her goods on that channel.

From business to pleasure, John and I flew to Paris for dinner in the apartment of Massimo Gargia, publisher of that same *Best* magazine which had so recently awarded John his citation for cuckolding the Duke of York. There, we met HRH Princess Esmeralda of Belgium and her partner, the journalist Albert Zarca, whom I dubbed 'the Reporter from Hell' but whom I was subsequently to introduce to the Duchess, to their mutual profit.

After dinner we moved on to a piano bar, on again to a gay disco, and then to Calvados, an after-hours place where the beautiful people eat spaghetti and drink therapeutic Bloody Marys to the accompaniment of a Mexican mariachi band. These poor simpletons recognized John but believed he was having an affair with the Princess of Wales, and duly changed the words of 'Guantanamera' to paint this picture:

He was a man from Texas
Then he came to London
John Bryan
Oh, oh, oh, John Bryan

Oh, oh, he went to the Palace
John Bryan
His name was Joo-oohn Bryan . . .

The song's subject found this awfully amusing. One of our party, a middle-aged socialite, invited us back to her apartment, which was in an elegant building across from the Plaza Athénée, but after some teasing conversation I realized my presence was no longer required. An exhausted playboy caught up with me four hours later, a sheepish grin on his face — the lady was old enough to be his mother.

A week later it was the Duchess's turn to claim me as her travelling companion. Her latest charity foray was to Split in Croatia, and on 11 February 1994 we joined our charter cargo plane full of supplies at Stansted airport, near London. At the back of the plane the Duchess and I sat under a waterfall of condensation, occupying two of the very few seats. Though the flight was long the conversation never flagged, and in no time we reached Split where, after a press conference, we made our way into Bosnia to a surprisingly clean refugee camp. Naturally, we had with us a journalist from *Hello!* magazine, and during the day this person complained that the monstrously large chief of police who was accompanying us had been surreptitiously taking pictures of HRH, and would I be kind enough to confiscate them? *Hello!* was supposed to have an exclusive on this trip.

When I made my request an argument broke out and the chief ordered me into his car. We drove to a deserted street where he turned off the ignition and kindly explained that he had killed many people in the civil war and had enjoyed it. He would not kill me, and he would even give me the film — but I must promise not to tell his men what had transpired. *Hello!* and the Duchess both profited from this strange transaction; all I was left with was an uneasy memory of that deserted street, and the silence as he switched off the car engine.

When I left HRH's hotel room that night I assumed the door would lock automatically as I closed it. It did not. The local body-guards who sat in the hallway between our rooms disappeared during the night, and someone then tried to get into the Duchess's room. Unable to lock the door quickly enough, she lay on the floor pushing against the door with her feet until her unwelcome visitor had departed.

The next day seemed as though it were the longest day in history. We visited a children's hospital where in one ward all the children had been shot below the waist so that, should they survive their wounds, and the war, they would be unable to reproduce. The horrors of ethnic cleansing were many and varied, it seemed. We also visited a ward which was a converted gymnasium, where Downs syndrome children were tied to the walls. The Duchess hugged and kissed these poor, filthy, abandoned creatures when the others in our party could not even bring themselves to enter the room because of the smell. This, for me, was Sarah at her finest.

Finally we made our way back to the hotel before flying Croatian Airlines back to Heathrow. The original plan had been to fly the American aid plane on to the States, where we had a Budgie marketing trip scheduled, but reason prevailed. After three hours' decompression in the Heathrow VIP lounge, with Sarah on the telephone to 'Dutch' (the Princess of Wales), we jumped aboard Concorde and idled away the next couple of hours with drinks and small talk: 'Allan, this is a two gin-and-tonic question: when we first spent time in Germany together, did you fall in love with me?' It was a good question. I ordered up the passenger list, and discovered my drinking partner was described as 'Sarah Starkie'.

At JFK we were met by a stretch limo filled with off-duty New York cops who were to be our bodyguards. One of the more attractive of these was a Puerto Rican named Sonia who had worked undercover in the Vice Squad and carried all manner of weapons concealed about her person. She, along with the others, had not been briefed on how to address a royal duchess, but she was at least aware that there might be a cultural gap between herself and the woman she was guarding. I told her, tongue in cheek: 'If you're really that interested, let me tell you. You should be curtsying to her.' She said, 'Wassaat?' so I explained this antediluvian social device to her and showed how it should be done. Sonia was delighted — 'Oh yeah, we all like her and we wanna do the right thing' — and at the next opportunity, a refined little get-together in a gilded salon at the Carlyle Hotel, she stumped over to the Duchess and rasped: 'Yo, Your Royal Highness, check it out!' then dipped into a deep curtsy, the weight of her many firearms tugging her downwards.

Sadly, Sarah was too distracted to see the charm of it all. She was ready to give herself up to the New York media and was understandably nervous. First through the door was a deeply unpleasant newspaper reporter who was blown off course by the Duchess's heavily ladled charm. Next it was the turn of the *Today* TV show: Sarah ran back to her suite where I discovered her a few minutes later blowdrying her armpits in preparation for the ordeal ahead. We'd had a long talk about John's need to be validated as her partner and she thought that the *Today* interview was the right place to do it. In the event, however, the footage was never used.

The moment the interview was over, we were off to a high-energy breakfast meeting to sell Budgie. Shoulder to shoulder round a conference table sat executives from a wide range of merchandising firms, all newly converted Budgie enthusiasts — Budgie prams, backpacks, pyjamas, sheets, indeed anything that could bear the logo, were either being produced or were on the drawing-board. One executive confessed that he could not get the Budgie theme song out of his head. all rose from the breakfast table having eaten nothing, but replete with enthusiasm.

Lunch was nearing and it was time to rendezvous with Bill Simon at his favorite restaurant, Le Cirque. William E. Simon, who was shortly to play a pivotal role in the futures of both Sarah and John, was a former US Secretary to the Treasury and a noted international financier. At lunch his noble profile looked well among the glitterati adorning other tables, including American TV's most powerful woman, Barbara Walters, and society's most seductive matron, Princess Elizabeth of Yugoslavia.

Bill Simon was rich, worldly, old and frank: 'I tell you, Sarah, all I want are another twenty years of the health and mobility I have now. I do a lot to keep it that way. Every year I go to the Black Forest where they inject my body with various extracts of sheep embryo — it's fantastic! My American doctor doesn't really approve so, hell, I flew my German doctor over and we all discussed it over dinner.' The Duchess, deadpan, responded, 'I hope you didn't eat lamb?' Bill missed it. 'Oh no, one is not allowed to eat lamb for six months after the procedure.'

Soon it was time to go. We had a date at Bloomingdale's, on Lexington Avenue — what was the point in being in New York if we could not shop? Accompanied by Christine Gallagher and Jane Dunn-Butler, who had flown on ahead of us, we were met at a side entrance by a saleslady named Ivy whom the Duchess already knew from her previous raids on this famous store. Ivy and an ever-burgeoning number of Bloomingdale's sales personnel followed our Pied Piper-style progress across the floor. We processed from designer to designer with Ivy halting periodically to whisper to the Duchess, 'It's new, it's fun . . . it's *you* . . .', and as we progressed an ever-mounting stack of these garments began to follow behind until we reached the changing room, where the Duchess tried everything on in record time. I sat outside the mirrored room giving the thumbs-up at the required moment.

There was only a short time until the store closed, so the Duchess headed for the children's clothes department where, with finger pointed frantically at anything she found appealing, she repeated firmly, 'In four and six'. Shopping for Beatrice and Eugenie, their identities as one in her mind, thus became relatively easy for my hard-pressed travelling companion.

On the way out the Duchess bought a solid gold pocketwatch for John — it was Valentine's Day. Earlier during our frenzied shopping, she had looked longingly at a silver necklace, but had moved on without asking the price. John had given her, in advance, a small ring for Valentine's Day which resembled a wedding band and did not particularly appeal to her, so I went back and bought the necklace on his behalf. Waiting until she was away from her room at the Carlyle, I wrote a note, employing his usual string of endearments and placed it and the necklace on her pillow. Later, John forgot that I had done this favour on his behalf and boasted about how clever he had been to make such a shrewd choice for her Valentine's Day gift.

During this trip I became aware for the first time that Sarah was interested in John Kennedy, Jr. We were in the Carlyle Hotel together and she had asked her secretaries to find out whether Kennedy was in New York at the same time and if he was, whether it was possible to find out where he was. She took me to one side and said, 'Don't tell your brother about this, but, you know, I find him so attractive.' From what I could deduce, this was simply a woman expressing an interest in a young, rich, handsome man; only later did I discover her obsessive belief that she would one day marry John Kennedy and become First Lady of America.

She got one of her staff to telephone Kennedy's apartment and discovered that he was in the neighbourhood. Finally she tracked him down and asked him if he would like to come round for drinks or dinner at the Carlyle Hotel. He agreed, and she was thrilled. She came beaming to me about this great coup, this first step in her latest madcap ambition. I felt awkward, however, on account of her clear intention: 'That's great, but you know he has a girlfriend, Daryl Hannah?'

'Yes, I know Starkie, but that's nothing,' she told me, her eyes lighting up. 'That's not going to bother me!'

Two hours later a message came from Kennedy's staff that he was busy and would have to cancel the date. The Duchess was furious. Turning to me, she said, 'It's quite clear what happened — Daryl Hannah obviously looked in his appointments book, saw my name, freaked out and made him cancel because she feels threatened.' But Sarah would not give up — she spent a lot of time working out other ways of trying to get hold of him; 'How do I get past this Daryl Hannah problem?' she'd ask me.

There had been no indication from Kennedy that her feelings were reciprocated; indeed, he barely knew who she was, had never met her, and was (at that time) perfectly happy in his relationship with the *Splash!* actress. This was a sad fantasy of Sarah's, but to her it was real — spookily real, as becomes clear towards the end of this story — and her feelings for America's crown prince only deepened when she heard that the Princess of Wales had also expressed a desire to meet him.

The competition between these two

women, which had lurked beneath the surface until this point, was suddenly made plain by Sarahs anger and jealousy at the fact that Diana might get to Kennedy before she did. It was an absurd situation. Both women had marriages that were on the rocks, both were looking for suitable partners, both found the welcome and the respect of the Americans infinitely preferable to those, such as they were, of their fellow countrymen, and both hankered after a new life in the States. But could it really be true that both Diana and Sarah had fixed their ambitions on this one man?

According to Sarah, it was true. It is my guess that to this day the unsuspecting Kennedy remains blissfully unaware that he might have taken his pick of Britain's discarded royal princesses.

That was not quite the end of this particular New York run. A day or so after our return I got a frenzied call from the manager of the Carlyle Hotel: 'The Duchess checked out and she owes us $12,000!' This, it turned out, was not for the cost of her room but for the incidentals run up by her, her staff and the various hangers-on who blew in — hairdressers, bodyguards, and so on. In the end someone picked up the bill: it wasn't the Duchess.

★ ★ ★

Within a few days, at the end of February, John showed up in Germany and I accompanied him to Munich to witness his TV appearance on the *Thomas Gottschalk Show*. John, of slightly less interest to the German people than his fellow guests Eva Herzigova and Roger Moore, strutted on stage to the Strains of 'My Way' and managed to attract viewers' attention by talking extremely frankly about his relationship with the Duchess. Rebuffed by Eva Herzigova, he spirited an attractive Oceonics employee to his hotel, where he performed one of his perfunctory sex acts. As usual, however, he also contrived to lose his suitcase somewhere along the line. He stuffed a note under my door next morning asking me to 'organize' his things; it was at times like this that one could see how much fame had gone to his head.

In late February I sent a letter to Sarah saying that her Olympic dream was beginning to come true. Robert Splaine had found a horse for her to ride called Midge; it was to be a substitute for Heather Blaze, and it would cost £15,000. I made her a gift of it. At the same time I encouraged her to close a deal with Sleepy Kids which would give her 21 per cent of the company, a rather better deal than the 35 per cent of net profits she was receiving.

On 5 March there was a message on my machine from Sarah, enthusing about the horse and saying she'd really like to talk to me about it. Seven days later, however, another message introduced a more sombre note: now both she and John needed to talk to me, it was crucial they did so, and above all, soon. It was not, she said, about them, for once — then John's voice broke in at the end: 'Help me, brother. . . .'

It *was* about them, of course. Sarah's sister Jane and her new husband, Reiner Luedecke, had discovered that John had kept back around £55,000 of the money *Hello!* magazine had put up to help pay for their wedding and honeymoon. Furious, they had instructed lawyers to sue John for the return of the money. When I finally called John and Sarah they begged me to intercede in what might turn into something extremely ugly unless it was nipped in the bud. So, although I had never met him, I called Reiner at Dummer Down Farm, Major Ferguson's house in Hampshire, where the couple were staying. I tried to impress on Reiner that this was a family matter, not something lawyers should be handling, and that a compromise should be reached. 'OK,' he said, 'the compromise is that John pays up in full, including our lawyers' fees, and then maybe we won't file criminal charges.' I begged him to think about it, but when I called him a little later he had spoken to his lawyers who also, not unsurprisingly, felt that the legal action should go ahead unless John settled in full. Though it was to take another two years, this inability to judge the depth of their anger was to bring about John's greatest moment of shame when Jane finally had him declared bankrupt in Britain. Inevitably, Sarah's loyalties were split, and a day later I found a very long and almost incoherent message from her on my machine, the gist of which was that John had unjustly accused her of not supporting him, that he was very depressed, that she could not talk to or reason with him when he was like this, that the row with Jane and her husband was 'a really frightening issue' — and would I please go to them as soon as I could? A second message two days later, shorter and calmer, seemed to indicate that while the problem had not gone away, it was not quite so pressing. We were due to meet on the following day, 16 March, so we would be able to discuss the matter then.

Next day, Sarah and I paid our second visit to Cork, to see Robert Splaine and to ride. Though so much else that was unsettling was going on in her life, the one thing the Duchess clung to was her new dream, an Olympic gold medal for show-jumping. Splaine was not slow to recognize this: I paid him the £15,000 for the Duchess's newly acquired second horse, Midge, only to discover that the cost of keeping the creature at his stable would be £90 a week, pretty much what one would have paid in London. But we had a lesson, had lunch with Robert and Eileen, and then flew back to Heathrow, where I changed planes and headed for Frankfurt. This time, we had managed to avoid the local press, and there were no further lies and subterfuge involving dying men.

A little while later, in April, I again accompanied Sarah to Cork for another riding lesson. Clearly, Robert Splaine was becoming increasingly important to the Duchess. Her Olympic ambitions provided both a diversion and a haven for her worried mind, and even if she was not going to be in Heather Blaze's saddle for the big contest, she could still demonstrate to the world her hidden depths. By now her short-term objective was for Robert to make her sufficiently competent so that she could ride at the Windsor Horse Show: she would surprise everybody, especially the Queen, by suddenly turning up and winning a medal.

This was now her dream, and she was constantly remonstrating with Robert that she had to be prepared for it. She was a talented horsewoman, no doubt; but anyone could see that if she was taking lessons only once every three or four weeks she wasn't going to get very far.

A few months before this, a new character had drifted into the Romenda Lodge drama. Clive Garrad was an East Ender, and he had a very fat chequebook; he was the garlic king of Britain, importing and distributing the stuff throughout the country, though he dabbled in a lot of other things as well. He was a very good fellow, but an extremely eccentric one.

Clive was, however, extremely astute when it came to business. He pretty quickly identified two important features. The first was that no matter how much the Duchess milked from him, it was worth it to him for the business contacts he would get from her and for the kudos of being seen with her; in this respect he was far more predatory than John Bryan. The second fact he recognized was that she needed to organize her life, and that if she did not do so she would be of no use to him, or to herself. As a result he supported me in my attempts to restructure the Duchess's life and divide it into three areas:

her charities, her business life, and her home life.

The apotheosis of this particular relationship came when Clive suggested buying up a number of old people's homes and renaming them Duchess of York Nursing Homes. Sarah would receive £1 per bed per night for each person in the homes, and it was calculated that the income in the first year of the scheme would be £30,000, rising to £200,000 within a few years and with a constant cashflow thereafter. In the end, although Sarah wanted the money, she did not want the homes named after her. As we were driving to Romenda one day she picked up the car phone and called Clive with her decision. He replied: 'Suits me,' and that was the end of that.

Nevertheless, Clive was extremely generous to the Duchess, and when she revealed that her great ambition was that Heather Blaze and Robert Splaine should win an Olympic gold medal, he was enthusiastic. I called Robert and told him to make an estimate of the cost of what he would need to prepare for the Olympic Games, because Clive was ready to back us and had promised to find others to sponsor us as well.

In some respects at least, things seemed to be looking up. It couldn't last.

Chapter 10

By April 1994 I had been chief executive officer of Oceonics Deutschland GmbH for over four years. When I arrived in Frankfurt in the winter of 1990 to take over, the company was a complete shambles — John had hired two men who were, in truth, little more than renovators of toilets in private houses on Long Island. But these men had talked John into allowing them to renovate the apartment of his former girlfriend, Geraldine Ogilvy; John liked what he saw, made a profit on the deal, and so brought them in to renovate the Oceonics Group offices in Aldershot.

As a result of these two minor successes John gave the men carte blanche to go anywhere in Europe at his expense, looking for customers eager to buy high-grade American interiors. The pair ended up in a Frankfurt bar called the Epsteiner Eck, where all too soon they found themselves getting on famously with the regular clients. One was an architect; together, these three decided to make a bid to dress the interior of the MesseTurm, the tallest building in Europe, which was going up practically on the door-step.

Such was the seriousness with which they took their quest that the bartender at Ep-steiner Eck was made secretary and project manager, and four or five other regulars who spent more time in the bar than at home were taken on as well. This happy group, albeit perhaps not quite in a state of equi-librium, proceeded to make a bid of DM 11.4 million to complete the MesseTurm interiors. Every other contractor who'd looked the job over had priced it at around DM 20 million, a more realistic figure. But these men, acting in the name of the Two Bryans, had absolutely no idea what they were doing — in some cases their bids ac-tually represented less than the cost of the raw materials. In other words, no matter how hard they tried, however well they did, they would come out at a loss. This, I hasten to add, had not been the Bryans' intention.

The work, when completed, cost DM 6 million more than the tender price, and al-most bankrupted the Oceonics Group. Hav-ing finally, and somewhat reluctantly, agreed to take on the chief executive's role, I found when I arrived that, from scratch, I had to create a company, piece together a manage-ment, and replace the workforce with one that was capable of doing the job.

Theoretically John Bryan was deputy Chairman of the parent company, Oceonics Group Plc, which had interests in the computer business, in offshore oil and in construction, and was working as an apprentice Chairman to his father. From the very first days, when Oceonics Deutschland had been in such financial difficulty, John and I had travelled round Europe and the rest of the world trying to find investors who would back the company or, better still, buy it from us. On the other hand, I did believe that with the right investment, we could still make a success of it, and so it proved: within eighteen months the company was profitable, and within the next four years it grew to be the fifth largest interior construction group in Germany.

In its brief life the company, which was to prove to be John's nemesis as well as Sarah's and my own, completed around four hundred interiors, including three of the largest such projects in Germany. Soon a second line of business, project management, was added: John and I worked on the American Hospital in the Costa del Sol, a hospital in Portugal, the International Business Centre in Poland, the American Medical Clinic in Moscow and the early development of the

Chernobyl Children's Hospital, also in Moscow. In Britain we took over the completion of a number of hospitals in Chertsey and Runnymede, and elsewhere; in addition, Lord Forte, head of Trust House Forte, awarded us a contract to help him secure petrol stations throughout the whole of the former East Germany. A third line, attempting to finance new developments as well as project-managing them, was also added, and for a time Oceonics was a soaraway success. By 1993 John could report a 4 per cent net profit with 28 per cent growth, and we were constantly searching for new capital in order to develop: we had pitched for the DM 800 million project to develop the University Clinic at Rostock, but all the time we were looking for more cash investment.

Despite a master's degree in business administration, John was learning as he went along. When I first met him in 1989 he was erratic, chaotic and very arrogant. His previous businesses, usually restaurants and discotheques, had all gone bust; his father lent him some money for a telecommunications business which also folded. But just at the time I met him he had made a paper profit out of his stockholding in the Oceonics parent company, and therefore felt that he had inherited what he and his father called 'the

Bryan Magic'. In those days he chartered helicopters to fly him around and spent a great deal of time jetting to and from Australia trying to buy a computer division.

John felt that he was a conglomerate bigshot, and he certainly presented the outward appearance of one, but the truth was that he was a very poor businessman. He went through secretaries almost on a weekly basis, and he kept track of nothing. When things went wrong it was his habit publicly to blame someone else; in private, however, he confessed his weaknesses to me. So I tried to organize his life: we would talk four or five times each day, and he would explain what was going on and ask me what to do. He became entirely dependent on me during this period; conversely, because he became more organized, had learned to focus his charm — his biggest asset — and had become a competent salesman, he started to be quite effective.

Ironically, when John first came to know the Duchess of York he wanted to do to her what I had done to him — make order out of her chaos, give a daily structure to her life, turn her into an efficient business unit. The downside was that, having so newly acquired these skills for himself, he was ready to ditch them in his headlong pursuit of Sarah. This was truly a case of the blind leading the blind.

At its peak, in May 1993, Oceonics Deutschland was employing 500 people, but John, the titular head of the company, had other things on his mind. From the moment he became involved with the Duchess in 1992 it was, at least for a while, as if Oceonics and I did not exist. We had liquidity, we were growing, we had enough money to acquire companies and diversify, and he let it all slip. John walked through the door of Sunninghill Park and away from his responsibilities.

From my own perspective, although his absence allowed me to shape the company, John had laid down guidelines that Oceonics should grow at 30 per cent a year, even though the building recession in Germany was already in full swing. To finance that growth we needed millions in new capital, and the bank was only willing to go so far, and certainly would not meet our full requirements. John's role was to find that finance, and in this he repeatedly failed to deliver.

As has been said, in the spring of 1993 the Hypo Bank in Germany showed interest in investing in Oceonics, but negotiations foundered. Our bank, Schröder Munchmeyer, put up some bridging finance while the Bryans tried to find new capital, but from that moment the company's cashflow began to dry up. Suddenly, with the DM 6 billion collapse later that year of one of the real-estate giants in Germany, our customers just stopped paying — and within weeks we were in a vicious cycle where, because we weren't getting paid properly, we in turn were unable to pay our sub-contractors properly. So the sub-contractors started pulling their men off jobs, materials were no longer being delivered because we couldn't pay the suppliers in full, the materials that were on site suddenly started to disappear, and we were getting thrown off jobs because of the chaos. Then, in the midst of all this, came the threats on my life.

In reunified Germany the workforce was filled with people from the former Eastern Bloc whose life-rules, until the recent collapse of communism, had been very different from our own. Because they had been involved in civil unrest and even war, death meant very little to them, and if they were owed money, they saw a simple way of making sure they got it. One day John and I were in our Frankfurt office when two very large armed men came in and said that unless we paid them at some time that day, they would kill us as we left the office. John, all ignorance and bravado, said, 'Let me make it easier for you!' — and picked up a silver letter-knife engraved with the message 'Lots of love, Sarah xxxx.' He handed it over to one of the men and urged, 'Stab me right now, I don't want to wait.'

Somehow we got out of that one, and had a bulletproof glass door installed in our reception area which could only be opened when the receptionist pressed a button. One day she opened the door to discover four men coming through at a run. As they raced down the hall my newly acquired bodyguard came out and, spotting that they were wearing shoulder holsters, drew his pistol; the police were called and the situation defused without a bullet being fired, but it was a close call.

To John, all this was a game. By 1994 he rarely visited Frankfurt, and never spent the night there — he had distanced himself from the everyday consequences of his running an undercapitalized company, but to me it was a continuing nightmare. Daily there would be between ten and fifteen threatening phone calls; people would try to storm into the office without appointments; there were fist fights breaking out all over the place; and there was the constant knowledge that a bullet could be waiting for you whenever you emerged from your office or home.

This turn-round in the company's fortunes had happened so quickly that we were all in a state of shock. I had taken Oceonics from less than nothing and made it into something that was considered to be enormously successful: an endless stream of articles appeared in business magazines in praise of our success, and I was working harder and harder to achieve increasingly impossible goals. While all this was going on, I was being drawn further and further into the spider's web that was John and Sarah's relationship. I was equally committed to both, and somehow felt that my presence could ease their increasingly bumpy path. On every trip John undertook it was essential to Sarah that I accompany him; then when she went away it was equally vital that I was by *her* side.

When the call came, as it did more and more often, I would usually put aside my work with Oceonics and fly to England. It was a huge relief momentarily to escape the daily pressure, but on the other hand I knew that I was running away, that it was wrong. John and I both needed to be there to do what we could to bail out our sinking ship, but when I suggested to him that, for the time being, he should move to Frankfurt, he disagreed: 'Allan, you're completely wrong, you're too close to the situation. I think it's great that you're so worried about our cash-flow, but it'll work itself out. In fact, I want you to move to England and spend only a couple of days a week in Germany — you'll see that the company will get on just as it always has. Nothing will change, except that we'll make millions together!'

Actually, what John wanted was my permanent assistance in his handling of the Duchess. She had become aware of the difficulties Oceonics was experiencing — it was all John talked about when they weren't discussing Sarah's business — and such was her interest that, as has been said, we had made her a director of the company. She asked for a director's fee of £40,000 a year but we said that instead we would pay her 10 per cent of any new capital she could raise for the company. Since we were looking for millions, this idea appealed to her greatly. She made approaches to a friend of hers, Peter Monk, one of the richest men in the world, but no deal emerged from their conversations. It may be that if she had tried harder with her many contacts, then Oceonics would have been saved. But she did not. We were so near to rescue, and yet so far from it.

Through March and April 1994 my main concern was to try to find new finance. We seemed to have achieved a breakthrough when Peter Simon, son of Bill, said that they would put several million into Oceonics if the Two Bryans would match the sum; and, thankful that a last-minute rescue deal might be in sight, we scheduled a meeting in New York for the end of April.

On the day before we were due to meet Bill and Peter Simon, I flew with John and Jeremy Scott to New York to see Tony Bryan at the Carlyle Hotel. Our meeting with the Simons was scheduled for the next morning, but when we rang to check the venue it emerged that, in true Two Bryans style, father and son had each thought the other had fixed the appointment. The Simons knew nothing about a meeting, and would not be able to attend one, since they were otherwise engaged that day.

This was heartstopping stuff, but worse was to come. We had invited along two investment bankers to witness us closing the deal, but the sight they carried away with them from this historic meeting was of the Two Bryans huddled over an extension phone in a hotel bedroom, grappling with their Simon counterparts, while I hovered in the sitting room on another extension actually doing the deal. Not that there was much of a deal — Peter Simon told me: 'There was no point in meeting you anyway — we want a third investor, and we want the third investor to put up a third of the money.' We had no third investor — just the Bryans and the Simons. It looked as though Oceonics was history, and in my mind I started writing a letter to our bank telling them the awful news.

Just then something extraordinary happened. The telephone rang and there was the Duchess on the other end. By one of those strange coincidences she, too, was in New York. Even stranger, she was staying in the same hotel, a couple of floors above us. 'How's it going, Starkie?' she asked. So I told her — 'Really, really bad' — and explained how, at the last minute, we had to come up with a third investor.

'Well, *I'm* your third investor!' she exclaimed.

'No,' I said. 'Don't do it, you don't want to get involved in this.'

'Too late, Starkie,' she said, and hung up.

I was to discover that she had called Bill Simon the moment our conversation had ended, and promised that she would put up the necessary money, raised from her share of the Budgie project. About an hour later I made a call to Peter Simon and he said, 'Yes, everything's fine, it's all been worked out.'

That night I wrote in my diary 'SHE HAS SAVED US.'

I could scarcely believe the generosity of her action. Though Sarah only half-understood what was going on at Oceonics Deutschland, she had learned enough to know that the company, bedevilled by the recession, was in deep trouble. Her offer seemed all the more generous because, as far as business decisions went, this was not a sound investment.

The reason became clear later, when she was to tell me: 'I've decided to leave John. It's just a question of time now and I don't want any loose ends. I don't want to feel I owe him anything.' The offer of nearly £1 million was John's kiss-off, only we didn't know it yet.

That night, wreathed in smiles and basking in joy and contentment at having saved our company, John and I, together with Mark Hallow, one of the investment bankers, went on a trawl of Manhattan's bars. In one of them, towards the end of the evening, two girls began looking over at us, and I said to John, to distract him, 'Let's send the Duchess some flowers.' (She had flown on to Washington, where she was staying at the Four Seasons Hotel.) 'Yeah,' he replied, 'we'll send her flowers, we'll fill her room with flowers,' and he went off to make the call. But by now he was so drunk that he was quite unable to order them; instead, he went back, smiled at the girls, and walked over to their table. I left.

The Duchess of York had just given John Bryan $1.5 million, yet the only way he could find in which to show his gratitude was to cheat on her with some cheap bar pick-up.

It was cheating of a different kind, however, which lay behind the next episode in this tale. A few days later a British newspaper reported: 'Fergie's Toe-Sucking Pal Faces Fraud Quiz — Riddle of Car Park Charges at Heathrow'. The story revealed that Scotland Yard detectives were chasing John to ask him about allegations that he had fiddled charges at one of the airport's long-stay car parks. As I have noted, John had a habit of trying to avoid paying excessive parking charges; usually it was a ruse that worked — but not on this occasion. The police had become involved after receiving a complaint from the car park's owners, and the *Daily Mirror* reported: 'An employee has claimed he [John] tried to evade paying a £400 bill by tendering a ticket which applied to another car.'

On 11 May the Duchess left a message on

my answering machine: she was watching the evening news on television, and had just heard that John had been arrested. Did I know what it was all about? Could I ring her?

John *had* been arrested. By arrangement with his lawyers he'd turned up at Heathrow police station and been submitted to a four-hour interrogation. At the end of this he accepted a police caution and, having paid the outstanding parking fee, was allowed to go free. His lawyer, Guy Martin, described the incident as 'a misunderstanding', but that fooled no one. John called me from a room in a cheap hotel at Heathrow and wailed: 'Allan, I need to move to a universe that's completely 180 degrees off this one, because I can't live in this universe. I can't function with the rules, I don't understand anything, I just don't fit. I just seem to do everything wrong all the time.' It was at moments like this that his true vulnerability showed — the pomposity and bullshit were stripped away, and underneath lay a layer of terrible self-hate. (Therapy, always the stick that the press used to beat Sarah with, was as much a part of John's life as hers: his diary for the Oceonics years shows regular visits to Lisa Glenn, John's particular sanity guru, but I never saw that she did any good.)

If this news came as an irritant to Sarah,

301

she had no time to discuss it with me. Far more vexing was the question of the burgeoning love affair between her brother-in-law, Prince Edward, and a blonde public relations girl, Sophie Rhys-Jones. Through the Buckingham Palace grapevine (for despite everything, she still maintained her office there), she had learned that Edward and Sophie were permitted by the Queen to spend nights together under the Palace roof, not a courtesy that had ever been extended to Sarah and Andrew before their wedding. She was furious, telling me how unfair it was — even though her marriage was history, and the whole business, therefore, an irrelevance.

By the beginning of May it had become apparent that something urgent needed to be done to try to rationalize the continuing chaos of the Duchess's life. There had been some loose conversation about her being given an office, which would be run as a subsidiary of Oceonics, in return for her having committed Budgie to help save the company, but although she was now a director, she preferred for the time being to keep this secret and remain non-active. Ultimately it was decided that she should establish her own company, which, in deference to the title I had given our unofficial business meetings all these months, would be called Fireside Communications Ltd.

This was a new beginning for Sarah, and as if to underline it, she decided it was time to find a new house. Romenda Lodge had many drawbacks, not least its size, but above all that it was a rented property. Sarah, with the backing of her separation settlement money, was in a position to buy, and started to look about for suitable properties. In the end, she settled on one in the Surrey country-side, not far from Romenda. It was a massive pile with stables, guest houses, and a price tag of around £1 million, though it probably needed the same amount again spent on re-furbishment.

The price was way beyond her means, but Sarah had set her heart on it. At that moment Clive Garrad came up with a suggestion: *he* would buy the house and repair it, Sarah would live in it rent-free for a year, then it would be sold as The Duchess of York's House, and they would split the profits. This idea initially appealed to Sarah, but in the end she could not bear the idea of the dis-ruption; also, she felt that she wanted to have something that was hers, and in any event did not want to be under too heavy an obli-gation to Clive.

We took another trip to Cork. I arrived first, to find Robert waiting to give me another lesson. It would be fair to say that Heather Blaze was now Sarah's great ambition, her dream: there was something pure and noble about her equestrian hopes, so very different from the makeweight nature of her everyday life, and she was prepared to put her all behind the plan to have Robert Splaine go for Olympic gold. For Robert, it must have been extremely worrying; suddenly he was being asked to drop all his other interests — his pupils, his horses, his breeding programme — and concentrate on becoming an Olympic athlete. That in turn meant his joining the international circuit, in itself an expensive proposition.

In addition, we were all conscious of the fact that the principal benefactor to this foolish ambition of Sarah's was Clive Garrad, and he had been suffering for some time from liver cancer: what would happen if he died? He was undergoing chemotherapy; sometimes the prognosis was good, sometimes not. I could see that, from Robert's standpoint, things looked a little shaky, especially when you took into account the way the pair had come to meet — with Sarah spotting him on television and saying, like a child in a toyshop, 'I want that!'

Robert and I had this conversation as we rode together through the woods. I had taken the Duchess's place as she had not yet arrived at the stables, but when she did turn up that evening she was ice-cold towards me. She was equally chilly the next day, and though I tried to confront her with it, she would not respond. Finally I talked to Jane Ambler, who told me: 'Well, Allan, you've got to understand — you went for a ride in the woods with Robert.'

'Yes?'

'Well, she went for a ride in the woods with Robert when she was here last week and Robert is *her* friend.'

We got through the next day well enough. Both Sarah and I competed in the local horse show: she went over without any faults, but I had trouble with one fence, having to attempt it twice before finally getting over. She was pleased with our performance, but still displeased with me. She had invited me to go back to Romenda after touchdown at Heathrow so that we could watch the video of the show which Jane Ambler had taken. But as we were packing our riding gear into the car, she very abruptly uninvited me and the companions I had brought along on this occasion.

Next day I called her and said, 'If you want to uninvite me in the future I'd appreciate it if you'd tell me why. It doesn't bother me

for myself, but there were other people involved here.' It had an electric effect on her
— I discovered later that she immediately
picked up the telephone and ordered from
her jeweller a magnificent silver plate with a
sterling silver man and horse jumping over a
fence. Engraved in her handwriting was the
legend: 'To my dearest Allan. Here's to
teamwork — love, Sarah xxx'. For my two
women companions she ordered sterling silver pens, and to get the work done (it was a
Sunday morning) someone had to be sent in
to the jeweller's specially. The cost, the
thought, and the effort involved were dispro-
portionate to the offence she had given; but
it was a response typical of the Duchess when
she felt she had been in the wrong. There
followed, inevitably, the placatory telephone
call — a message left on my machine on 14
May, bubbling over with affection, and telling me how much she would like to talk to
me.

My troubles with the Duchess might have
been resolved, at least for the time being, but
the problems with Oceonics remained. Sarah
had pledged her money, but along with the
difficulties I was facing in keeping the bank
happy and keeping Bill Simon happy, there
was always lurking in the back of my mind
one other question. Will the Duchess really

do what she said she would do? Without her help, the company would be dead inside three months. I looked forward to the fact that she was coming to Frankfurt on an official visit for the first time: I felt that, once here, any lingering doubts she might have had about supporting Oceonics would disappear. A nervous message on 17 May, the day before she was due in Frankfurt, asking what the arrangements were and whether I would be there, underlined her essential lack of confidence, at least in a setting out of the usual run of her experience.

In the event, the occasion was a great success. Sarah visited the Oceonics offices, and was given the red carpet treatment when she met the Polish Ambassador and Graf Krockow — the man whose absence at Annabel's, so many months ago, had led to my meeting her. Graf Krockow offered to donate money, throw charity balls, and in every way do anything to help the Duchess's charity work; he was even prepared to contribute to a development fund for her commercial projects. It was extraordinary how people warmed to her, wanted to see the good side of her, believed in the royal myth.

Afterwards we drove out to the airport — I was flying back to London with her — and on the plane she gave me her 'Honour

Bright' confession (meaning the absolute truth): she was going to leave John, a decision which, to be honest, was no longer a surprise. To me it was just a matter of whether she could see it through — the intention was there, but did she have the will actually to go through with it?

The Duchess and I came back to Britain reasonably satisfied with the way things had gone. It was now her ambition to establish a children's charity in Germany, a country she had barely known before she had encountered John and me. With this she would now be able to tread the world stage, thereby gaining access to the world's most lucrative markets, where the high profile created by her charitable works would assist in her personal business ventures. Certainly, the lines between her business and personal activities were often blurred; but then, if a Concorde flight, paid for so that she could execute charitable duties, also whisked her to a place where she could set up profitable business deals, who was going to complain?

We arrived back in London in time to make our way out to the city's Docklands area, where the Duke of York's ship lay. As always, Prince Andrew was willing to assist Sarah in any way that he could, and right now, impressing Clive Garrad was what the

Duchess needed. The Duke's ship was paying a courtesy call to the Tower of London and, having sailed up the Thames estuary, now bobbed at rest in the West India Dock, awaiting guests for an early evening cocktail party.

Sarah and I arrived early and went below to the Duke's cabin. As I sat on a chair I was suddenly grabbed from behind and wrestled to the ground — it was the Duke, indulging in a little Royal Navy horseplay. As a former serving officer, I found it difficult to know how to respond. Wrestle back? Or allow him to win? The protocol here was beyond me, but we soon separated, got up and dusted ourselves off. It was this kind of behaviour which made knowing Prince Andrew very difficult — moments of high informality would be followed by a chilling and regal formality, as if he felt he had gone too far and needed to retreat behind the royal façade. Sure enough, later that night, when we all found ourselves in Annabel's again, he barely spoke to me.

Before too long, Clive would be put on trial for evasion of VAT, and would be convicted and sent to gaol. His manners were rough, his clothes were awful, his jokes were in the poorest possible taste, but in Annabel's that night the Duke levelled his attention and his charm at this man, because that was what Sarah wanted. She needed to secure her Heather Blaze dream, and Clive was the man to help her in that. He had promised his backing verbally, but we weren't quite there yet.

Next day, whatever jollity we had managed to salvage from this dire evening evaporated in an instant. We learned that the owners of the rights in *Hector the Helicopter*, a children's book too eerily similar to Budgie, though published a good number of years before, were about to launch a lawsuit for plagiarism. My diary entry for that day reads: 'The fatal blow came. Killed by *Hector the Helicopter.*' Laughable as that may now seem, the implications of this lawsuit were very serious: Sarah had pledged one-third of her share of the Budgie property to Oceonics. If legal action were started, it would have the effect of preventing her liquidating Budgie; and Oceonics, without that vital financial prop, would collapse. Even in my despair, after weeks and months of agonized negotiation to keep my company afloat, I could not help but see the black humour of the situation. In the end, however, the Duchess's prediction that Hector's people would not sue turned out to be correct, even though it was wishful thinking, not logic, which had put the words in her mouth.

Since his emergence in his own right (so he thought) in the international jet set, John was constantly in demand these days. Sarah preferred it, if he was asked to dinner or a party in some European capital, that I go with him: she believed that he was unlikely to be unfaithful if I was in tow. But I was not my brother's keeper and he always did exactly what he wanted. Such was the strain in John and Sarah's relationship by now that she knew he would, once again, be using his sex as a weapon against her. On 29 May he was in Munich at a jet-set party whose guests included his middle-aged lover from Paris, and Sarah was telephoning his room until dawn and getting no reply. Predictably, that night brought an agonized message from the Duchess. Where was John? Was he out with some woman? Could she talk to me about it, as she found his behaviour really strange? This, it must be remembered, from a woman who had ostensibly decided that she was going to rid herself of the errant jet-setter.

It was her own fault. Feeling guilty at her continuing determination not to be photographed with John, it was she who had encouraged him to step out on his own in society. Soon she was to regret this, as he was feverishly taken up by the international jet set after his triumph at the Best awards in Paris. John already had connections with the royal family of Monaco, having dated Princess Stephanie when she was officially going out with Rob Lowe; at Grand Prix time he would be in the company of Prince Albert.

In Paris, Princess Hermine de Clermont-Tonnerre, descended from a royal family which lives on in French minds if not in the French constitution, introduced us to that country's Prince Michael; while the Duc d'Orléans, the son of the pretender to the French throne, took a particular liking to us. The scions of the Italian royal family, every bit as dispossessed as their northern counterparts but carrying on as though the House of Savoy still ruled, took us under their wing, and Princess Esmeralda, a relation of the King of the Belgians, was always around.

Until now Sarah had taken the view that John's social life was generated by and through her, but in fact he had suddenly acquired a momentum all of his own and no longer needed her as his lifeline in society. For her part, she believed that his newfound acceptability must in large measure be due to her makeover campaign: shoes from Lobb, cream dress shirts instead of white, a sharper

Savile Row cut, the proper kind of cufflinks. What neither of them realized was that the gilded and tanned Eurotrash adored John simply because he had cuckolded the Queen's second son. To them, it was *très amusant* to have this bad boy around.

One day, John and I were in my office in Frankfurt when my secretary came in to announce, 'Her Royal Highness is on the telephone.' Because of our new and seemingly endless string of Euro-royal contacts, I asked her, 'Which one?' and we all laughed. Unfortunately, it was Sarah on the line, and on overhearing this aside she burst into tears. John grabbed the phone and tried to soothe her: 'Oh, Linky, he didn't mean anything, he didn't mean anything, it's all right sweetheart. . . .' Then he ordered me, 'Call her up! She is so upset!'

So I called the Duchess who, still crying, spluttered: 'I used to be the only Royal Highness in your life — and now you've got another one! I don't count any more! You don't care about me! You've got all these other people!' I had to assure her that, really, she was the only Royal Highness that counted in the lives of both John and me.

If there was nothing I could do to rein in John's behaviour, at least I could continue to further the Duchess's business career.

Some time earlier she had been asked by *Family Circle* magazine in the US to write an article about motherhood, and we had written the piece together. The project was fraught with difficulties, however, because under the terms of her Deed of Separation from Prince Andrew, Sarah had made various undertakings to protect the royal family's privacy. Among other things, she had pledged that she would not disclose any information relating to her marriage or to the royal family.

This draconian agreement was to prove an immense hindrance to Sarah in the early months of 1996 when she was trying to write her own autobiography, but in 1994 there seemed a possibility that the material contained in the motherhood article could be dispersed by Princess Esmeralda and her partner, Albert Zarca, among the Continental press, where it would be unlikely to be drawn to the attention of Buckingham Palace — or the British press. The Princess and Albert had recently interviewed John for *Gala* magazine in Germany, and the resultant piece had gone down particularly well with its subject. It had included such statements as 'I have never considered myself as financial adviser of the Duchess of York,' and that he was 'much offended' by accusations that he was a playboy who sought 'success with women because of their money'. 'My upbringing and my religious education,' he intoned 'prevent me from doing anything like that.'

John got £25,000 for this ego-polishing tissue of lies, and Albert and Esmeralda were deemed to be 'safe'. Certainly they were to prove a useful source of income to the Duchess in the coming months and years, selling articles from which they all shared the profits. They also engaged in a number of other money-making enterprises, one of which involved shifting Clive Garrad's idea of a 'Duchess of York's House' to France, where Sarah would buy a property, stay for the summer, paint some murals on the walls and leave some of her furniture behind, then move on, taking the profit with her as she went. As with Clive's original plan, this one came to nothing, but it was treated seriously as a potential income-earner for some time.

All these business deals, as well as others, were discussed in our Fireside Chats. Now, however, we were ready to create a company to exploit these projects, so Fireside Communications Ltd was born. What most worried me in the case of Sarah's new company, though, was that John was jealous of her apparent move away from him in terms of business. I noted in my diary: 'The rift between JB and the Duchess is so great that it seems hopeless to believe that ultimately the great potential can be achieved. A potential Budgie investor wants nothing to do with John, as many people. I will stand by him, however, and try to control his destructive behaviour and her insensitivities.'

But controlling John was a well-nigh impossible task. At the next Fireside Chat he sent chills down everyone's spine: 'I just want you to know that before you start structuring Fireside Communications and all these other projects, that if you and I do break up, Sarah, I'm going to destroy the whole structure and I'll take all my people with me. You won't have any of these people, they're *my* people. You'll have nothing.' Warming to his theme, he added self-importantly: 'I like to have business dealings with my women and if they're not interested in being my woman any more, then they shouldn't have any dealings with me businesswise.' Sarah sat there, white-faced and appalled.

The truth of the matter was that several wealthy contacts wanted to do business with HRH, but only if John was out of the way. He knew it, and was scared that Sarah was set on a path whereby he would be eased out — which, of course, she was. One day, as we were walking along the street, John said to me: 'You're about to knock me out of the box and replace me as her chief adviser, chief partner, chief everything. With this Fireside Communications, you're going to be the managing director and I'm just going to be a non-executive nobody — but do you believe for one moment that this will continue?' Knowing Sarah's true intentions, the best I could do by way of answer was, 'I know she's hard to get along with, John.'

'It's worse than that, Allan, you cannot finish a deal with her. The only deal I was able to finish for her was Budgie, and that was because she didn't care about it and turned it over to me completely.' He voiced his frustration over the business side of Sarah's life, but his real worry now was the emotional side. She was being extremely inventive with her reasons for not going ahead with the divorce from Andrew. John had no choice but to swallow these excuses, not least because he was not privy to information passing between the Duchess and Duke, but he no longer believed her.

His defence mechanism was to fantasize that Sarah wanted to marry him more than he wanted to marry her, and often at this time, when I warned him that his relationship with her was nearing its end, he responded angrily, 'She's never been more committed to it than she is now.'

Intrigued, I asked, 'So do you think you're going to marry her?' and he said, 'Well, let's put it this way. I could marry her, but the question ultimately is, do I want to marry her? Quite frankly I'm not sure. She hasn't proved that she is an ethical, moral enough person for me to spend the rest of my life with, and I'm just not sure any more.'

Like teenagers, Sarah and John tried to spend time apart, but kept racing back to each other. Now, however, their sex life, which had been the focus of their relationship, had become sporadic: at times in the past they had made love four or five times a day, now they were seeing each other a couple of times a week. The whole relationship was unravelling, and they were both drinking a lot. Their affair had become a shadow of what it had been before.

Then suddenly the Duchess decided, once again, that she was going to divorce Andrew after all. She had come to believe that the royal family no longer wanted anything to do with her. She called me and said, 'You know, Allan, it's as if my eyes have been opened. I don't know what I've been doing, I don't know why I've been holding off, it's crazy.

It has taken something like this to make me realize I'm deluding myself.' Two days later, however, she had decided it would be better to wait until after the Prince and Princess of Wales had divorced.

In one respect, however, she was resolute: she had decided that her life-saving loan to Oceonics should be turned into a gift to John. In effect, it was to be the kiss-off. She told me this and we got John on a conference call. 'Oh no, Linky, I can't accept that money from you,' he said. 'It goes in, you get 26 per cent of Oceonics in return and you'll make a lot of money. I can't take the money from you.' But Sarah was firm, 'Look, I'm happy to be a director of Oceonics, but I don't want to make any money from this. I want to give you this money so we're clear of any problems over Budgie, and everything that is left over on Budgie belongs to me.' I ordered John to accept, and he did so meekly. I was witness to that agreement, an agreement which the Duchess never honoured. To this day, she still owes John Bryan $1.5 million.

Chapter 11

With Coutts Bank chafing for a reduction in her overdraft, still rising by between £30,000 and £50,000 a month, Sarah needed to make some quick decisions about how to raise cash. My suggestion that she turn herself, in business terms, into 'Duchess of York Plc' and call her company Fireside Communications was now given top priority, and Sarah asked me if I would quit Oceonics and become Fireside's full-time chief executive.

The offer was, I suppose, tempting, but I found it resistible. 'I've been an army officer and I've run a construction company, but I've never been involved in developing miniseries and movies, and the only book I ever worked on was the one we did together. You need someone with broader experience,' was my response. My true reasons were that, even though by now I hated my life in Germany, and that trying to salvage Oceonics was a nightmare, I felt it morally wrong to usurp John. To become chief executive of Fireside Communications would be fine with me, provided that John were made an equal partner. I argued to myself that, but for John,

I would never have come to know the Duchess: I could not leapfrog over one friend to get closer to another.

On the other hand, I was very conscious of the fact that Sarah could make a great deal of money. Many of the projects we had chosen in our Fireside Chats were well targeted, and for the most part easily achievable, and such was the goodwill she engendered that it would have been virtually impossible not to have created a highly profitable business. Sarah benefited from the fact that people liked her (or her status) so much that they would give her cash for nothing. Earning it was almost as easy.

All that was needed was the organization around her. In the end we finally agreed that, since I was spending so much time with her anyway, I would devote 40 per cent of my time to Fireside and the rest to Oceonics. In return I would take only a small stake in the company — she had offered me 30 per cent, with nothing for John, but I said I would split that percentage with him.

All of which was well and good so far as business projects went. Personal relationships were another matter, however. As usual, my answering machine caught the next broadside of the Duchess's thoughts and concerns and hopes. On 12 June came two messages: I must look after my brother, he came first and foremost, and she utterly respected that. But I was allowed to have my own life, too — why didn't I jump on a plane and join her in England or Ireland, and we could be happy, and all would be well? Then the second message, shorter and more sombre: where was John? He was supposed to be lunching with her. It was clear that she thought that even if I wasn't my brother's keeper, then I ought to be.

A couple of days later, on 14 June, Sarah came to stay with me in my apartment in Frankfurt. It was there that her money-spinning liaison with Princess Esmeralda and Albert Zarca was clinched, though not without difficulty. The fashionable pair had driven across Europe to be with the Duchess that night, but as the doorbell rang, she became typically defensive: 'Why are we meeting these people? Who are they anyway? Can't you make them go away?' I went to the door and started making her apologies — a headache, so sorry — when she bounded past me: 'Ah! You must be Esmeralda! How lovely!' It was typical *volte-face* behaviour from the Duchess, calculated to bring out the best in her guests and the worst in her host.

Among the half-dozen money-spinning

ideas the four of us discussed was a planned series of books about Amanda, a seven-year-old freckled redhead who gets lost in Buckingham Palace. This was clearly good autobiographical stuff, and extremely marketable as such. Sarah had written a short synopsis and character description, and I had developed the material and flown to New York to clinch a deal. One publisher offered $90,000 a book, which, considering that the project was still in its early development stages, without a word having been written, was not bad. As I started negotiations, I had a call from Sarah: 'Can we change the venue? I don't think it should be Buckingham Palace.' I was furious, and called up John to complain: 'All the Duchess has come up with is a piece of paper saying we've got this fool girl Amanda who gets lost in Buckingham Palace, and already half of it has been changed.' John said, 'Didn't you hear? The little girl isn't a freckled redhead any more, she's a black-haired Hispanic.' To those who were trying to help her, Sarah's fickleness was infuriating.

By now I had also become an arbiter of their quarrels. Sarah would call me in the middle of the night and scream: 'Allan, I can't communicate with him! You've got to explain to him! I'm going to tell you now what my problem is and you explain it to him!' Then she would run through the argument. I would think about it, then she'd pass the telephone over to John and I would tell him what I thought she really meant to say. It was a ludicrous situation, but instead of seeing the absurdity of it John was more and more beginning to resent my presence in Sarah's life.

He had reached a low moral point in his life. Among other things, he now looked at money in an obsessional way, and was fond of quoting to me the phrase, 'There is no such thing as dirty money.' The differing moral codes which governed our lives were forcing us apart, even though we retained, on the surface at least, a camaraderie and a certain joviality. Then, in late June 1994, we flew to New York, to celebrate John's mother's seventieth birthday. Before the party began I took John outside where, beside his mother's swimming pool, I gave him the hard facts about Fireside Communications. There were a number of projects under way, and we were looking for an office. This surprised him: 'Who's putting up the money?' So I told him that two wealthy investors had given Sarah money to help to set herself up. He was shocked, because he suddenly realized that things were happening in

Sarah's life about which he knew nothing.

Nor could he wait to wreak his revenge. Back in Britain he screamed at Sarah: I was good, he said, good at what I did, but I was basically only a manager. She could find managers on every street corner, she could find a hundred Allan Starkies, she could find a thousand if she really wanted them. But he was the only person she couldn't replace. In clinging to his own increasingly tenuous position, he was quite ready to stab me in the back.

Sarah, freeing herself more each day from the yoke of John, concentrated on her German charity. Graf Krockow, who had expressed great interest in it, is one of the richest men in Europe, and the Duchess was quick to see the advantages of creating an alliance with him, and with the Sal Oppenheim bank, one of the most influential private banks in Germany, and among whose family members just happened to be Krockow's wife. He offered a property in Poland for Sarah's charity Children in Crisis, thereby adding lustre to her charitable reputation, and it was clear that further donations were not far behind. All this pleased Sarah — but not my bank manager, Herr Meyer at Schröder Munchmeyer, who was, after all, shouldering the burden of the Oceonics debts while still waiting to see the colour of Sarah's Budgie money. 'This is unbelievable,' he raged, when he heard of her German charity plans. 'We do all the suffering and Sal Oppenheim get all the benefits!' He told me his own bank managed millions of charity money and that he could do a much better job for us because he knew us all. I pointed out the logic of this to the Duchess, and she instructed that Herr Meyer and I should fly to London, where she would meet him in her Buckingham Palace office — 'That should impress and tame him.'

If Herr Meyer was a worry of mine, he was clearly not one of hers. Her next message, on 21 June, welcomed me back to England, and told me that she needed to talk to me about a fall she had taken on the previous day, while riding Midge.

Riding was not the only love we shared. Sarah and I talked about painting, and writing, and projects and dreams — abstract as well as material things. On the other hand, her conversations with John were becoming more basic all the time. She was frightened of him now, and one day described to me her fear of being alone with him. On our trips together I would see her rise out of herself and blossom as the plane took her away from Romenda Lodge; then I would watch the tension and black moods return as we came down through the cloudbase to land at Heathrow. She told me about the abusive language John employed, and I remarked, 'You know, when you talk, you sound like a beaten woman.' She replied, 'That's what I am Starkie — emotionally, I'm just a beaten woman.' Often she blamed herself for it, arguing that if she hadn't said this, or done that, then perhaps he wouldn't have reacted the way he did. Maybe, she argued, in common with thousands of beaten women, it was all her fault. I told her she had to snap out of it. 'Starkie,' she responded, 'I just need to get stronger, I need to pull myself together and just get rid of him.'

The children started noticing the gradual disintegration of the relationship. John, who had always been so good with them, no longer minded if his rows with their mother were overheard by Beatrice and Eugenie. Beatrice yelled at him one day, 'Don't shout at Mummy!' and this in turn upset Sarah even more.

And yet he still had some bizarre magical hold on her. Their sex life became rougher, and after one particularly brutish session Sarah was left bleeding; for a time it was thought she would have to be hospitalized, but she was terrified of what would be said if the cause of her injuries was discovered.

On 3 July her voice, distorted by my answering machine, told me how sorry she was that I had been feeling ill. Mostly, though, it told me how difficult John was being. She had to go her own way, businesswise, and she knew that he was hurt by this. Could I ring her? Please could I ring her? . . . Then Christine Gallagher's voice cut in to tell me how deeply upset the Duchess was — they were, she thought, at crisis point.

If he was to be prevented from doing business with or for the Duchess, John wanted to show her that he was, as ever, a Master of the Universe. Still basking in the (as he saw it) glory of being nominated one of the Best people in the world — that heady evening in Paris remained fresh in his mind — he was moving with a new set of people totally unconnected with Sarah and the British way of life. Through Massimo Gargia he had met Irene and Franco Majorie: she was Russian and he was Italian, and they had made a massive fortune out of exporting aluminium from Siberia. The Majories, said John, were going to make him immensely wealthy, and stimulated as much by this thought as by Irene's beauty, he visited them in Monte Carlo, where he flirted unabashedly with her.

None the less, the friendship flourished, the Majories eager to introduce John to all sorts of business opportunities in the former USSR. In July we flew to Moscow with the couple and they introduced us to some people who were going to sell us raw diamonds — the 'motherlode' that John had been searching for all his life. 'We're going to the bowels of Russia and we'll get them for a song and then bring them out and sell them for a fortune!' he fantasized. Then the Majories improved on this by suggesting that we import from Germany tankers full of petrol, which would then be sold, via the vehicles' hoses, on the streets of Moscow. We could acquire building sites by squatters' rights — parking a broken-down car on the plot usually did the trick — and turn them into petrol stations. We attended one dizzying meeting after another with Irene and her husband, in an exhausting and, as it turned out, wholly unproductive merry-go-round: nothing ever came of a single suggestion of theirs.

I came back from Russia convinced that for every hundred opportunities offered us, perhaps one might be lucrative. The country was in a state of flux, and nothing could be guaranteed as either safe or predictable — the risk of opening up a Moscow arm of Oceonics simply wasn't worth taking. In spite of my doubts however, John thought differently; fascinated by the Siberian aluminium deposits, he decided to see them for himself. Some friends decided to charter a jet, Dewi Sukarno even flying in from Jakarta to join the party. The idea of a sable-clad jet set visiting the Siberian plains for a week of fun and frolicking is hard to picture, but that was their plan.

Before he left, we had had a Fireside meeting, at which he had told the Duchess once again, 'I'm not happy with the way all this is going. I will tear this whole thing apart if you leave me.' I took him and Jeremy Scott — now an equal partner in Fireside with John and me — to Foxtrot Oscar, the fashionable Chelsea restaurant close to the Bryans' apartment. Over dinner, I warned them of the difficulties ahead if we three were not able to present a united front to our fourth partner, the Duchess. We all shook hands and symbolically drank to our new brotherhood, but before the glasses were in the dishwasher John was back at Romenda Lodge, tearing into the Duchess, ripping down her defences and telling her how worthless the whole Fireside project was.

While John was in Siberia the Duchess hired an independent lawyer to review our plans, with the result that she came to the conclusion that Fireside Communications would be too unstable if John were involved. She called me and asked once again if I would drop my work with Oceonics and go to work with her full time. I told her it would be a breach of my loyalty, to which she replied sadly, 'Starkie, we are both such ethical and loyal people that sometimes we hurt ourselves.' For the next three days I could not reach her: she ceased her non-stop round of calls to me, and would not return mine. Then I started to receive strange messages from her staff — a sure pointer to an imminent mood-swing. When she finally called, I could tell from her tone that she had decided that in her need to cut free of John she required me to go to her completely, leaving John to his own devices. It was obvious to her that I could not do this. Realizing this, I told her that I understood, and that there would be no hard feelings; I would still be her best friend and travelling companion and brother. She said, 'Oh, Starkie, you're the greatest person I know. You're a real gentleman — thank you so much.'

We ended the conversation in an atmosphere of mutual respect and jollity, but I felt upset that things had turned out this way. She had eclipsed John as my best friend; as my relationship with her matured, so my friendship with him deteriorated.

When we had redrawn her life-plan and split it into three, we had agreed that, apart from the business side (Fireside Communications) and her home life, there would also be a Duchess of York Foundation, into which all her charitable efforts would be gathered. It had been assumed that I would play a leading role in that, and now, as we said our farewells at the end of that fateful telephone conversation, Sarah asked me if I would still like to be involved. I said that I would.

A couple of days later she was once again bombarding me with calls as though nothing had happened. Her plan that she would shed John at some time in the summer seemed to be nearing fruition. 'How sad it will be for the children,' she said to me, 'when JB has gone, and with Sally [the nanny] leaving this summer; too.' I put down the phone, only to receive a call from an irascible JB in person: 'Frankly, I am sick and tired of you always saying the relationship is on the rocks.' Round and round the calls went, getting ever more complex. 'I really love him,' Sarah now said. I just shook my head.

They both gave me their version of Sarah's proposal of marriage. Needless to say their two accounts of this momentous occasion varied more than somewhat. They had attended a party given by the comedienne Ruby Wax. Later I took a call from a jubilant John: 'Guess what? Sarah's asked me to marry her — she begged!' Apparently an extremely attractive female guest at the party had hung round John all evening, making sure he knew how sexy she thought he was, and this had prompted a precipitate action from the Duchess. He told me that after the party was over Sarah had begged: 'Oh please, will you please marry me? Marry me as soon as we can?' I could picture John's beaming countenance as he bragged. 'I told her we would but I don't know. . . .'

It was sensational news. John, against all odds, in fading light and against a strong headwind, had turned the relationship round. He had found an accommodation whereby he and Sarah could live their lives happily unencumbered by the anxieties of a business relationship. Sarah had lost that hidden yearning for her great love, Steve Wyatt, and was ready to settle down to a new life. Or that, at least, was how things appeared.

I rang the Duchess. 'Congratulations! You two have finally taken the step forward!'

There was a silence at the other end of the line. Then, 'What are you talking about?'

'You and John — getting married!'

'Whaaaa-aaat?'

'Well, you asked John to marry you. At the Ruby Wax party.'

There was another pause. 'Oh — that,' said Sarah. 'That wasn't serious, Starkie — yes, I said something. Yes, I *did* say something, but I wasn't serious.'

As it happened, however, this was no time to pass on the news to John. The London *Evening Standard* reported that night:

> The Duchess of York's friend John Bryan has been ordered to pay £55,000 plus interest and costs to her sister for receiving secret commissions from *Hello!* over the magazine's coverage of her wedding.
>
> The High Court ruling is likely to deepen the Royal Family's already considerable embarrassment over the American businessman's relationship with the Duchess.
>
> Mr Bryan negotiated extensive *Hello!* coverage of Jane Makim's marriage to Reiner Luedecke earlier this year, at which all the Ferguson family were reunited in Australia. But a writ taken out against him by the couple in March accused him of breaching his duties on

their behalf and a High Court case was found in their favour in chambers yesterday.

'There were secret commissions. Some of the *Hello!* money had been paid to him,' solicitor Kathryn Garbutt said on behalf of the Luedeckes today. 'He had extra money on top which they didn't know about — the £55,000 he has been ordered to pay.'

This looked like a typical piece of Bryan sleight-of-hand, but the facts were rather different. The Luedeckes would have received no money at all if John had not brokered the deal; instead they were given a significant sum by *Hello!* John and Sarah paid for the honeymoon — and for the flights to Australia of members of the Ferguson family so that they could be reunited. Jane and Reiner's pursuit of John was, in my view, mean-spirited, and not least because he ended up with nothing from the deal personally.

Sarah called me to say she was appalled by the judgment, and that she would stand by John. Fifteen minutes later I switched on CNN to hear her words being repeated by a newscaster. She had rung me to make sure that John knew she was going public for him.

That, however, did not stop her from turning up at Prince Andrew's side on a number of public occasions. Though separated, they would turn out together for their children's sports days and other such events. But Sarah seemed determined to be photographed with her husband on other occasions: at golf matches or dining informally at a pub or, as on this occasion, attending a fireworks display. John, who had not been told that she was yet again going to be pictured in the press with her husband, was furious. Even now, he was banned from being photographed in public with Sarah — but it was her habit of blithely dismissing him when with Andrew which filled him with impotent rage.

For Sarah there were tactical reasons as to why she should cosy up to her husband, but every time they were pictured together it prompted another spate of newspaper articles speculating on the possibility of a reconciliation. Yet after the fireworks display, Sarah had rung me to state her position — she would never return to Andrew. She wished she were not titled, and she wished she could go back to living a normal life. I asked her when she had last been happy. 'Last time we flew to Ireland together,' she said. 'Or the time we flew to New York together and we had a *laugh*.' She invited me to accompany her on a trip to Nice with no apparent agenda apart from having fun, but I said no: there was no business reason or charity reason or horse reason to go, and I knew that John would think I was trying to steal his girlfriend if I did accept.

A few weeks later, as she flew away on holiday with her children to a villa near Grasse, an interview appeared in the Australian *Woman's Day* magazine in which she admitted that the publication of the South of France photographs of her with John had been 'the most humbling experience of her life'. Ironically enough, John had not been invited on this French holiday, and with good reason, since she had asked the Duke instead. So he and I accepted an invitation to go to Sardinia, but even as we set off Sarah called me to say that she and John had agreed to a two-week communications blackout between them. It was to be a trial period of silence, to give both of them a chance to reassess their relationship, and it turned out to be a complete farce. HRH called John three times on the first day alone, and me twice, to reconfirm that there was to be a communications moratorium. By the third day she was calling as frequently as ever, often leaving messages for him with the concierge of our hotel. On the fourth day she left a message for John which she later regretted, so she woke me in the small hours and asked me to snatch it away from the concierge before John could read it.

It hardly mattered: John's attention was diverted elsewhere and he barely had time to respond to this bizarre form of non-communication. He found himself knocked off-balance by the attentions of Princess Hermine de Clermont-Tonnerre, to whom we had been introduced in a piano bar in Paris during the winter. Hermine, for whatever reasons of her own, had targeted John, and meant to make the most of his stay at the Hotel Pietra Blanca.

John was in seventh heaven. We were surrounded by the *crème de la crème* of European society — so much more amusing, so much more beautiful, so much richer and sexier than their dowdy British counterparts, or so he perceived it — and they seemed to be extremely interested in him. Sergio Montagasse was said to be seventeenth richest man in Europe; there was a batch of lesbian women, including an Italian government minister; wives of envoys and marquises abounded; a brace of princes graced us with their presence; Buzz Aldrin was reminiscing about his moon-walk; and there was Ivana Trump who, unlike the rest of us, was not on holiday. She had a mobile phone clamped to her ear the whole time, talking deals.

It took no more than forty-eight hours for Princess Hermine and John to connect, and when it happened there were fireworks. At lunch by the pool next day he and Hermine, mouths almost touching, tied spaghetti in a knot with their tongues. Their next public display could be viewed through John's bedroom window, and culminated in the man himself appearing, naked and in full view, cooling himself off, and using the billowing curtain to wipe himself down.

Here, in Sardinia, the title 'Duchess of York' carried less weight than it did elsewhere. In Europe John was a star in his own right, though the screwy logic was that he was only famous for being with someone whom Sardinia could easily do without. Princess Hermine liked being around this star. Out by the pool, she clung to him like a limpet, and staged photos which John thought were for the hotel's brochure. The inevitable photographs were wired around the world, to appear in newspapers and magazines everywhere. They looked suspiciously like the pictures of JB and HRH taken by another poolside two years earlier. They also looked suspiciously like a set-up.

Not that Sarah, an hour's flight away in

Grasse, had the wit to work that one out. She simply saw John and a topless girl in a savage replay of the worst moment in her life, then read the text which went with the pictures. 'Hermine is a very sexy-looking girl and knows how to have fun,' ran one caption. 'She is a Princess from both sides of her family which, I think, is a little better than a Duchess by marriage.'

John, of course, was beyond blame. So Sarah turned her fury on me — it was I who had betrayed her, I who had let her down. 'You were supposed to be watching John!' she howled. 'That's what you do with him on these trips — you watch him and you keep him out of trouble! And you promised me, Starkie, you promised me that nothing was going on with Hermine.' In this last, she was right. A British newspaper had alerted her to the poolside frolics and she had called me, asking if there was anything in it. I said no, but I had reckoned without the camera crew Hermine had brought with her, as eager as she to capture every second of this elaborately constructed sting.

A month passed before Sarah and I were on speaking terms again. Money, and her need for backup and support, finally brought her round, though the call came through a third person — if my answering machine could be so described. The message said that she was dying to see me, and that she had found the perfect destination for one of her projects — Romania. She was, she said, faxing the details to my office.

Among the many business propositions we had discussed, one was a plan for a TV miniseries Albert had originally dubbed *Leave Them Smiling*. The idea was that the Duchess would travel into Eastern Europe and find some hellish place in some way associated with children. Via the cameras, she would draw public attention to its plight, raise money for its sick or starving or dispossessed, and then go back and graciously hand the cheque over. After a time we decided a more palatable name would be *The Envoy*, and since we had fixed on the idea Sarah had been looking round for a place with the worst conditions we had yet encountered — worse than Albania and Bosnia. Finally she had found this place in Romania, and had become energized at the prospect of her latest mercy dash.

If this seemed cynical, at least at the end of the line someone would benefit. John, seduced by the jet set, had gone to play in Monte Carlo, where the only beneficiaries would be the room-service waiters and the bellhops. His beaming face — sandwiched between those of arms dealer Adnan Kha-shoggi, socialite Luis del Camp Bacardi, of the rum family, and his wife Angela, and the omnipresent former First Lady of Indonesia, Dewi Sukarno, adorned the gossip columns and glossy magazines for days and weeks afterwards.

In New York, word leaked out that Sarah was looking for a $5 million deal for two (ghostwritten) novels set in London and based on a royal theme. John was said to be brokering the deal, and one report stated that he had hinted that the novels would contain 'veiled autobiographical references' — a sort of grown-up *Amanda*. Then the London *Sunday Times* reported: 'Only one serious offer was made of about $400,000 (£270,000) for a series of two or three mystery novels. The Duchess has rejected the offer and dispensed with Bryan's services as her personal literary representative.' The tenor of the piece was that John had blown it.

Sarah was not the only member of her family with literary ambitions at this time. Her father, not previously known as a man of letters, burst into print with his memoirs. In his book, he claimed that Andrew and Sarah would be reconciled, and offered the ingenuous observation on his first marriage, 'Prince Philip had an eye for Susie. Certainly, they remain friends to this day.'

Princess Esmeralda and her boyfriend Albert Zarca circled Sarah like bees round a honeypot. They sold the feature we had concocted on the theme of 'Motherhood and A Day in the Life of the Duchess' to *Paris Match* and *Point de Vue* and a number of other Continental magazines. *Hello!* wanted to buy the British rights, and if the deal had come off the total sum raised from that one piece of journalism would have been around £450,000. Sarah, however, had fallen out with *Hello!* over the business of her sister Jane suing John, and so refused to allow them the British rights. Albert, whose commission was 40 per cent of whatever the Duchess received, could see his share of *Hello!*'s £200,000 offer disappearing in smoke and came to me, begging that I should intercede with her.

Sarah said she might agree as long as certain conditions were met, of which the principal stipulation was that it should be made known that the money was going to charity. This, however, was not true. The feature had already earned over £200,000 abroad, and that she had kept. Although the icing on the cake — the £200,000 from *Hello!* — never materialized because of poor timing, she had made sure that the magazines signed their contracts with Albert's and Esmeralda's company, Presse Impact Italia, so that it would be virtually impossible to find out whether she had received any money at all from exposing herself to the public gaze. The article itself, though anodyne, probably broke the terms of the Deed of Separation she had signed, which forbade her to write or speak about her immediate family, including her own daughters.

Sarah then told me that none of the proceeds would be going to charity, not even to her own Children in Crisis. I was shocked: it was necessary to make some kind of gesture, both practically and morally. In the end I persuaded her to give something, but it was a fraction of the overall fee. I compared her attitude on this occasion with a conversation I had with her a couple of days later, when she was in one of her recurring religious-ethical moods following a verbal attack by John. 'Honesty is my middle name,' she said, her eyes and conscience clear. I felt that to have reminded her of our previous conversation about giving to charity would have been like waking a sleepwalker.

I don't think John ever claimed honesty to be his middle name. Though he had done nothing towards the writing, selling or publication of this one money-spinning article —

indeed, he had lambasted its author to the point of tears, telling her not to go ahead with it — he now felt that he was entitled to some share of the proceeds. Sarah, rightly appalled by this, asked me to handle the problem — eventually he received £20,000 from Esmeralda's company in the form of a cheque to cover his latest American Express bill.

The time had come for a parting of the ways between John and me. He had neglected Oceonics in his pursuit of Sarah and the jet-set life; he had sabotaged the relationship between me and Sarah; and he had ceased to behave as a friend. I wrote him a letter saying that I did not want to do anything destructive to the company, but that I was giving him ninety days in which to find my successor as chief executive. It shouldn't be a problem, I added sourly, since every street corner had a thousand Allan Starkies — as he had pointed out to the Duchess.

This letter, I later learned, threw John into an emotional upheaval — he began crying and demanding that something be done to get me back. I had flown to Paris, and was greeted at the airport by a humbled partner falling over himself with apologies. He told me that he simply hadn't realized that I had given so much for so long. An observer does not need to be particularly cynical to understand that John was frightened of being left in sole control of an ailing company he did not know how to run. His life now was in England, with Sarah, and he could not bear the thought of having to relocate to Frankfurt to preside over the funeral of Oceonics.

Princess Esmeralda and Albert came knocking at Sarah's door again, this time with two more propositions, together worth £400,000. But Sarah, sorely tempted though she was by the idea of another quick and painless transfusion of cash, felt that the proposals for two more magazine articles blatantly exploited her children. She was, perhaps, less concerned that the princesses might suffer from overexposure in the press, than that she would be seen to be flouting the confidentiality clause of her Deed of Separation, thereby incurring massive Palace displeasure. In the end, the Palace had the whip hand, and despite her apparently rebellious behaviour, Sarah knew it.

This displeased the ambitious Esmeralda and Albert, who saw the prospect of millions emanating from their association with Sarah. Though I was no longer officially the Duchess's business partner or manager, they thought that the best way of securing their own ends was to try to recruit me to their team, and made me a series of offers, all of which I refused. They accepted this, but pointed out that though Sarah paid lip-service to making money in this way, every project they put up was either killed by her or died a natural death, not because she didn't need or want the money, but simply because of her vacillating nature. I was inclined to help — I was very fond of the Duchess by this time and saw that, if it was well handled, no harm and some good could come from a properly orchestrated publicity campaign. She was by now getting no help from John, whose negativism led him to shoot down every money-raising project in flames, and what she needed in her life now was some financial independence. Where money was concerned, the terms of her separation were unrealistic, however — Buckingham Palace wanted to keep her 'barefoot and pregnant', to use John's phrase, which is to say utterly reliant on them — and indeed John agreed with that principle. But although the Duchess overspent, in truth she did not have enough money from Andrew and the royal family to live in a way befitting her station as mother of the fifth and sixth in line to the throne.

Watching with horror as her overdraft spiralled out of control — just as ours was doing at Oceonics — I felt a great deal of sympathy with her. The money was just sitting around, waiting to be shovelled into her bank account — all she had to do was agree to the deals that were being put to her — and it seemed a crime not to take advantage of that state of affairs. I drew up a short list of projects which could be executed with elegance, and when I added up what they would pay, the figure came to around $1 million.

The Sleepy Kids deal, from which Sarah would have received around £3 million in return for surrendering her shareholding, had gone cold, and we were left in a situation where we needed the sale of that precious asset — Sarah because of her overdraft, and John and I because of her pledge to support Oceonics. If she honoured that pledge, Oceonics would survive the recession; if she did not, the company would be dead by next spring.

I therefore suggested a tie-up, using Sarah's shareholding in Sleepy Kids, with the company which had the licence for Budgie in the US, Launey Hachman and Harris: by a complex restructuring it would be possible to raise $6 million this way. Meanwhile Clive Garrad was working with his friends in the Far East, including David Tang, to raise the capital to buy Sarah's slice of Budgie. Clive set up an offshore company for her called Gracious Lady, through which she would receive £4 million for just 49 per cent of her Budgie shareholding. These two deals, therefore, would increase the value of the asset she held, and would be more than sufficient to wipe out her bank overdraft and honour her commitment to Oceonics.

The real beauty of these deals was that they would provide cash fast — cash the company urgently needed. To her and to John I tried to present a calm and unruffled exterior, but I was succumbing to the pressure. I had never suffered mood swings or depression before, but now I was taking Valium, as well as a strong sleeping pill of which I needed constantly to increase the dosage in order for it to have any effect. I had recurring nightmares, while the physical effect of the combination of drugs was such as to lower my resistance so that I suffered sore throats and constant fever. Part of me wanted to quit, and I had warned John that I was going to do so, but I could not forget that the employees of Oceonics relied on me — they would never be able to rely on John.

There were still lighter moments to look forward to. Sarah celebrated her thirty-fifth birthday on 15 October, and a party was held for her at Mosimann's. The party itself was a great success, but hanging over it was the shadow of a row between John and Sarah involving the Princess of Wales, who had recently visited them at Romenda Lodge.

Diana was envious of Sarah's relationship with John, and of the fact that her sister-in-law had someone to help her with the transition from being inside the royal family to being on the outside; she herself lacked a man who would give her the emotional and financial support she needed. So, believing that he provided such support for Sarah, she admired John, and John admired her, and when he came into the room on this particular visit the Princess said how much she liked the shirt he was wearing. This had been a gift from Sarah, but she now denied having bought it for him. One could only conclude from this rather odd disavowal that she didn't want Diana to think that she and John were that close.

After the Princess had left, there was a row, John demanding, 'Why are you always trying to deny me?' Sarah said that this wasn't the case, but in truth it was. Their relationship was nearly three years old, but John was still the Prisoner of Romenda — he could kiss her only when the curtains were closed, he had to wear a baseball hat when on the way to Romenda Lodge, he had to adhere to strict instructions on which route to follow when driving to and from the house. Once, when she discovered he had not kept to her prescribed route, she called him on his mobile phone and screamed, 'Dammit, I told you we've got to be careful, we can't afford to make stupid mistakes!' John felt diminished and angry on all these occasions, though by the end of Sarah's birthday party he had recovered his usual buoyancy.

At this time John was in Romenda Lodge every day, and so too was Jeremy Scott, who was working full-time as her administrator. If there was a lack of communication between the two men it would not have taken much for Sarah to bring them to their senses. Instead, she turned to me — several hundred miles away and struggling with my ailing company — to sort out their differences. On 16 October; the day after her birthday, my machine held an effusive message in thanks for my 'beautiful and thoughtful' presents to her. A second message a day or so later, however, asked me to brief Jeremy on what was happening, and to find out from John what was going on with Budgie.

This I did, though John, in jet-set mode, was barely able to pay attention. He was back in Sardinia dancing the night away aboard *Kalizma*, the yacht once owned by Elizabeth

Taylor and Richard Burton, which we had both visited in August. The guest list was a round-up of the usual suspects, including Princess Hermine de Clermont-Tonnerre. The latest issue of *Hello!*, more familiar with his status than most, chose to disabuse its readership by describing John as a 'former' adviser to the Duchess. In a sense, of course, the magazine was right.

Although the public view of the Duchess of York was by now largely critical, not everyone dwelt on her shortcomings. She inspired fierce loyalty, especially among some of her women employees, of whom I would particularly single out Jane Ambler and Christine Gallagher. But it was at around this time that she suddenly found herself in receipt of one of the most charming, and deserved, tributes from a former member of her staff.

She had found Pemba Gyaldzen, whom she immediately dubbed 'Yeltsin', on her trek to the Himalayas the year before, when he had acted as her guide and porter. Through her own efforts he was brought to England, where he worked for six months at Romenda Lodge. Although, as I noted earlier, he had difficulty in answering the telephone, his removal to the other side of the world changed his life. 'Fergie is like my God and my mother. She has given me opportunities in life others can only dream about,' he told a startled reporter. 'She gave me what my father could not, because we are a poor family and cannot afford to go out of Nepal.' Until two years before his encounter with the Duchess he had never seen a television or a car; now Sarah had paid for him to have driving lessons, computer lessons and skiing instruction. The first two would prove to be vital assets on his return to Nepal, for they dramatically increased his earning power in the impoverished kingdom. So, while this may have been a strange episode for both Yeltsin and Sarah, it was one from which only good came.

Another person who still felt warmly towards Sarah was Robert Splaine. At about this time — that is, the early autumn of 1994 — she persuaded Simon Brooks-Ward, an extremely influential figure in that world, to write to the organizers of the nation's show-jumping events: 'The Duchess of York is championing the cause of Robert Splaine of Ireland. HRH is prepared to help publicize the show by attending, and speaking to the press about her love of horses and show-jumping, if you were able to invite him to your event.' Brooks-Ward also sent a similar letter begging a place for Robert at the forth-coming show-jumping championships in Brussels. The reality, however, was that Robert Splaine was an above-average rider who was not quite good enough to make his national team. Strings had had to be pulled even to get him on to the international jumping circuit, but the Duchess was prepared to do whatever it took in order to see Heather Blaze win Olympic gold. Our efforts verged on the ridiculous: at one stage we talked about going back to Albania and suggesting to her friend the President that Robert become their show-jumping representative at the Olympics. She was incapable of seeing that neither horse nor rider were up to the task she had set them.

Nevertheless, she managed to enthuse Princess Esmeralda sufficiently for her to use her contacts to get Robert an entry at the Paris Horse Show early in December, and by similar methods we also procured a place for him at the Frankfurt show a week earlier. I noted in my diary, 'She will not give up the idea of making Robert Splaine and Heather Blaze Olympic champions despite the age of the horse and the performance of the rider.' Whenever I queried the viability of this ambition, I would get a highly emotional reaction from her; others were less questioning.

Clive Garrad had pledged £100,000 for Heather Blaze's first year in the Duchess of York's colours, to cover operating costs and the purchase of a horse transporter, but now there was another call for money. The Duchess telephoned me in a state of panic to say that Heather Blaze, who was only rented by Robert, was to be sold by her owners to some Americans.

Robert had previously told me that the horse could probably be bought for £150,000, but Sarah was now saying that the price stood at between £350,000 and £400,000. I suspected that the vendors had been told of her Olympic ambitions and accused them of opportunism, but she would have none of it, telling me that she could not bear to lose Heather Blaze and that the money had to be found somehow. It was an absurd situation for a woman with an overdraft hovering at £2 million, and I repeated that I thought it was a foolish idea and that she was being pressured into buying what was an inadequate horse. All she replied was that she would fix it.

One day not much later, as we were watching Heather Blaze and Robert Splaine knock down yet another fence, Sarah leaned across and whispered excitedly in my ear, 'And she's two-thirds mine now!' I had had no idea that she had managed to raise the money, but I was told that the ever-generous Clive Garrad had come up with £100,000 in cash, and had secured all but one-third of Heather Blaze.

Early in November, Sarah was back in New York — the third time that year — preparing the ground for the launch of Chances for Children, her third children's charity. The advance publicity said that she was starting the appeal with £50,000 of her own cash, and that she was setting up her own office in the city which would deal with her business and charitable affairs. These two merging interests came together in a flying visit to the Midwest, where she met a roomful of patients at the Kansas City Children's Mercy Hospital who, coincidentally, as it were, just happened to be surrounded by Budgie products for the benefit of the cameras. On 9 November she left a message asking me to ring her; she was dying to talk to me about Budgie, which she thought was 'going extremely well'. Back in New York she happily faced queues of autograph-hunters clutching Budgie books, toys and T-shirts: America, which had clasped the Princess of Wales to its bosom for the past decade, was warming to Sarah in a big way.

Sarah returned to London on 15 November, an excited message on my machine enthusing about Budgie, but adding, ominously, that John was being 'a jerk' again. The US trip had been a triumph, and she had ended up right where she needed to be — talking to Hollywood giants like Steven Spielberg and David Geffen. This was too much for John, who reacted to the news that Spielberg had expressed interest, real or feigned, in Budgie with an angry tirade. No matter what she did, or however happy she might be with the results, John would always second-guess her, exclaiming, 'No, Linky! That's not the way to do it!' He had his own idea of how to get Budgie accepted in Hollywood — but then, this was easy for him, since he was not there actually doing the deals.

It was at about this time that a journalist called Stephen Wright came knocking on my door. He had been dispatched to write a profile on the Duchess — would I help? Before too long I had established that his mission was to reveal that Sarah was misusing funds from her charities in order to pay for her exotic lifestyle. Although I assured him that this was not the case, my answer was only partially true. Sarah would very often pay out of her own purse for her flights on charity business, and then forget to claim the money back from the charities in question. She would also combine business and charity in a perfectly justifiable way — as when she had linked Menschen in Not ('People in Need', the name she had finally chosen for her German charity), Schröder Munchmeyer and Oceonics during her visit to Germany — but, inevitably, that would be miscon-strued by some members of the public, who would see darker forces at play. Later, the British TV programme *World in Action* would make a documentary on this theme, but the result was an aimless potshot at the Duchess and Oceonics which failed to find any evi-dence of wrongdoing.

Where the Duchess did err, however, was in saying, when *Budgie* was first published, that money from the book would go to her husband's charitable trust. And she would try to confuse the public into believing that a charitable trip was purely that, while the truth was that if *Hello!* magazine came along, she would be making money for herself out of the trip. She never tried to misuse charity funds, but she would deduct her expenses, which sometimes could be thousands of pounds, before the charity in question saw any of the money which she had raised. When it came to the ethics of charitable fundraising, the Duchess of York walked a very fine line.

By now winter was with us, and John's relationship with Sarah had survived, despite her attempts to choke it off back in the summer. On reflection it was remarkable that Sarah, who had worked herself up to a point at which she was ready to dump him, and had deliberately gone on holiday with her husband, would want to continue the affair after the pictures of him with a topless Princess Hermine had been published, but it tottered on. John, despite the fact that he had been hoodwinked into being photographed with Hermine, seemed to bear her no ill will, and when he and I sauntered into a party at the Ritz Club in Paris that November, we found her waiting for us with open arms.

Later that night we moved on to Calvados, the club with the Mexican mariachi band which, a year ago, had played their cockeyed version of 'Guantanamera' to celebrate John's entrance. In recognition of this famous figure, they struck up their tune again, but he was less fascinated by their musicianship on this occasion — he and a woman disappeared into the unisex toilet, from which sounds of intense pleasure began to emanate. The musicians looked at the door nervously, then played louder, hoping to drown the noise. As the pounding and stifled screams began to reach a crescendo, the band gave up their attempts, set down their instruments, and took a break. One of my fellow guests looked around and asked innocently, 'Where is John?' Madame Merci, another guest, answered in bored and jaded tones, 'Oh, he's fucking in the toilet.'

If that was one form of revenge, Sarah had her own way of fighting back. By now, Gracious Lady, the offshore company set up by Clive Garrad, had done its paperwork and was prepared to give her a cheque for her shareholding in Budgie. Time was ticking on, and there was just one month left before Oceonics went under — unless the bank kept it afloat, and there seemed less and less chance of that. All Sarah had to do was fly to Hong Kong to pick up the money, and an appropriate moment even presented itself when she was invited to a party in the colony. But instead, she flew to New York again for another Chances for Children meeting.

Slowly the realization began to dawn on me that Sarah was playing a waiting game: she was delaying liquidating Budgie until Oceonics had ceased to exist. This upset me deeply, not least because every day I was fighting to keep the company alive and its employees paid. From New York she had flown on to Australia for a reconciliation with her sister Jane, their differences over John's £55,000 court judgment apparently reconciled, but was due back in Frankfurt on the following Friday, 2 December, for the official launch of Menschen in Not.

This should have been an embarrassment for her, but strangely it was not. The bankers for MIN, waiting to welcome their royal patron, were also the bankers for Oceonics to whom she had pledged $1.5 million — a sum that was overdue, and with no evidence that it was any nearer being deposited with them. I was the one who was agonizing over what would be said that day, but worse was to follow. Sarah, in her offhand way, had invited John along to the launch of MIN, fully aware that the bankers wanted nothing more to do with him. Now she was asking me to uninvite him, as a message left on my machine on 28 November made all too plain. She had only asked him along because she 'just thought it would be nice', but if he didn't come, 'then so much the better'. Needless to say, however, she left the decision — and the privilege of telling him he was uninvited — to me; she knew I would 'make the right decision about our brother — just push him off on Friday'.

The Duchess arrived in Frankfurt to a rapturous welcome for the official opening of her Germany charity, and the bankers had the good grace — and good manners — not to mention her outstanding pledge to them of the money for Oceonics. The crowds turned out for her everywhere, applauding and waving and shouting and whistling; at one point she turned to me and said, 'Starkie, this is fantastic! It's only in my own country that I'm not loved.' The date for her visit had been wisely chosen, since she could also officially open the Frankfurt Horse Show, into which I had managed to enter Robert Splaine, and after she had read the speech I'd written for her we sat down to watch Robert bravely but unsuccessfully pursue the championship. The performance did not dismay Sarah at all: afterwards we went behind the scenes where she produced a beautifully arranged bunch of carrots, looking more like a bouquet of flowers than a common root vegetable, which she fed to her darling horse.

Back in Britain, the press had caught up with a John Bryan story that was over a month old. They did not even tell it very well:

The Texan millionaire was seen cuddling busty Italian movie star Francesca Dellera, whose near-naked picture adorns advertising billboards all over her native country.

John smooched all night with the Latin beauty at an awards ceremony in Rome. He then whisked her off to a top nightclub.

The actress, who recently stripped off for the cover of an Italian magazine, once dated hunky Highlander star Christopher Lambert. Earlier she was engaged to Italian Prince Emanuel Filiberto — and had a fling with rock star Prince.

She said: 'Johnny's a lovely person. I like men who are young, good-looking and dangerous.'

In the wake of this came a timely but none the less electrifying statement from Sarah that she had twice submitted to an AIDS test. She made the announcement on a visit to Portugal, where she was supporting an AIDS charity. She disclosed that she had had one test before she married Prince Andrew in 1986, and another in 1993 'in order to take out life insurance'. By coincidence, that test came soon after it had been revealed that

Peggy Caskie, a former sexual partner of John's, had been diagnosed as HIV positive. Sarah's frankness was praised by the AIDS lobby but brought forth a sigh of disgust from an unnamed Buckingham Palace official: 'These personal and delicate matters should not be debated openly by royalty. God knows what she'll say next.'

The year ended with John a lost soul. The Duchess did her usual routine of going to Sandringham for the royal Christmas, even through she was pretty much an outcast by that stage, then flying off with Beatrice and Eugenie on a skiing trip. John was not invited to accompany them, and had to face the chilly truth that his presence was no longer essential to Sarah.

Always in the past there had been an open invitation for him to spend Christmas at the house of his stepmother, Josephine Abercrombie, in Vail, Colorado. This year, however, his secretary Julia received a call from Josephine's office: 'We would just like to confirm that John won't be coming to Vail for Christmas, because we have no room for him.' He had to console himself with another visit to Paris where, jet-setter that he now was, he received an automatic invitation to the Best awards. Even here, though, he could not escape a sense of hopelessness. Last year he may have been Best, but this year he was just another member of the rootless, bored, bejewelled audience who turned up because they had nothing better to do that night.

Chapter 12

A wiser man might, by this stage, have reviewed his situation and drawn some useful conclusions. John's attempts to be publicly accepted as Sarah's life-partner had been squashed. He had been marginalized in her business life, and the prospects of marriage to her looked bleaker than at any time. He was now unfaithful to her at every available opportunity, and yet felt insecure and abandoned by her.

But some strange force still held them together and kept me close to them as well. After Christmas I sent Sarah a note of thanks for the present she had sent, wrongly describing it as a candlestick. Early in January Sarah and John were out driving when she called to leave a message on my machine. First she pulled me up, slightly resentful, for having thought her present was a candlestick, when it was 'actually a *matchstick holder*', and thus '*slightly more* special'. But all the time she was becoming more and more furious with John, who was driving, and occasionally butting in with comments of his own for my ever-sympathetic mechanical ear. 'Why should he take such pleasure in seeing me suffer and take control of my life to such a degree?' she complained, while he cut in with a denial.

This call summed up our relationship — Sarah and John ('nightmare man in a leather jacket being a nightmare') arguing, and calling on me to arbitrate between them; Sarah appealing to me, saying that John should not always be putting her down; John laughing at her and encouraging me to do so too. The only weird thing was that they were in a car, and talking to my answering machine as if it were me. In the early days of 1995 things had become very strange. They were to become a lot stranger.

Sarah came to Frankfurt to meet the Schröder Munchmeyer bankers and some of the board members of her newly created German charity. It might be supposed that the bankers would have asked her where the Budgie money was, since Oceonics was now virtually dead in the water and was only being kept afloat by the very men to whom she was talking in that room. Instead, they scrambled around like children, asking her to sign photographs — in which they also featured — of her last visit. The meeting itself was a complete shambles, and after a while Sarah stood up and laid it on the line — she would not be messed about by people who had no firm agenda and no forward plan, apart from a scheme to hold a charity ball to raise funds. It was not the way she did business. If they wanted her to continue, they must brighten up their ideas.

It was an astonishing performance, given that she owed some of these men — or at least, had pledged them — the best part of $1.5 million. Afterwards Herr Kling, one of the managing directors of Schröder Munchmeyer, asked me to thank her for disciplining him in the way she had. The whole thing was bizarre. Just as bizarre was the Germans' idea that HRH should put out a statement about her concern for the people of that country who had suffered loss as a result of the recent flooding of the River Main. This was MIN's first appeal for funds — but it was done in such a pathetic way that it resulted in netting just two contributions which, together, amounted to some £15.

Still there was no sign of the Budgie money coming in, and by now even John was suspicious that Sarah was not trying as hard as she might to cash in her shareholding. The two deals designed to give her very generous sums for her slice of Budgie were still in place, one in the US, one in Hong Kong. It now turned out, however, that built into the US deal was a substantial cut for John. When

Jeremy Scott pointed this out to the Duchess she wanted to confront John about it, but was too scared to do so alone. A dinner was therefore arranged at Mosimann's, to which Clive Garrad (who had an interest in the Hong Kong deal), Jeremy, John and I were invited. As the discussion progressed Sarah threw out several half-veiled hints that she didn't trust John and felt that he was still trying to control her.

There was more talk and then, like a great ocean liner emerging out of the fog, John's deal became clearer and clearer. This was not just a deal for Budgie, but for all the Duchess's future projects. For a man who had been consigned to a 15 per cent stake in Fireside Communications and told to go off and pursue his own business career, this was a bold move — and nothing less than a bid single-handedly to take back control of Sarah's business. Once again she quizzed John, on a different tack this time, and he realized that she was accusing him of taking backhanders through investment bankers' fees. Jumping up, he shouted at her: 'Oh, I see what you're accusing me of! Well, you can just fuck off!'

I tried to calm him down, but he was raging. He went on: 'You just let the Queen shit all over you! You like being shitted on! You enjoy it! You think that's all you're good for! And, you know, she's just going to keep on shitting on you — do you know why? Because she doesn't care about you, she doesn't care anything about you!'

This was no longer a meeting about how we were going to manage Budgie in the future — it was about mistrust, control, and the hidden agenda to which Sarah had been working for the past year in order to write John Bryan out of her life. Underlying this was her lover's biggest resentment — why haven't you divorced your husband and married me? — and his whole hatred of the royal system to which Sarah still clung poured out in his vitriolic statements about the Queen.

I had never seen the Duchess in such a state. Hunched over the table in an almost catatonic state and with a lighted cigarette drooping from her lips, she started to make a speech in a low, flat monotone. As she sat there motionless with her hands folded in her lap, tears started to cascade down her face, sometimes hitting the cigarette as they fell, then splattering on her plate in front of her. She talked of how the monarch had sat on the throne since she was twenty-one (not true: she was twenty-five), how she had given up her life for her duties, how she was the most powerful head of state in the world, and how people had died for her.

Still motionless, still weeping, Sarah went on to talk of how the Queen had stood by her, how she had paid for her wardrobe when she became engaged to Prince Andrew because she could not afford one herself, and how Her Majesty met her at Christmas because she wanted Sarah to beat the system. As has been said, this last conviction was a recurring theme of Sarah's — she truly believed that the Queen was backing her against the royal system, without ever being able to explain why Her Majesty was unable to change the system to allow her back in.

Nobody, she went on, understood her or understood what she was trying to do. It had never been done before in history, and she must be taken seriously. Her vulnerability at that moment caused me to say how very sorry I was, how this whole scenario was unnecessary — at which point she turned on me. Eyes blazing, her cheeks flushing, she shouted at me: 'You know nothing of what I'm going through. You're not a member of the royal family, how can you understand? You Americans think you know everything, but don't understand *anything*.' I was appalled: I had done nothing that evening except try to calm them both down, and I watched in dismay as Sarah strode angrily from the room.

John reacted as he always did in such circumstances: taking me with him, he went off in search of a party, then ended up in Tramp, the Jermyn Street nightclub, where he wasted no time in picking up the sister of the girl on whom he had performed a perfunctory sex act in Rhode Island the previous year. Given his mood, it was likely he would be even more perfunctory on this occasion, but before we had raised a drink to our lips the telephone in Tramp's lobby started to ring: it was the Duchess. 'Go and talk to her — I can't talk to her,' John barked, and over the deafening disco music that emanated from the dancefloor I shouted to Sarah that he was as upset as she was about the whole incident. She ordered me to bring him to the phone, but when John strode over he simply slammed the receiver down. She called the club three or four more times, but John refused to talk to her on each occasion.

He also refused, whenever he could, to talk to our bankers in Frankfurt. He believed that they would not push us into receivership, and indeed it was true they were doing their best to accommodate Oceonics' difficulties. But they were furious with John's lighthearted approach to the situation, and it was then, in February, that they refused to honour his monthly cheque. In part this was an act of revenge on Tony Bryan, who had come to Frankfurt to promise the bank that a merger was possible between Oceonics and a hospital company, but had gone away and 'forgotten' to provide the necessary paperwork.

Our credibility with the bank by now was zero, and worse than zero. John would come back from his latest 'motherlode' trip to Russia and brief the increasingly cynical bankers about how a massive new project was about to come off and how our debts would be settled. But all the bank could see was a no-hope partnership between an elusive father and an off-the-rails son, neither of whom had the will to see Oceonics survive. I was battling on myself and trying to protect my employees, but since the Two Bryans would not concentrate their efforts on what was, after all, their company, it would all be over in a matter of days.

John refused to push his father, and also refused to push Sarah to spring the cash she'd pledged — partly because he wanted to control her in her new, restructured, US-based company, the one which had been the cause of their blazing row at Mosimann's but for which he still had high hopes. He — and his father — ignored another bid by the bank to save us, whereby Oceonics would close and a new company be created; they did not show up for the meeting. The bank cancelled a promissory note we had issued, and suddenly everybody pulled off the jobs we were doing and the trade creditors cancelled their credit. We were insolvent.

The Duchess called up brightly and told me she was having a house-warming party at her new home, Kingsbourne, and would I like to come? I said I could not leave Germany at that moment because my staff would have thought I was abandoning them. John was too frightened to come to Germany, too embarrassed to face the people who worked for him, and too busy moving his few things into Kingsbourne and setting up a mini-office in a vestibule next to one of the Duchess's walk-in wardrobes.

In Germany there was a staff of thirty in the Oceonics office, and there had been many sub-contractors who had worked for the company, perhaps five hundred in all. It may not have been glamorous, but it was a worthy business which, in the good old days, had generated a remarkable amount of money. But John knew virtually none of his workforce and cared nothing about the contracts we were involved in — his perpetual search for the 'motherlode', for the limelight, for international social acceptance, had by now ruined whatever self-discipline he might once have had.

I had ten days left in which to find the money to pay the bank, or I could be criminally liable for having kept my company trading longer than German law permitted. Once more I pleaded with Sarah for the Budgie money, and once more with the Two Bryans for help. To no avail. The Duchess, it appeared, was prepared to help me in any way she could except honour her promise. My last plea to her to liquidate Budgie came too late — she had flown to Puerto Rico and was uncontactable. John did not return my calls — he was in Moscow, fooling around with models from an agency which, or so he convinced the pliant girls, he was going to buy. Tony Bryan did not return my calls, and Bill Simon — the only other major investor in the company — was beyond reach. In fact, it was not until many weeks later that the former Secretary to the US Treasury discovered that a company in which he had a substantial stake had gone to the wall — and then only from a chance telephone conversation with the Duchess. She asked: 'He's fired all the staff and is selling all the furniture. Is that liquidation, Bill?'

My diary entry for 25 February 1995

summed up the death of Oceonics Deutsch-land GmbH: 'It's all fallen apart. I am left alone to face it.'

Faced with her massive unconcern for her pledge, I spoke to the Duchess less and less. The truth was, however, that things had chilled between us. She now refused to give me any fresh information about her liquidating Budgie, nor would she come to Frankfurt to tell the bank what was happening with her plans to liquidate, nor would she talk to the bankers about their mutual charity, MIN. Her only concession was to ask me to invite Herr Meyer from Schröder Munchmeyer to come to London as a sop. Meanwhile the lawyers were now warning that I risked being arrested if I kept Oceonics open any longer; John was telling me that I was not allowed to close Oceonics because the shareholders and the bank would not sanction it; and the Duchess refused to help in any material way. It was not surprising that I had given up returning, or even answering, her calls. This infuriated her, and on 12 March she left a message, which while ostensibly sympathetic, nevertheless made it clear that my behaviour, and especially my failure to return her calls, was unacceptable. I was to ring her; we were to talk about it.

There was nothing to talk about, though:

Sarah knew what the problem was, but was not prepared to do anything about it. Obliterating from her mind what was happening in Frankfurt, she was diverting her attention elsewhere, making plans for the future. For her, that future looked rosy and she was in partying mood. It just so happened that the next time she left a message, on 15 March, was the day five armed men burst into the Oceonics office to make an attempt on my life. They were emissaries of a sub-contractor who had not been paid, just as Oceonics had not been paid: but these men were not about to show their disappointment with mere words. They wanted to shoot me.

The situation was defused and I went home, only to learn, via the ever-faithful machine, how 'damned fucking irritating' the Duchess found the fact that I had not talked to her, and that I didn't return her calls. I could not even begin to formulate a reply. On the day on which I had nearly been killed — in part because of her failure to support Oceonics, as she had promised — there were no words left to express my feelings.

Five days later, on 20 March, she left another complaining message. Next day she called Karen, my secretary, in Frankfurt and put Beatrice and Eugenie on the phone: 'Please tell our cousin that we want him to

377

come over. We miss him — pleeeeeease . . .'
When I got into the office Karen told me that the Duchess had ordered tickets from British Airways, and had instructed her over the telephone to insist that I flew to London immediately — otherwise she would come to Frankfurt personally and take me back with her. 'You know I will,' was her message, but I knew she wouldn't. And she didn't.

It had not yet been made public that Oceonics was finished, and so I was astonished when I picked up a newspaper on 26 March to read the headline 'Bryan Goes Bust'. When I looked closer, however, I realized that the story related to John's first interest, not his second — he was back in the States, judging a bevy of big-breasted girls who had entered the Miss Hawaiian Tropic contest in Daytona Beach. He rang me almost immediately, and proceeded to call with periodic updates on how many of the finalists he had slept with. I told him that he was needed in Frankfurt to meet officials from the bank, but his response was: 'Allan, I can't do that right now. You can't believe how many of these girls I've fucked — I fucked a previous winner and they keep on sending more up. With luck I'm going to get a threesome on the beach tonight — how can I come today when the finals are in two days' time?' I insisted, and somehow he managed to find his way from Daytona Beach to Frankfurt, and together we went to meet the bank. Schröder Munchmeyer had been bending over backwards to try to keep Oceonics afloat, and even at the last gasp had put forward various proposals which might have worked. But when one of the directors told John that he and the Duchess of York would surely not want the publicity attendant on Oceonics going bankrupt, John launched into a tirade against the bank. Herr Meyer winced, then looked at him. 'Very well, Mr Bryan. If that is how you feel, you had better file for bankruptcy.' Two days later, we did.

There is one word in my diary for 30 March 1995: 'Dead'.

John, who had flown back to England after our meeting with the bank, had reluctantly turned up that morning, walked self-consciously round the offices, written a horrible one-paragraph notice to the remaining staff saying how honoured we should all be by the accomplishments of Oceonics, made a brief appearance at the bankruptcy court, stopped off at McDonald's for a Big Mac, then jumped on the next plane and gone home to Sarah. As far as he was concerned, the collapse and bankruptcy of his company was about as inconvenient and painful as a visit to the dentist.

The next day I confronted the Duchess as I had never done before. I told her that this was the last day her Budgie money could save Oceonics: 'Do you have it?'

'Of course not,' she said.

'When are you going to have it? Because the bank still wants the money — it's owed to them.'

'No, no, Starkie,' she laughed. 'Did you think I was stupid enough to pour money into a company that was going down the tubes? Jeremy Scott told me Oceonics was like an octopus, cutting off its own arms to survive — why should I put money into it?'

She paused, then added: 'Do you really think I should give that money to John? Why should I give nearly £1 million after his diabolical behaviour towards me?' Then, perhaps thinking she had gone too far, she added: 'Well, I *will* give him some money, but he can wait for it.'

She went on to say that I had done the honourable thing and that I should be rewarded: 'I want you to know that now you can really devote yourself to our charity. Now you're free from our obligations to John, you can concentrate on that, take a salary from it if you want.'

If I was depressed and upset by losing the greatest battle of my life, I was at least consoled by the fact that the Duchess had lost none of her enthusiasm for Menschen in Not; that my five-year sojourn in a foreign country had not been a complete waste. Sooner or later I would leave Germany, I reasoned, but if I left behind a strong and vital charity which enhanced the lives of those it embraced, my time there would have been worth it. These may seem pious sentiments, but at that moment I was clutching at straws: within five years I had seen a company grow from less than nothing to being one of the most powerful in its field in Germany, through the efforts of myself and those dedicated enough to stick at it, and now it was dead. Small wonder that Sarah's softly spoken words gave me comfort.

I had assumed responsibility for collecting the debts, amounting to millions of marks, still owing to Oceonics: the money would go to the bank, but at least our retreat would be an orderly one. I asked the Duchess if I could take two of my key staff from the company into MIN with me, and when she agreed we moved into a tiny office in the MesseTurm, where years before Oceonics had started its interiors business.

John now attempted a new money-making

scheme, in Las Vegas, of all places, which managed to be both potentially illegal and dangerous at the same time. I had been involved, and so had Bill Simon's European manager, Peter Bougdanos. When we learned of John's machinations, however, we withdrew, as did all the other investors. In retaliation he started in on the Duchess, attempting seriously to undermine the German charity. In this she was an easy target, for she had decided that she never wanted to meet the people from Schröder Munchmeyer ever again. They were her charity's bankers, they had seats on the board of MIN, and each of its meetings would carry with it the same unspoken but never-to-go-away question: *where is our money?* John pressed his point home — what value was there in having a German charity when we were all going to be sued in that country? The lawsuits would be an embarrassment, and would damage the charity. Next he targeted her health, telling her he was concerned that she was overtaxing herself. Sarah, who only half listened to John these days, nevertheless listened hard to this because it was what she wanted to hear.

Though by this stage I no longer wanted to spend any time with John, my relationship with the Duchess had repaired itself somewhat, recovering something of its earlier warmth. Soon after the collapse of John's Las Vegas venture, however, I had a call from her assistant, Deborah Oxley, now in charge of Children in Crisis, which made me doubt whether the relationship was as warm as I hoped and believed. Deborah told me, 'The Duchess is so busy and I don't think it's fair for you to keep pushing her to stay involved in this German charity.' Tight-lipped, I pointed out that MIN had nothing to do with her, and explained that there were a number of reasons, not the least of them being the charity's bankers, Schröder Munchmeyer, why the Duchess would want to see MIN flourish. Then I had a call from her secretary, Jane Ambler, saying pretty much the same thing, to which I replied: 'If the Duchess wants to get out of her charitable responsibilities in Germany, she must call me herself.'

It was, of course, the same old story. When Sarah commits herself to something she later regrets, a typical pattern of behaviour occurs: she is not available for your calls, she either leaves messages when she thinks you are not around, or she gets her people to call. Sarah had demonstrated exactly this pattern when she had got cold feet about several other projects, including the *Amanda* deal — now she was doing the same with the German charity. I called her, therefore, and told her that I wanted to come over to England to show her the reasons why we should keep MIN.

I flew in on 7 May and drove to Kingsbourne, Sarah's new rented home. Once there, I confronted her, saying: 'You and I started this charity for all the right reasons — because we wanted to help people, because we wanted to get more involved in Eastern Europe, and also because it was an opportunity to spend time together on something worthwhile. None of these things have changed, have they?'

'No, Starkie, they haven't.'

I carried on: 'I want you not to back out of this. You backed out of a lot of things in our relationship and the relationship has been hurt, and I don't want you to walk out of this.' My friend looked me in the eye and said: 'I was never going to withdraw. I just wanted to restructure it — so this is what I want you do to: go back and get the finance for the first three months.' A while later I left, happy that I had persuaded her not to abandon her commitment to Germany and its children in need.

A couple of weeks later she called me, but not about the charity. Secure in the knowledge that Oceonics was a dead duck, she was now prepared to liquidate her share of Budgie, and was preparing to fly to Hong Kong where Clive Garrad's consortium, Gracious Lady, was ready to hand over a substantial cheque. Then she wanted to fly back via Paris, her brain still crowded with memories of better times there with John, and where she felt she could celebrate her new-found wealth in some style. She wanted to go dancing in Paris, and I said I would be there. In the end, however, and partly because the messages I received from or about her over the next few days were equivocal, I decided not to go. She was furious.

I had no time for dancing anyway. The sub-contractor to whom Oceonics owed the most money managed to get into my office in the MesseTurm accompanied by a strange-looking man who would not stop staring at me. Finally I asked, 'Is this man with you a lawyer? Because if so, I don't think it is fair for me to talk to you without my having my own lawyer present.'

The sub-contractor said, 'He's not a lawyer. He's a purchasing agent.'

'Purchasing agent? Of what?'

The sub-contractor smiled. 'Body parts. He's taking a look at how healthy you are to see if he is going to buy your body parts.' And he was not joking — in Eastern Europe they have made a highly lucrative industry out of kidnapping people and removing their vital organs for use in transplant operations. I got him out of the office, pushing his lugubrious friend with him, then sat down at my desk to reflect. I was alone in Frankfurt, left with the very dangerous task of mopping up Oceonics, while Sarah was catching the sun in Bermuda and John was partying the night away in Monte Carlo. It was, perhaps, the moment to question the value of their friendship and commitment, but that was not something I wanted to think about just then.

At the beginning of June I accompanied Sarah and her entourage on a Children in Crisis trip to Poland, taking with me, at her request, Peter Bougdanos, whom she had been trying to meet for some time. Peter had money, and she could smell it.

In the month since I had seen her last, when I had gone to Kingsbourne, I had been hearing more and more rumours that she wanted to kill her German charity, and I was anxious to hear once more from her that she was as committed to it as she had been a year ago. Towards the end of the trip, as we travelled by train from Warsaw to Cracow, Sarah held a committee meeting for Children in Crisis during which, I later discovered, the future of Menschen in Not was also discussed. Afterwards she told me that there would be a breakfast meeting next day, at which the main topic would be MIN. That night, however, she was as sweet-natured, as generous, and as joyous as only she could be.

At the meeting next morning I found that the entire board of Children in Crisis was also present, which seemed strange since CIC and MIN shared nothing apart from the Duchess as their figurehead. Sarah looked at me coolly and said, 'My board has something to say,' whereupon one of its members took up her theme: 'The Duchess has sought our advice and we have recommended to her that she dissolve the German charity because she simply does not have time for it.'

Stunned by what I had heard, I still managed to point out that CIC had no jurisdiction over MIN. In Germany, MIN had its own board, which included the bankers from Schröder Munchmeyer; if Sarah wished to dissolve the charity she had helped to create, she would have to come to Germany and face her board there. 'You can say that, and it is technically right, but this is the decision we have reached,' I was told. 'This is what the Duchess wishes to do.'

I looked at Sarah. Shamefacedly, she said,

'I have to defer to their decision.' Then she ordered me, on my word of honour, never to bring up the question of Menschen in Not in any subsequent private conversations we might have: 'All you will do is convince me to go the other way. I want your word of honour in front of these other people that you'll never mention the charity again.'

And so ended the Duchess of York's shabby foray into charity fundraising in Germany and Eastern Europe. After the fall of the Berlin Wall four years earlier, West Germany had suddenly had to accept responsibility for an additional 18 million people, most of whom lived in poverty. Of these unhappy people, many were children without homes or parents, living in abject poverty, and with no hope of ever forging a decent life for themselves.

Here — more than in Britain, more than in the US, in which countries the Duchess's other charities were situated — was the chance to do some real good; a chance too, to do work which was not being duplicated by other charities, as so often happens in the more developed countries. Sarah had bravely told the German people in her speech a year earlier that she would spend time with them, she would learn the language, she would devote herself to this good cause. After that last conversation with me in Poland, however, she has not set foot in Germany again.

At the back of her mind, always, was the almost £1 million which she still owed, through John Bryan, to the Schröder Munchmeyer bank; and now there was the knowledge that if she ever returned she would have to face those same bankers across the boardroom table of the charity she had abandoned. Personal interests, always perilously close to her charitable interests, had finally triumphed. She would kill her German charity — and thereby deny the thousands of impoverished, malnourished and diseased children who might have expected its help and succour — because of an outstanding debt to the bank. Nor was it, by this stage, a matter of Can't Pay. Her decision, cynically, was Won't Pay.

I left the room and flew back to Frankfurt. Waiting for me on the answering machine was a vitriolic message from John, in which he accused me of betraying him. He said, 'You and Sarah expect everything to be brought to you on a silver platter. Now you expect the platter to be carried by starving orphans.' It seemed that, within the space of a few hours, I had lost the love and affection of the two people who were — with the exception of Edda, to whom I was by now engaged — my dearest friends.

It was when, not long after my return, Edda told me that she no longer wanted to marry me that I decided to kill myself.

Chapter 13

My best friend Starkie, I miss you so much, I miss your laughter, honesty, and your pure, kind heart. I love my brother/best friend relationship and RE-ALLY REALLY cherish and treasure it. Thank you, my friend. . . .

Dedication to the author from HRH the Duchess of York

By the time they got me to hospital, my friend had called twice. The first time was to ask how I was, the second to ask whether she should come. Then came a third call: sorry, she couldn't find anyone to look after the children and wouldn't be able to come.

It didn't matter. For the first few days I was in intensive care, and then I slept. After a fortnight I moved to a private clinic in the mountains outside Frankfurt and gradually began to regain my strength. Three weeks after that dreadful day I received a call from Herr Meyer at the Schröder Munchmeyer Bank. If I was feeling well enough, would I come and have lunch with him? There were a few matters concerning Oceonics still out-standing that he would like to discuss with me.

My doctors argued against it, but I drove into Frankfurt and to the restaurant. Halfway through lunch Herr Meyer said casually, 'By the way, whenever a company declares bankruptcy the file automatically goes from the bankruptcy court to the District Attorney. When we have finished lunch, would you kindly go to your office, as some people from the Attorney's department will be there?' Though I was not feeling tremendously well, I agreed, and Herr Meyer advised me, 'Just be friendly to them and say you'll co-operate. Naturally the bank will back you up.'

There were fourteen of them at my office. At the same time an unknown number of them broke into my apartment, and simul-taneously these two teams started to rifle through my papers. The afternoon wore on, and as they bundled up more and more of my papers, a terrible realization began to dawn on me. Finally one of them said, 'We will not handcuff you here in the office, Dr Starkie, we will allow you to travel down to the street before we put the handcuffs on.'

At the police station I was put in a holding cell, but they were unable to remand me to prison because of my recent medical record:

a doctor's certificate saying I was fit to be imprisoned was required. I was driven around Frankfurt that evening from one doctor's premises to another, and ordered to stand, still handcuffed, in the queues in a succession of shabby waiting rooms until I was seen. Naturally no doctor wanted to take the responsibility for imprisoning a recently-failed suicide, so on we would drive to another surgery, where the process would be repeated.

Finally I was driven back to the University Clinic, to which I had originally been taken after having been discovered. The doctors there were appalled at my treatment. I was moved to a criminal psychiatric clinic, then finally allowed to go back to the private clinic I had left many hours earlier; here I was told that I would be allowed to stay for the next couple of months. I called my luncheon partner, Herr Meyer, to tell him where I was — and my friend of all these months and years, my co-director of the MIN charity, the man I had taken to Paris to show the nightlife, responded by calling the District Attorney's office and declaring that the bank did not want me to have my freedom. I must be locked up immediately.

I was handcuffed again and taken from the clinic back into Frankfurt. At the police station I was told I could be detained because there was a suspicion that I had kept Oceonics running too long, that I might have misled people by saying that I had good reason to think that the company was solvent. What was that reason, they asked me?

The reason, I hardly needed to remind myself, was the Duchess of York's eternal promise of DM 2,100,000, although I refused to name her in a court document. I was encouraged again and again to change my mind, but I shook my head: I would not name her.

I went to gaol, without charge, for five months.

When I was finally able to call and speak to Sarah and John, their reactions to what had happened were mixed. John had learned that there was likely to be an international arrest warrant issued against him, with the result that he jumped on a plane and headed for Los Angeles. From there he called me and said, 'Poor you, Allan — but don't worry, I'm going to turn myself in, too, and we can fight this thing together!' He called again to tell me that, actually, he'd decided not to turn himself in. Then he called once more, just as I was about to be rearrested, and said, 'Allan, we're in damage-control mode!' He had to think about his reputation, he said. To that end he had hired an image consultant — could I please call him and help him come up with a press statement? Sadly, I was unable to oblige, for just at that moment my wrists were pinned behind my back and a pair of heavy handcuffs clamped roughly around my wrists.

Sarah's reaction to my suicide attempt was unnerving: 'Oh you poor chap . . . when they told me what you'd done, and that you botched it up, I felt so sorry for you. There can't be anything worse, can there, than screwing up a suicide attempt? You know, I spoke to Rita* about it and she said, yes, he is going to survive this attempt but he'll do it again soon and he won't survive the next one. Allan — when are you going to do it next? Are you going to do it now, or wait till they release you and do it at home?'

It was hard to know what to say. 'I haven't given it a lot of thought,' I replied, and put down the phone. Later, John's secretary, Julia Delves Broughton, suggested to me that this bizarre response to what was, after all, a human tragedy was the Duchess playing at being an amateur psychiatrist. I hope, although I am not sure, that Julia was right.

*Rita Rogers, clairvoyant

Sarah said one other thing — even more hurtful, even more bizarre — regarding my attempt at suicide. If on the next occasion I was successful, would I undertake a mission on her behalf? She begged me: 'Would you do me a favour, Starkie? When you're dead, would you find JFK and explain to him that I am destined to marry John-John and become the First Lady of the United States? But I would like him to help me with this and approach John-John in his dreams and try to explain it to him and convince him.' This is what she expected of me; not only was I to serve her in life, but I had to serve her in death, as well.

Back in England, speculation about the future of Sarah's relationship with John continued to grow. So successfully had she kept him out of sight that very few journalists — if any — knew the full extent of their affair. At the end of the ill-fated Polish trip she had told a British reporter, 'He's not involved any more. I can't say anything else because I'm a very loyal person. Totally loyal.' But not totally truthful: when in England, John was still living with her at Kingsbourne, and even an optimistic newspaper piece a month later saying the affair really, *truly* WAS over, was still wide of the mark.

A fortnight after my arrest the police had

announced that John would be arrested if he returned to Germany, and he had relocated to the Peninsular Hotel in Los Angeles; he had been in such a hurry to get out of England that he left his wallet behind. For some time he had owed relatively small amounts to various creditors in Britain, but when they heard of the collapse of Oceonics there was a sudden surge in demands for repayment. He had, however, made the mistake of leaving unpaid a bill for £6,414 owed to his solicitors, Penningtons, and also the residue of the money he owed Sarah's sister Jane and her husband from the court case which had followed the *Hello!* article featuring their wedding. These two bills would ultimately bring about John's bankruptcy and social disgrace in Britain — but not yet.

The overall effect of all this, however, was enough to dissuade him from returning to Britain. Since Sarah only visited the States for brief periods, they were spending more and more time apart. She wrote to me saying that he was feeling lonely and isolated, and added that she had taken a one-week holiday with Prince Andrew which had infuriated John when he read about it in the American newspapers. 'He is so special and I am 100 per cent loyal to him,' she said, but I thought her sentiments now sounded increasingly unsure.

By now I had been locked up in Höchst Prison, along with around a hundred and forty prisoners. It was, I imagine, like many other prisons across Europe, with three levels of cells constructed around an atrium lit by a skylight through which daylight oozed, filtered by layers of dirt. As I was hurried into the building for the first time I saw a group of about fifteen prisoners walking around a barred corridor. One face was immediately familiar — that of Nick Leeson, the 'Man Who Broke The Bank'.* I later learned that when I first saw him, Nick was enjoying the privilege, afforded four times a week, of circling the corridor for an hour before taking a shower.

In my cell, three metres square, I had to climb on to the desk in order to look out of the barred and heavily grilled window.

But it was those first minutes in the cell that were to remain with me. My heart was pounding with a rhythm that seemed to say 'Let me out, let me out!', and I was certain that my blood pressure had climbed to dangerous levels. Once, when I was a child, play-

---

*Barings Bank had collapsed earlier in 1995 with losses of £850 million, in large measure because of the Far East trading activities of one of its employees — Leeson.

ing hide-and-seek with my parents, I hid in a clothes hamper, and my father sat on the lid as a joke. I will never forget that terror, that feeling of being buried alive. It took more than thirty years before I had cause to remember that feeling — in Höchst. 'Calm down,' I told myself out loud. I tried to control my breathing, tried to relax. Without my watch I was not sure what time it was, and on my first night every time the guard switched on my light — which he did regularly — I sprang up and dressed, not knowing what was expected of me.

Breakfast was dispensed in the hallway by prisoners lucky enough to be offered work. Anything that gets you out of your cell is highly valued, and prison jobs are a privilege for which you have to wait. These lucky colleagues dished out three pieces of brown bread and a glob of greasy, indestructible margarine on to our white ceramic plates, and filled our white plastic pitchers with a syrupy coffee-coloured liquid. That was to remain standard breakfast, sometimes supplemented with wurst and, twice a month, with a hard-boiled egg — but essentially it never changed. I found it almost impossible to eat the stuff. Breakfast lasts about five minutes, and one requires about an equal amount of time to fight with the margarine;

then you are confronted with the unpleasant reality that it is 6.10 A.M., you are dressed, awake, and have an entirely empty day ahead of you.

That is the real horror of prison. If I could explain the hopelessness of that feeling I will have accomplished something. For the fact is that you are smothered alive with your own fears, regrets and doubts, and with nothing but an endless, oppressively open-ended span of time with which to confront them. All the while you are trying to adjust to living in a tiny room in which the door does not open. Time becomes your tormentor. Time, you see, is the real punishment.

So you are left alone to fence with time. You try to tame it by breaking it up into units around which you create an agenda. You structure your day around the skeleton of preprogrammed activities — the three meals, the arrival of the 3.30 P.M. cold drink in summer, the ninety minutes of circling the prison yard like hamsters on an exercise wheel, and the four hourly sessions of 'open station' when you can shower. You fill the massive holes between these events with reading the same books until your eyes hurt, with writing letters of apology for all your sins which seem so overwhelming as you sit alone, and you speculate about your case.

400

Soon you abandon the question of innocence or guilt; your thoughts and conversations centre around estimations of likely punishments. Then you take part in frantic discussions, conducted with almost religious fervour, with other inmates about whether you must serve the whole sentence, or receive parole for the last third. Time is your preoccupation: combating it alone, dissecting it, speculating about its length, wishing for it to stop.

The Duchess did not forget me. Through the early months of my imprisonment she wrote me notes and letters of such sweet tenderness that it was easy to forget that, but for her procrastination, I might not be in gaol at all. '*Please,* in moments of anxiety and fear remember the laughter, Annabel's, good dancing and the love of friends,' she wrote. 'Most of all remember Concorde.' I had plenty of time to remember Concorde. On board we would sit together drinking too many gin and tonics, swishing at supersonic speed between London and New York, the only sounds our laughter and the rattle of ice in our glasses.

She wrote to me about John, obliquely referring to the danger surrounding his Las Vegas project, '. . . very frightened about the cowboys giving him the boot', and presaging, at last the end of the affair: 'He seems to be in his house on the peninsula[*] the whole time, so I never see him.'

Despite the absurdity of her continuing hopes for an Olympic gold medal, Sarah wrote fondly and proudly of Heather Blaze's occasional successes: 'She won the biggest competition in this country last month and the whole family[‡] were over to see it. Certainly the father[†] did brilliantly and we were all so proud. . . .'

The days slowly turned into months, and during the daily walk around the prison yard Nick Leeson and I became friends. As we walked in endless circles we passed the time telling each other our stories and on returning to my cell I began to write mine down. So too did he. In his book *Rogue Trader* (Little, Brown, 1996) he tells how he called me 'Lord Starkie' because I wore a silk dressing-gown and velvet slippers. He describes, in amused tones, my encounter in the shower rooms with an enormous Turk who had been keeping us awake at night by kicking his cell door.

[*]The Peninsular Hotel.
[‡]i.e. the Queen and other members of the royal family, probably at the Windsor Horse Show.
[†]Robert Splaine.

'Starkie threw himself at the Turk and pummelled him to the ground. . . . The Turk lay there groaning, bleeding from the nose. . . .

' "Don't kick your door again," Starkie shouted as he was taken away by the guards, his tiny legs swinging beneath him . . . his slippers still immaculate on his feet.'

Not every day was as eventful. The mood of the prison seemed to function on a collective consciousness tuned to predictable cycles. Friday afternoons were sombre: we mustered our nerves to survive the weekend depression which came to a crescendo on Sunday, the day of twenty-three hours of unbroken solitary confinement. Mondays were quiet as we began to recover our spirits from the weekend, Tuesdays were calm. Wednesdays and Thursdays were manic and inexpressibly painful; for these were visiting days, when the door opened a crack to expose the living world. Reality rushed in for a frantic, hurried, thirty-minute visitation. The night before was generally sleepless, the day of the visit (if you had one) agonizing, the next two days a time of recovery.

Sarah continued to write, her letters overflowing with news of her daughters, her husband, her part-time lover and — most excitedly — Heather Blaze. As I lay on my bunk and reflected upon my situation, I asked myself which was more bizarre: that I should find myself locked up in a gaol several thousand miles from home, without charge and without having done anything illegal; or that Sarah, prisoner of another regime, should spend her waking days not plotting her escape, but dreaming of Olympic gold. Heather Blaze was an obsession into which she poured her frustrations, her heartache, her lost ambition, and her love.

Then one day another letter arrived, rubber-stamped with the familiar red Buckingham Palace cipher. It said, bleakly, 'I thought you ought to know Heather Blaze had to be shot. She broke her leg at the Dublin Horse Show in a final jump-off at the water-jump.' As with everyone and everything else in her life, Sarah had pushed Heather Blaze too far, and the poor horse had paid the price.

The Duchess was devastated. Her life was in a state of flux — her lover trapped on another continent, fearful of travelling in case he should be arrested; her 'best friend' in jail with no prospect of release — there were no longer any constants. If she was to have any peace of mind in the future, some decisions had to be taken. She wrote: 'Your brother is no longer with his girlfriend. She eventually took the courage and said she could no longer accept such diabolical abuse. However I know she misses him terribly and sometimes they talk on the telephone.'

It took the death of a horse she had not known long, and which she did not even wholly own, for Sarah to take the decision to rid herself of John's increasingly malign influence. Her association with him had caused both her and the British royal family irreparable damage; in the latter case, damage already being compared by historians with the House of Windsor's previous flirtation with another American, Wallis Simpson.

Two months after Heather Blaze's death, Sarah was still mourning. She regretted, too, the passing of her affair with John: 'Your brother and his girlfriend have remained apart, and actually he seems to be happier in some extraordinary way. As though he was expecting it for the last year and now respects her for having had the courage where he didn't.'

In fact, it had taken eighteen months for Sarah finally to say goodbye. She had known since the beginning of 1994 that the relationship was doomed. By then they had been together for two years, and the best had passed; the two cherry trees, growing intertwined towards the sun, had parted and withered. For John, it would mean moving from a quasi-stable relationship back into the rampant bachelorhood to which he was more suited. For Sarah, however, it was the beginning of a journey down a long and lonely road — for the first time in her adult life she was without a man. From Kim Smith-Bingham, her first serious love, to Paddy McNally, from Paddy to Prince Andrew, from Andrew to Steve Wyatt, from Steve to John Bryan — there had always been someone. Now there was no one.

She wrote: 'Your brother swings up and down like a pendulum, and poor Rose[*] is battling on, picking up all the pieces dropped over four years.' And from Concorde, that delightful fantasy in the sky, she added, 'Off for another crazy adventure in trying to get my goal of financial freedom.' I knew, though I could not say it to her, that Sarah would spend the rest of her life searching for the pot of gold at the end of the rainbow.

Autumn turned to winter, and the investigations against me continued. There was, amongst the German authorities, a decided air of embarrassment about my continued incarceration, but the bank wanted blood. Schröder Munchmeyer calculated that its best

*Herself.

chance of suing Tony Bryan and Bill Simon successfully for the outstanding DM 12 million lay in its being able to prove that there had been some sort of wrongdoing. The bank had been working with the District Attorney's office for months, trying to demonstrate that the Simons and the Bryans had misled them. If anyone was at fault on this score, however, it was the bank itself which, dazzled by its new association with the Duchess of York, had let Oceonics' credit mount up to unacceptable levels.

On the day on which I was sent to Höchst Prison, the authorities set my bail at DM 12 million — the sum owed by the shareholders of Oceonics to the Schröder Munchmeyer bank. But as time wore on and the embarrassment at my continued imprisonment without charge grew, that figure reduced — first to DM 5 million, then to DM 1 million, then to DM 500,000. Dennis Sokol, Tony Bryan's partner, came to visit me and told me he was ready to post the DM 500,000 — that promise evaporated, however, after he had returned to the States and been talked out of it by the Bryans.

Though the two Bryans presented themselves as being fabulously wealthy, when it came to raising the bail they suddenly discovered that they had no cash, or very little:

the best they could do was DM 150,000. Even that came neither graciously or quickly; indeed, it only materialized after my mother, who had been fobbed off by the Bryans whenever she had asked what they were doing to secure my release, threatened to go to the American television programme *60 Minutes*. It seemed to her that they were in no hurry at all to set me free, a suspicion confirmed by a telephone conversation she had with John, who coldly suggested that if she needed to raise money for my bail then she should take a begging bowl around the churches and other religious establishments of Manhattan.

Though bail had by now been set at DM 300,000, the best we could come up with was DM 200,000. By now it was mid-November, and the German authorities had realized that I was turning from an embarrassment into a major problem: they could find no evidence of wrongdoing, and would rather that I simply got on a plane and flew away from their country, preferably for ever. A court hearing was arranged to review my case and early one morning, tightly handcuffed, I was led out of Höchst to a prison van. I looked up in amazement because for the first time in five months I caught sight of the moon and the stars, but the guards, not understanding my need to pause and drink in this glorious sight, pulled me roughly into the van.

I was told by the judge that I would be released on surety of DM 200,000, on condition that I came up with another DM 100,000 by January, and that I would be free to go home to the States for Christmas as long as I came up with the extra money. I replied that I was unable to accept his terms because I did not have DM 100,000, and I did not think my former partners were going to put it up for me. I added that I felt I would be misrepresenting myself and misleading the court if I agreed to my release on those terms.

I was re-handcuffed and taken down to a holding cell. Just as the prison van was due to arrive to take me back to Höchst, I learned that Frau Hohn, the District Attorney, had been alerted to my honest declaration, and had conceded the point. Bail, which all those months ago had been set at DM 12 million, was now just DM 200,000.

I was given the equivalent of £1, and turned out on the street.

I was free.

Afterword

John Bryan was declared bankrupt in Britain on 6 August 1996.

The debt which had nagged at him for so long — the £55,000 he had kept for brokering the *Hello!* article about Jane Luedecke's wedding back in January 1994 — had been paid. But John sank under the burden of Jane's £30,000 court costs, weighed down by the petitions of two other creditors, American Express and his erstwhile solicitors, Penningtons. All of them, if he had ordered his finances right, could have been paid. But they were abandoned — along with his suits, his papers, and his wallet — in his headlong flight from responsibility. He did not attend the twenty-minute hearing in the High Court before Mr Deputy Registrar Brettle because in recent months he had come to find England an alien land, full of snarling creditors and baying pressmen.

He found no one to replace the Duchess of York in his life. Since their separation he had been photographed with a number of younger escorts, and seemed to have little taste for establishing another one-to-one relationship. His zest for travel had diminished; he was no longer the toast of the European jet set, and he did not venture back into Germany. In Los Angeles, where he had relocated to start his new business empire away from the petty irritation of people demanding money, his electricity was shut off over an unpaid $500 bill.

The Duchess was revealed to have debts of between £4 million and £5 million. Interest charges on her bank overdraft of around £40,000 a month were unavoidable, but her continued outgoings on a permanent staff of thirteen, including a cook, a driver, a maid, a butler, a dresser, a nanny, a personal assistant, three secretaries and an accountant, were perhaps a little unnecessary, given her new status. She and the Duke of York were now finally divorced; he never became Regent, and she was no longer Her Royal Highness. No one need curtsy to her any more.

In love, she was no luckier than John. Defying the predictions of her many clairvoyants, John Kennedy, Jr — the man she knew she was destined to marry — went and married someone else.

And then the world finally learned, in words which could not have been put more clearly, how the royal family viewed the woman who, for ten years, had been One of

Them. A letter to Sarah from Princess Margaret, the Queen's sister, read: 'You have done more to bring shame on the family than could ever have been imagined. Not once have you hung your head in embarrassment even for a minute. . . . Clearly you have never considered the damage you are causing us all. How dare you discredit us?'

Speculation grew as to her future. At its height, it suggested that the Queen wanted Sarah stripped of her title and her children taken away from her. Among the many headlines were a few references to the fact that Sarah wanted to ban publication of this book. In this though, as with so many other enterprises in her life, her ambition remained unfulfilled.

I still keep a picture in my mind of Sarah, Duchess of York, at her finest — magnificent in her crimson Ralph Lauren dress, her blue-grey eyes sparkling, her brilliant red hair a glorious contrast to the faded grandeur of Buckingham Palace on a summer's afternoon.

It does no harm to keep a snapshot of the person you once loved, but love no more.

Glossary

Linky	JB's pet name for the Duchess
Otto, Mr Beam, your brother	The Duchess's pet names for JB
Mrs Beam, Sally Metcalf, your aunt	The Duchess's names for herself
Your sick aunt, your very sick aunt	The Duchess as she described herself in increasing stages of depression
Billy	The Duke of York
Mama	The Queen
Pa	The Duke of Edinburgh
The Blonde, Dutch, Goody Two-Shoes	The Princess of Wales
Cherry trees	I love you
Potatoes	Money

Honour Bright	I swear
Royal Honour Bright	More emphatic version of above
BP	Buckingham Palace
Reptiles	Journalists
Metronome	Jim Hughes
Barney Rubble	Barney Lindley

We hope you have enjoyed this Large Print book. Other Thorndike Press or Chivers Press Large Print books are available at your library or directly from the publishers.

For more information about current and upcoming titles, please call or write, without obligation, to:

Thorndike Press
P.O. Box 159
Thorndike, Maine 04986 USA
Tel. (800) 223-2336

OR

Chivers Press Limited
Windsor Bridge Road
Bath BA2 3AX
England
Tel. (0225) 335336

All our Large Print titles are designed for easy reading, and all our books are made to last.